MODEL LIBRARY LEGISLATION

CONCEPTS IN COMMUNICATION INFORMATICS & LIBRARIANSHIP
(CICIL)

For a list of titles in this series, *see* pp. 309 at the end of the book

---

Dr Velaga Venkatappaiah is a well-known librarian, administrator, bibliophile, writer, and above all a research scholar in library and information science. He authored about 42 books; edited 15 volumes; 16 souvenirs and special numbers in library and information science; compiled 18 bibliographies and 3 indices; prepared more than 300 papers; and reviewed about 200 books or journals in English and Telugu in various periodicals. He has written the largest number of books on library science in any regional language in India. He was awarded many prizes and citations for his books by the Southern Languages Books Trust, Government of India (thrice), Andhra Pradesh Sahitya Academy, Andhra Pradesh Bolala Academy, Telugu University and the Andhra University. He is the Secretary of the Prof. Kaula Endowment for Library and Information Science. He served as a member on several expert Committees set up by the Government of Andhra Pradesh, and was nominated as Chairman of the Central Sectional Committee on Public Libraries of the Indian Library Association twice 1988-90 and 1990-92. Recently he was elected as Vice-President, ILA.

He participated in, and organised several conferences, seminars and workshops, and lecture programmes on library and information science. He visited the USSR and browsed extensively among books in some of the major libraries and scientific information centres.

He specialised in library legislation and is recognised as an expert in library legislation and service matters.

Concepts in Communication
Informatics & Librarianship-58

General Editor: **S.P. Agrawal**

MODEL LIBRARY LEGISLATION

Model Public Library Act and Rules made therein for the Constituent States and Union Territories

VELAGA VENKATAPPAIAH

Vice President (SZ)
Indian Library Associatior
DELHI

CONCEPT PUBLISHING COMPANY, NEW DELHI 110059

ISBN 81-7022-518-3

First Published 1994

Published and Printed by
Ashok Kumar Mittal
Concept Publishing Company
A/15-16, Commercial Block, Mohan Garden
NEW DELHI-110059 (India)

Lasertypeset by
Printing Express,
H-13, Bali Nagar,
NEW DELHI-110015

To

"I am thankful for warm good earth,

The morning sun,

A new day's birth"

and

DR S.R. RANGANATHAN

EXCELLENT DOCUMENT

The Model Public Libraries Act
drafted by Dr. Velaga Venkatappaiah
is an excellent document. He has
done commendable job in a short time.
On behalf of the Indian Library Association,
I extend him our sincere thanks.

Delhi
Date : 14-2-1990

Prof Krishan Kumar
President
Indian Library Association

GENERAL EDITOR'S INTRODUCTION

Despite literacy drive and various non-formal education programmes and even after the elapse of more than forty years of Independence, the largest democracy of the world has not been able to wipe out the ugly spot of illiteracy from its face. For an effective functioning of democracy and for economic progress and prosperity it is necessary that majority of its people are at least literate and are aware of the new moving wheels of the changing modern world. True, that the successive Five-year Plans, new methods of farming, improved transportation, mass communication and various governmental measures for improving the living condition of villagers have considerably changed the rural scenario. But then, it is also a fact that in the sphere of literacy and health-care and progress in the rural areas is painfully slow. Moreover, the deplorable fact is that whatever is achieved in the direction of literacy, is more or less thwarted by the non-availability of facility for continuing education in the absence of rural public libraries which alone can provide reading materials to the neo-literates in order to prevent them from relapsing and also help change shadow of their stereo-type and irrationally rigid attitude towards basic issues of life. Even in urban areas the public libraries are woefully inadequate in some of the States of India. In order to make literacy drive a success what is needed most is the establishment of a large network of libraries in rural and urban areas. It would be naive to think such a large number of public libraries, which we need today, can be established and run on individuals munificence and philanthropists' donations or on blissfully irregular funds provided by the State Governments and the local bodies. Quite naturally, therefore, through library legislation, the public libraries could have adequate funds on permanent basis, could be developed on proper lines, and administered by the competent library authority in the light of the rules framed for the purpose. UNESCO has also repeatedly stressed the need for setting up the public libraries 'under the clear mandate of law, so framed as to ensure nation-wide provision of public library service'.

While in the West, Edward Edwards, the notable British librarian, had been the pioneer of library legislation, in India it was Dr. S.R. Ranganathan – the doyen of library science – who first gave the call for library legislation and drafted a Model Libraries Act which was approved at the First All Asia Conference held at Varanasi in 1930 and which proved to be a great source for enactment of library laws in some of the States which have such Acts. It was mainly through his efforts that the first Library Act came into existence in Tamil Nadu in 1948. At present, following eight States have enacted and adopted library legislation: Tamil Nadu (1948), Andhra Pradesh (1960), Karnataka (1965), Maharashtra (1967), Manipur (1968), West Bengal (1979), Kerala (1989) and Haryana (1989). Thus, most of the States and the Union Territories are as such without the Library Acts. These States do have libraries both at the State and district levels, but their functioning leaves much to be desired. Efforts are being made by the associations of the librarians and supporters of the library movement to exert pressure on these States to enact such laws for proper functioning and development of their public libraries.

Revised version of the Model Public Libraries Act (1972) of Dr. Ranganathan is there, for the guidance of the States for enactment of the library laws. On the recommendation of the Advisory Committee on Libraries, Union Ministry of Education set up a Committee under the Chairmanship of Dr. M.D. Sen with a view to preparing a Model Library Bill for the States. The Bill drafted by the committee was circulated to the States for consideration and necessary action. This Model Bill was also discussed and approved with certain amendments in a 'Seminar on Library Legislation', organised by the 14th All India Library Conference held at Patna in April 1964. Similarly Planning Commission constituted a 'Working Group on Libraries' to advise the Commission on the development of libraries in the Fourth Five-year-Plan. This Working Group too produced a draft Model Public Libraries Bill in 1965. This Bill was also circulated to all the States for their consideration. But, as it is, no response was there from any of the States on the subject. Recently Indian Library Association, in its Council meeting in June 1989 in New Delhi, resolved to prepare a Model Library Act, in the light of the recent developments and on the basis of the experience gained through the existing Library Acts. This Act, drafted by Dr. V. Venkatappaiah – the Chairman of Central Sectional Committee Public Libraries of ILA – was discussed in a National Seminar on February 14, 1990. The Draft Act, incorporating changes suggested by the participants was adopted by the Seminar.

The focus of the present book is on this Draft Model Public Libraries Act along with the Draft Rules, much as it could be adopted by any State desiring to enact such a law. Of course with changes suited to its corresponding needs and circumstances.

After giving a brief overview of the public libraries in India, the guidelines for library legislation and its essential features are discussed in detail. It also traces the history of library legislation in India with particular reference to Model Public Libraries Acts drafted by Dr. Ranganathan, the Committees constituted by the Union Ministry of Education, the Planning Commission and also by Dr. Venkatappaiah – senior professional and an expert in his own right – under the umbrella of Indian Library Association.

S.P. AGRAWAL

PREFACE

This is a Model Public Libraries Act drafted by me and is quite suitable for adoption in any State or Union Territory where there is no library legislation and useful for those who are interested in library legislation. It is an established fact that library legislation only can empower appropriate authorities to provide a network of library service and ensure adequate financial support and efficient functioning of the public libraries. So, for a good public library system, library legislation is essential. Those who are planning to have library legislation may adopt this draft or modify it according to the needs of the State or Union Territory.

I cannot claim this as my creative work. What I did was the collection of material on library legislation published during the past sixty years in India and made use of :

1. my experience working with the Library Act for more than thirty years,
2. my participation in the official meetings with administrators at various levels, and
3. my organising and attending the library seminars and conferences, particularly on library legislation.

The main provocation for drafting the Act was the resolution of the Council meeting on 23rd June, 1989 of the Indian Library Association, which assigned me the task of preparing a Model Public Libraries Act "keeping in view of the recent developments and the experiences gained from the existing library Acts". Taking this as a great opportunity, I have drafted this Model Public Libraries Act, for which I must be ever grateful to Prof Krishan Kumar, President, Shri C.P. Vashishth, General Secretary and Thiru T.S. Rajagopalan, the past President of the Indian Library Association and other members. Based on this draft, the Indian Library Association, in collaboration with the Raja Rammohun Roy Library Foundation, organised a NATIONAL SEMINAR ON MODEL PUBLIC LIBRARIES ACT, on 14th February, 1990 at New Delhi. The proceedings of this Seminar have been given in Chapter 7 of this book.

I express my deep sense of gratitude to Shri Gopal Rao Ekbote, retired Chief Justice, Andhra Pradesh, who was a great source of inspiration for me in drafting this Model Act, Prof. P.N. Kaula, Emeritus Professor of Library and Information Science, University of Lucknow and Dr. P.S.G Kumar, Head, Department of Library and Information Science, Nagpur University, for their valuable support and guidance in drafting this Model Act and to Dr B.P. Barua, Director, Raja Rammohun Roy Library Foundation, for permitting me to reprint my paper.

I am grateful to Shri Ashok Kumar Mittal of M/s Concept Publishing Company for bringing this work to light.

I will be the happiest person, if the Model Act or any of its sections or sub-sections, and the draft Rules or Sub-rules made there under, are of any use to the people, who are in need of them, in their efforts towards enacting an effective legislation for systematic library service.

V. VENKATAPPAIAH

CONTENTS

ABBREVIATIONS

BDC	Book Deposit Centre
BL	Branch Library
CCL	City Central Library
CLA	City Library Authority
CPL	City Public Library
DL	Director of Libraries
DCL	District Central Library
DL	District Library
DLA	District Library Authority
DLO	District Library Officer
DLS	District Library System
DPL	Director of Public Libraries
DP Lib	District Public Library
Deptt PL	Department of Public Libraries
ILA	Indian Library Association
LC	Library Cess
LLA	Local Library Authority
ML	Mobile Library
NAPLIS	National Policy on Library and Information System
RPL	Regional Public Library
RRRLF	Raja Rammohun Roy Library Foundation
SCL	State Central Library
SLA	State Library Authority
SPL	State Public Library
SLC	State Library Council
SLC	State Library Committee
SRL	State Regional Library
VL	Village Library

1

INDIA AND PUBLIC LIBRARIES : An Overview

India, a federal union of States attained Independence on 15th August, 1947, and became a Sovereign Socialist Secular Democratic Republic on 26th January, 1950. It covers an area of 32,87,263 sq.km, expanding from the snow-covered Himalayan heights to tropical forests of the South. India is the largest democratic country in the Commonwealth and seventh largest country in the world. "India is well-marked off from the rest of Asia by mountains and the sea, which give the country a distinct geographical entity".[1]

Indian Republic is governed in terms of the Constitution. The executive powers of the country rest with the Council of Ministers with Prime Minister as its head, who are collectively responsible to the House of the People (Lok Sabha). Similarly in the States, the executive powers rest with the Council of Ministers, who are collectively responsible to the State legislature. In the Indian Union there are 26 States, 6 Union Territories as mentioned below–

States

1. Andhra Pradesh
2. Arunachal Pradesh
3. Assam
4. Bihar
5. Delhi
6. Goa
7. Gujarat
8. Haryana
9. Himachal Pradesh
10. Jammu and Kashmir
11. Karnataka
12. Kerala
13. Madhya Pradesh
14. Maharashtra
15. Manipur
16. Meghalaya
17. Mizoram
18. Nagaland
19. Orissa
20. Punjab
21. Rajasthan
22. Sikkim

23. Tamil Nadu
24. Tripura
25. Uttar Pradesh
26. West Bengal

Union Territories

1. Andaman and Nicobar Islands
2. Chandigarh
3. Dadra and Nagar Haveli
4. Daman and Diu
5. Lakshadweep
6. Pondicherry

In most of the States Municipal Corporations and Municipalities have been established under various Acts of the States. These are run by elected representatives. Similarly, a three tier structure of local self-government has been established at village, block and district level in most of the States.

According to 1991 census, the total population of India was 84,39,30,861. Out of this the rural population was 76.79 per cent and urban population was 23.31 per cent. The overall literacy rate was 52.11 per cent and out of this 63.86 per cent males and 39.42 per cent females are illiterates. Table 1.1 presents the literacy rates in the country.

TABLE 1.1: Literacy Rates in India

Year	Percentage (overall)	Males (%)	Females (%)
1901	5.35	9.83	0.60
1911	5.92	10.56	1.05
1921	7.16	12.21	1.81
1931	9.50	15.59	2.93
1941	16.10	24.90	7.30
1951	16.67	24.95	7.93
1961	24.02	34.44	12.95
1971	29.45	39.45	18.69
1981	36.17	46.74	24.88
1991	52.11	63.86	39.42

In working, the literacy rates mentioned above in 1951 Jammu and Kashmir and in 1981 Assam were excluded for various reasons.

Public Libraries

India has a rich tradition of public libraries. All these libraries were maintained by kings, queens, *Mathas*, temples and universities. Only during 18th and 19th centuries enthusiastic young men voluntarily came forward to start public libraries for the benefit of common man. Added to this, the social political conditions, printing of books on popular subjects in vernacular languages paved the way for the spreading of public libraries in India. At the beginning public libraries were started to cater to the recreation of the people. During the freedom struggle public libraries played a vital role in creating awareness in the common man. With the framework of library legislation a concept of Public Library System has been developed which comprises a network of public libraries at different levels, freely available to all, catering to the general and more specialised needs of the members of the community.

As per the Constitution of India, the subject 'libraries' was included in the State List and the Centre has no jurisdiction over the libraries established by the States. Consequently, the nine States passed Library Acts during 1948-1993.

1. Andhra Pradesh (1960)
2. Haryana (1989)
3. Karnataka (1965)
4. Kerala (1989)
5. Maharashtra (1967)
6. Manipur (1968)
7. Mizoram (1993)
8. Tamil Nadu (1948)
9. West Bengal (1979)

In the pre-independent India, the princely State Kolhapur passed library act in 1945, and after Independence the Princely State Hyderabad passed library act in 1955. However, these two acts are merged in new acts passed after the States' reorganisation. In all the nine States, where the library legislation is in force about five thousand libraries are functioning, under direct control of the Library Authorities or State Governments, as the case may be. There may be some more private libraries for which the Library Authority or Government sanctions grant-in-aid for their maintenance. According to the "India-Reference Annual 1990" "there are more than sixty thousand libraries in the country".[2] The validity of this figure is questioned in the absence of a consolidated directory of public libraries in the country. Secondly, there is a doubt that the concept of a public library on an international standard was not followed, while arriving at the figure of number of libraries in the country. Long back, Advisory Committee for Libraries (1958) in its report, deplored about the situation and recorded that – "In India the phrase 'public libraries' is used in a very loose sense. It is used to denote any library which permits members of the public to use its material for reference or borrowing on payment of fees or rent. In this sense, all kinds of libraries, national, university, schools and subscription libraries, etc., would be public libraries. Because of the loose connotation of the term, it would appear from the statistics published by UNESCO in 1956 that India leads the world in the number of public libraries, which is given as 24,086, while figures for the United Kingdom, the United States of America, Denmark and Sweden are given as 618; 7,500; 1,329 and 3,507 respectively. The statistics are flattering; they express the aspiration rather than the achievement of the country".[3] The concept of a public library is to be judged with international standard only. A public library is one which is opened to the public without any distinction of caste, creed or sex etc., and which is financed by the public funds. A public library should preserve all types of reading and learning materials which should be available for consultation and lending. With this guidelines only, the number of public libraries are to be counted.

National Libraries

To serve as a permanent repository of reading materials produced in India and to function as reference and research libraries on the concerned subject, the following national libraries are functioning in the country, as a symbol of India's culture and learning':

1. National Library, Calcutta
2. National Science Library, New Delhi
3. National Medical Library, New Delhi
4. Indian Agricultural Research Institute, New Delhi.

In addition to these, there are four copyright libraries which are entitled to receive one copy of every book and magazine or newspaper published in the country, as per the Delivery of Books and News Papers Act, 1954. These are:

1. Central Reference Library

c/o National Library, Calcutta
2. Central Library
c/o Royal Asiatic Society, Bombay
3. Connemara Public Library
(State Central Library), Madras
4. Delhi Public Library, Delhi.

Still there are three more libraries functioning under statutory provision. These are:

1. Khuda Baksh Oriental Public Library, Patna (Bihar)
2. Rampur Raza Library, Rampur (U.P.)
3. Asiatic Society Library, Calcutta.

All the above-mentioned prominent libraries of India are being maintained mainly with the funds of the Government of India and other sources. The Thanjore Maharaja Serfaji's Sarasvati Mahal Library, Thanjavur (Tamil Nadu) is registered under Societies Registration Act, and functioning as a voluntary organisation with the munificent grants of the Government of India and the Government of Tamil Nadu. Still there are some more great libraries working with the assistance of the Centre, State, and other resources. In all most all the States there are State Libraries and District Libraries functioning under the legislation or administrative orders of the State Governments.

Raja Rammohun Roy Library Foundation

Raja Rammohun Roy Library Foundation (RRRLF), a non-statutory autonomous organisation sponsored by Government of India, came into being in May 1972 on the occasion of bicentennial birth anniversary of Raja Rammohun Roy. The main objective of the Foundation is the promotion and support of the library movement in the country and the development of reading habits. Of course this objective will be fulfilled with the active cooperation of the State Governments and Union Territories. The Memorandum of the Foundation has listed a number of the objectives, which includes the "enunciation of a national library policy and working towards its adoption by the Central and State Governments and persuading them to enact library legislation where such legislation does not exist."[4]

The RRRLF is doing its best in public library legislation. The

RRRLF circulated the Model Public Libraries Bill of the Ministry of Education, Government of India to all the States and Union Territories, where there is no library legislation. Again the RRRLF collaborated with the Indian Library Association in organising a National Seminar on Model Public Libraries Act, on 14 February, 1990 at New Delhi with the working document prepared by Dr. V. Venkatappaiah. The details of this Model Act are available in various chapters of this book.

National Policy on Libraries

One of the objectives of Raja Rammohun Roy Library Foundation is to work for National Library Policy and its adoption by Union and State Governments. In pursuance of the objectives of the Foundation, the Government of India constituted a Committee with Prof. D.P. Chattopadhyaya as Chairman, for the formulation of National Policy on Library and Information System (NAPLIS). This Committee submitted its report to the Hon'ble Minister of Human Resource Development, Government of India for approval on 30th May, 1986. This report is pending with the Government of India. As per the recommendation of the NAPLIS, "the most important task before the Government is to establish, maintain, and strengthen the free public libraries in the country and enable them to work as a system."[5] The profession and the public are anxiously awaiting the acceptance of the NAPLIS Report and its implementation.

NOTES

1. *India 1990* — A Reference Annual, p. 1.
2. *Ibid.*, p. 117
3. Report of the Advisory Committee for Libraries, 1958. Delhi: Manager of Publications, Government of India, 1961. 2nd Ed. pp. 6, 155.
4. Books for The Millions At Their Door Steps – information manual, Calcutta: RRRLF, 1988. p. 1.
5. National Policy on Library and Information System – a presentation, May 1986. New Delhi : Committee on National Policy on Library and Information System, Department of Culture, Ministry of Human Resource Development, Government of India, 1986. p. 5.

2

PUBLIC LIBRARIES UNDER MANDATE OF LAW

The concept of a Public Library is an outcome of Vedic ideal that "Dissemination of knowledge is charity par excellence".[1] It stimulated the progressive youth to start library service voluntarily, in different provinces and princely States of pre-Independent India. Subscriptions from the members and the donations from the philanthropists were the main source of income of these libraries. There was no State support for them. These libraries functioned as long as the initial enthusiasm remained and afterwards slowly decayed and closed down.

In the second half of this century the UNESCO in its Manifesto declared the "public library as a living force for education, culture and information and an essential agent for the fostering of peace and understanding between the people and between the nations".[2] A public library will serve as a centre for informal self-education. A public library opens its doors to all sections of the people of a community irrespective of any consideration. "This open door policy helps an individual to develop his potentialities and abilities which otherwise would go waste for lack of proper resources, equipment or atmosphere. A public library attracts such an individual by means of its varied activities and provides him with material for self-education".[3]

To fulfil this objective, a public library should equip itself with the latest reading materials, audio, video cassettes computerized systems etc. to suit the changing needs of the readers. Advisory Committee on Libraries appointed by the Government of India (1958) advocated the internationally accepted definition of a public library. A public library is one:

1. "which is financed for the most part out of public funds;
2. which charges no fees from readers and yet is open for full use by the public without distinction of caste, creed or sex;

legislation, it may possible with rudimentary library systems to render library service through some administrative orders. But they will not be so effective. Further in the coming years it is also presumed that the number of philanthropists and the enthusiastic individuals will dwindle and the Governmental involvement will become absolutely necessary.

In this situation UNESCO manifesto states that "the public library should be established under clear mandate of law, so framed as to ensure nationwide provisions of public library service".[10] So the public library should be wholly maintained from public funds, and no direct charge should be made to anyone for its service. To fulfil this objective there is no alternative to it.

This manifesto is also "concerned to establish man's right of access to knowledge and information". This objective has been powerfully reinforced in the NATIS Report which declares that" information is an essential part of nation's resources and access to it is one of the basic human rights".[11] In this connection it is noted that information networks are not only meant for scientists, technologists and scholars but also equally important for all citizens of the country to have access to the knowledge and information. If this objective is to be achieved, an effective public library system must be established under legislation.

NOTES

1. V. Venkatappaiah, *Public Library System in A.P.*, Waltair: Andhra University, 1982, p.6.
2. UNESCO, Public Library Manifesto. Paris: UNESCO, 1949, p. 2.
3. Robert D. Leigh, *The Public Library in the United States*, New York: Columbia University Press, 1950, p. 12.
4. *Report of Advisory Committee for Libraries, 1958*. Delhi: Manager of Publications, Govt. of India, 1961 2nd Ed. p. 31.
5. S.R. Ranganathan, Model State Library Act. *Her Lib Sc.*, 11(3) 1972, p. 236.
6. Model Public Libraries Bill, Ministry of Education, Government of India, 1963.
7. Model Public Libraries Bill, Planning Commission, Government of India, 1965.
8. V. Venkatappaiah, National Seminar on Model Public Libraries Act, Working Document. Delhi: Indian Library Association, 1990.
9. Development of Public Libraries in Africa: The Ibadan Seminar. Paris: UNESCO, 1954.
10. UNESCO Manifesto.
11. Establishing Legislative Framework for the Implementation of NATIS. Paris: UNESCO, 1977. p. 36.

equally levied and responsibly expended". The revised and restructured British Act i.e. British Public Libraries and Museums Act of England and Wales, 1964, presents the preamble as "An Act to plan the public library service provided by local authorities in England and Wales under the superintendence of the Secretary of State, and to make new provision for regulating and improving the service. . . ." In the Danish Act 'The purpose of public libraries is to promote the spread of knowledge, education and culture by making books and other suitable materials free of charge.' The purpose of this Act is to foster and promote the establishment and operation of multicounty free public libraries' service throughout the State in order to give to all of its citizens equal opportunity of access to comprehensive library collections. . . .'.[3]

In the nine acts, which are in operation in India the preamble is not so exhaustive. The essential elements like access to information, right to learn, socio-economic aspirations of the people, culture etc. are missing in the preamble.

Ekbote Committee while suggesting the amendments to the Andhra Pradesh Public Libraries Act, 1960 recommended the following preamble: "Whereas it is expedient to organise a State Library system for the purpose of fostering and promoting the spread of knowledge, education and culture, for strengthening the forces of socialism, secularism, democracy and rule of law and by fostering and promoting the establishment and operation of free public libraries comprehensive and efficient service, providing to all the citizens of the State, equal opportunity of access, in rural as well as urban areas freely and for matters connected therewith".[4] So far this seems to be a comprehensive preamble.

The Model Act of Dr. Venkatappaiah spells out the following preamble "An Act to provide for the establishment and operations of an integrated, comprehensive and efficient rural and urban public library service and the recognition of *Right to Learn* including the access to information and educational resources in the State for the socio-economic and cultural aspirations of the people, and the matters connected herewith".[5] This preamble may be acceptable by one and all since it is drafted to suit the changing needs of the society.

Administrative Authority at State Level

Every act should have a focus on Government responsibilities. So much so it is also desirable to keep the responsibility on the Head of the State. If this is not possible, the minister incharge of public libraries shall be held responsible for the development of public libraries. UNESCO document recommends the following ministerial powers:

> An Act must designate the Minister responsible. He will have power normally to :
>
> (i) superintend, promote and secure proper discharge of duties of subordinate bodies;
> (ii) call for information;
> (iii) require entry to premises by his officers;
> (iv) appoint boards and advisory councils and chairmen thereof;
> (v) make schemes for facilitating co-operation and co-ordination;
> (vi) appoint, make or dissolve joint bodies;
> (vii) act as an arbitrator in relation to the service;
> (viii) exercise default powers;
> (ix) exercise reserve powers e.g. in relation to the allocation and use of finance;
> (x) determine level of fees to be charged for specific exceptional services; and
> (xi) establish minimum standards of service.

It is relevant to point out here that the Public Libraries and Museums Act, 1964 of England and Wales stated that "it shall be the duty of the Secretary of State (now Minister of Education) to superintend and promote the improvement of Public Library services provided by local authorities in England and Wales, and secure proper discharge by local authorities the functions in relation to libraries conferred on them as Library Authorities by or under this Act".[7] This section confers wide powers to the Secretary of State for implementing the Act which includes inspection, administrative and fiscal powers. Mr. F.M. Gardner in his book on 'Public Library Legislation' observes that "a responsible Minister or Department of State shall be named for implementation of the Act, with powers to make regulation under it. . .". Similarly Dr. S.R. Ranganathan, in his Model Public Libraries Act, stressed the need for a State Library Authority, with a specific duty "to provide for an adequate library service in the state GRANTHAJAGAT and for the progressive development of institutions devoted to the purpose, and to secure other effective execution by Local Library

Authorities, of the National policy for providing adequate library service to the people"[8] for every locality. On this background Dr. Venkatappaiah proposed the functions of the State Library Authority as mentioned below:

1. He shall promote the public library service in the State.
2. He shall sanction the opening of new branch libraries, village libraries etc., and also taking over the private libraries.
3. He shall overview the functioning of the libraries under the Act, and Act in default, or failure, and to perform any duty by any library authority.
4. He is authorised to make Rules under the Act.
5. He shall develop infrastructural facilities such as buildings, furniture, equipment to all public libraries.
6. He shall arrange subsidy paid to authors in respect of books lent out for home reading from public libraries.
7. He shall also specify, lay down and publish the standards of library service, and see that these standards are strictly observed and that he shall keep the standards under continuous review.
8. Ultimately, he must establish one's right of access to knowledge and information.

The State Library Authority shall be a body corporate, having perpetual succession on a common seal with powers subject to the provisions of this Act, and rules made hereunder, to acquire, hold and dispose of the property and to enter into contracts and shall by the said name sue and be sued.

Keeping this background in view the Model Act of Dr. Venkatappaiah also reiterated that the Minister for Libraries shall be the State Library Authority charged with the responsibility of implementing the provisions of the Act.

Union Library Authority

Dr. Ranganathan recommended for a National Library Authority in the Model Union Libraries Act that the "Union Minister for Education shall be the National Library Authority,"[9] with the functions to establish, maintain and manage system of National Central Libraries and promote and stimulate the establishment of libraries in each constituent State.

State Level Advisory Body

In every Act there is a need for an advisory body at State level to advise the State Government on all matters about library and information services in the State. In all the four Model Acts/Bills there is provision for State Library Council/Committee as advisory body to the government. In the Model Act of Dr. Ranganathan and the Model Bills of the Ministry of Education and Planning Commission the Minister for Education shall be declared as the ex-officio Chairman of the State Library Council/Committee. Dr Venkatappaiah in his Model Act stated that an elected non-official member shall be the Chairman of the State Library Council. Since the Minister is the Chairman of the State Library Authority, with statutory powers it may not be desirable that he should also head the advisory body. If an elected non-official happens to the Chairman of the advisory body, he can tender fair and frank advice on the matters referred to him under the Act or bring the matters to the notice of the Minister. If the advice is to be effective, the body should be independent. If the Minister happens to be the Chairman of an advisory body, the official members will naturally be silent, when discussing a controversial issue and even refrain if voting situation arises, or at some issues they will fall in line with the Minister. So, the experience of the Advisory Committees of the existing Acts warrants that an advisory body must be headed by an elected non-official, with a balanced temperament endowed with a wisdom of learning and culture.

Directorate of Public Libraries

There must be provision in the Act for an independent Directorate of Public Libraries, headed by a professional expert. If this is not clearly stated in the Act, there is every possibility for an appointment of a non-professional as head of the Department, like in Andhra Pradesh and Tamil Nadu States and so on. A professional only can think and plan for the betterment of the profession in a broader perspective. Just as a medical expert is appointed to head a Department of Medical and Health Services, so also a library and information science expert should be appointed to head a Department of Public Libraries. This is a natural justice.

The Directorate of Public Libraries should supervise and control the State Public Library System in the State. It should promote the establishment of Public Library Service so as to achieve the purpose of this Act and ensure proper utilisation of the library fund and also man-power. It should submit to the Government every year through the State Library Council, a descriptive and critical report on working of Public Libraries in the State and give publicity for the progress of libraries in the State including the findings of the inspection and audit parties.

State Library System

As stated in the preamble, the public library system should be comprehensive for providing library service including access to information both in the urban and the rural areas. An effective system should have a State Public Library at the appex. Regional Libraries may be necessary, if the conditions warrant the same. Establishment of a District Public Library is essential at district level. Provision should be made to start as many branches as funds permit. There should also be a provision to start Reference and Research libraries, mobile libraries and book deposit centres.

The structural set-up of the State Public Library system shall be as follows:

1. The State Public Library
2. The Regional Public Library
3. The City Public Libraries
4. The District Public Libraries
5. The Divisional Public Libraries
6. The Mobile Libraries
7. Block Public Libraries
8. The Book Deposit Centres

Administrative Authority at City/District Level

There must be a provision in the Act to constitute City/District Library Authority one for each Municipal Corporation and one for each District for rendering library service in their jurisdiction. These are the corporate bodies having perpetual succession and common seal with power to acquire, hold, dispose of property and to enter into contracts and shall by the said name sue or be sued. The Authorities shall have the elected Chairman and District Librarian or District Library Officer, as the case may be, as the ex-officio Secretary.

Other Boards

There must be some provision in the Act to constitute the following boards and councils on such terms and conditions as the Government may prescribe from time to time:

1. Staff Welfare Board
2. Board of Library Education
3. Book Development Council
4. Adult Education Council
5. Board of Coordination and Standards

The efficient functioning of these boards and councils will help the functioning of libraries on sound lines.

Ignoring the Illiterates

The irony of the library legislation is the collection of library cess even from the illiterates and to spend it only for the benefit of literates. There is a provision in the Model Acts and the Acts of Tamil Nadu, Andhra Pradesh, Karnataka and Haryana about the library cess to be collected under various sub-sections. But it is surprising that there is no stress (except a casual mention) of spending proportionate amount for the benefit of illiterates. Even top level administrators never bothered to spend a single pie for the cause of illiterates.

As per the estimate of the Government of India "the number of literates in the age-group of 15—35 increased in 1981. On the basis of trend analysis the number of illiterates of this age-group is likely to go up to 116 millions by 1991 and decline 110 millions by A D 2001. By 1955 the Government of India has planned to educate 50 millions through massive adult education programme". So it is obligatory on the part of library legislation to provide a legitimate portion of the library cess for the benefit of illiterates.

Financial Resources

The success of the library legislation depends on the financial resources, which it gets through statutory obligation. The generally accepted pattern of financial support is from public fund i.e. library cess from the local bodies. Basically the libraries should not collect any fee directly from the users, since as per the concept of the public libraries service should be free. The experts like Edward Edwards, Dr. S.R. Ranganathan advocated for the collection of library cess, even though it is an additional burden on the public. The Advisory Committee for Libraries (Government of India) headed by Shri K.P. Sinha, examined this issue and opined that "in spite of a strong body of opinion against library cess, the Committee has come to the conclusion that only a cess can provide a stable base of library finance. . . There is also a doubt that library cess alone cannot make the bill, but a simultaneous provision from general revenues could be linked with it so as to share with it an assured annual budget". Experience also proved that library cess collected in Tamil Nadu, Andhra Pradesh and Karnataka States helped for the proper and smooth functioning of the Library Authority in the States. This fact is also to be examined that library legislation is quite successful in the West Bengal State even without collection of a single pie as library cess and at the same time it is to be appreciated that West Bengal Government is allocating the highest budget provision in the country for library service. Having much said and done, it is advisable to have library cess as surcharge on house tax, property tax and other leviable taxes. The State Government should also contribute a matching share to get a stable income to the library authorities for smooth functioning of the Act. For this purpose at State level 'State Library Fund', at district level 'District Library Fund' and in the Union level 'Union Library Fund' are essential. The provisions to this effect should be made while drafting the Bill for the Constituent States or Union Territories.

Accountability

Every Local Library Authority or State Library Authority must have a provision for maintenance of accounts. The accounts of the authority shall be open to the public inspection, and shall be subject to audit, dis-allowance, and surcharge and shall be dealt with in all other respect in such a manner, as may be prescribed.

Again, every Authority must be obliged to submit such reports and returns and furnish such information to the Director or any person authorised by him on his behalf as prescribed in the Act. All the institutions managed by the Authority shall be subject to inspection by an officer for the purpose of satisfying himself that the provisions of the Act and rules and the bye-laws made thereunder are carried out.

Saving Clauses

Any Act, which needs smooth functioning, shall have the following saving clauses. These clauses must be inserted at suitable places.

1. *Delays in the Constitution of City/District Library Authorities:* At times there may be delay in the constitution of the City/District Library Authorities. In such a case there must be some provision in the Act, to appoint the Secretary, Library Authority as Special Officer to manage the affairs of the Authority and to perform the functions of the Chairman, as the case may be, for a period not exceeding six months and they may in the like manner from time to time extend such period beyond six months and the aggregate period including the extended period, if any, shall not exceed two years. The person or persons so appointed shall, subject to the control of the Government and to such instructions or directions as they may issue from time to time, exercise the powers, discharge the duties and perform the functions of the Library Authority and its Chairman, as the case may be, and take all such action as may be required in the interests of the Library Authority.
2. *Action of the Council or Authority not to be Invalidated:* At times there may be same vacancies in the State Library Council or City/District Library Authority for various reasons. In such a case there must be a provision in the Act as saving clause that no action of the Council or Authority shall be deemed to be invalidated by reason only on the existence of any vacancy in or any plan in the constitution of the body.
3. *Removal of Difficulties while Implementing the Act:* There may be some difficulties in working of the Act. In such cases there shall be a provision in the Act to empower the Government to do any thing not inconsistent with such provisions which appear to them to be necessary or expedient for the purpose of removing the difficulty. Every order so made shall be laid, as soon as may be after it is made, before the Legislative Assembly.

NOTES

1. Establishing a Legislative Framework for the Implementation of NATIS. Paris : UNESCO, 1977.

2. Ibid, p. 42
3. Frank M. Gardner, Public Library Legislation: A comparative study, Paris : UNESCO, 1971, p. 276.
4. Report of the Committee to review the working of the APPL Act, 1960 and to suggest amendments to the Act. Hyderabad : Government of Andhra Pradesh, 1978.
5. V. Venkatappaiah. *Working Document of the National Seminar on Model Public Libraries Act*, 1990. Delhi : Indian Library Association, p. 1
6. Ibid, p. 44.
7. Public Libraries and Museums Act of England and Wales, 1964.
8. S.R. Ranganathan, *Indian Library Manifesto*. New Delhi : A B C Publishing House, 1990, pp. 67-68.
9. Ibid, p. 55.

4

MODEL PUBLIC LIBRARIES ACTS : A Historical Study

During the past sixty years of library legislation in India five Model Public Libraries Acts/Bills were drafted as mentioned below:

1.	1930	Model Public Libraries Act, drafted by Dr. S.R. Ranganathan and revised by him many times till his last breath (1972).
2.	1950	Model Union Libraries Act, drafted by Dr. S.R. Ranganathan and revised by him during 1957 and 1972.
3.	1963	Model Public Libraries Bill, drafted by the Ministry of Education, Government of India.
4.	1965	Model Public Libraries Bill, drafted by the Planning Commission, Government of India.
5.	1989	Model Public Libraries Act, drafted by Dr. V. Venkatappaiah and revised by him in 1992.

While studying the historical study of the five Model Acts/Bills mentioned above, we have to study the following items:

1. Historical background
2. Salient features
3. Specialities incorporated
4. Structure of governance and management
5. Feasibility of implementation

The credit of library legislation in India goes to Dr. S.R. Ranganathan, who spared no efforts to enter the library Act in the Statute book of the States. Till his last moments he worked for library legislation. We will now go into details of the first Model Public Libraries Act.

Model Act of Dr. Ranganathan

Madras Library Association founded in 1928 was responsible for library legislation in the Madras province. This Association provided a platform to discuss about the development of library services. The group discussions at the summer schools paved the way for the drafting of Model Public Libraries Act by Dr. S.R. Ranganathan. This draft was discussed thoroughly in the First All Asia Educational Conference held at Varanasi during 26-30 December, 1930 and was accorded general approval.

Changing the Draft

Dr. Ranganathan during his life time improved his Model Act many times, whenever there was an occasion for it. In fact, he had even changed the title of the Model Acts drafted by him.

TABLE 4.1 Improved Model Acts Drafted by Dr. Ranganatan

S.No.	Title	Source
1.	Draft Model Public Libraries Bill	*Five Laws of Library Science* by Dr. S.R. Ranganathan, 1931, p. 256.
2.	State Library Act	*Five Laws of Library Science* by Dr. S.R. Ranganathan, 2nd ed., 1957, p. 208.
3.	Model Public Libraries Act	*Public Library System*, edited by Dr. S.R. Ranganathan and A. Neelameghan, 1972, pp. 39-70.
4.	Model State Libraries Act	1. *Herald of Library Science*, edited by P.N. Kaula, 1972, Vol. No. 11(3). 2. *Indian Library Manifesto by Dr. S.R. Ranganathan*, New Delhi: ABC Publishing House, 1990, pp. 63-96.

In every draft he made some changes in the sections to suit the present needs. However, he did not compromise about the salient features like the following:

1. Constitution of the State Library Authority.
2. Constitution of the District Library Authority.
3. Collection of Library Cess.

4. Autonomy of the Local Bodies.
5. Tapping the local potentialities wherever possible and needed.

The draft of Model Library Act prepared by Dr. Ranganathan contains a number of compulsory clauses. In it library rate was compulsory, library grant was compulsory and library cess from local bodies was compulsory. These compulsory clauses gave hindrance for its enactment in the early days. The salient features of this Model Act are given below:

1. It provides a system of public libraries for the cities, rural and other areas;
2. The constitution of State Library Authority with Minister of Education as the State Library Authority, to provide for adequate library service in the State;
3. The constitution of the State Library Committee for the purpose of advising the State Library Authority on all matters arising out of the Act;
4. The constitution of a Local Library Authority, one for each city and one for each district; and
5. Powers to raise the library cess by the State Library Authority and with the previous sanction of the Government.

Except the Kerala Public Libraries Act, 1989, all the Acts passed from 1948 to 1990 have the influence of Model Public Libraries Act drafted by Dr. Ranganathan.

Model Bill of the Ministry of Education

The Government of India appointed an Advisory Committee on Libraries under Chairmanship of Shri K.P. Sinha, the former Director of Public Instruction, Bihar which was a mile-stone in the planning of library development in India. This Committee submitted its report to the Government of India in 1958. This report suggested to the constituent States a few guidelines regarding public library service and library legislation:

(a) Free public library service with the following objectives:

(i) to house material giving reliable information and wholesome recreation;

(ii) to organise them so as to promote their use; and

(iii) to stimulate non-readers to be readers and readers to be purposive students.

(b) A library rate of 6 *naya paise* in a rupee of property tax to be levied by local bodies and panchayats.

(c) The State Government will aid the local bodies by a matching formula. The law may be brought into operation gradually....

(d) There will be Block Library Funds and the Municipal Library Funds, but the district would be regarded as a unit of library service.

(e) The various units of library service will have their own library committees, as recommended in this Report.

(f) The State will organise a Department of Libraries. The functions of the Department will be generally on lines indicated in the Report.

(g) The State Governments will recognise Library Associations and provide for adequate assistance to them.

(h) Books will form the bulk of library stocks, which must also include newer media of mass communication like audio-visual materials, etc.

As followup action of the Advisory Committee Report, the Ministry of Education, Government of India, constituted a Committee under the Chairmanship of Dr. M.D. Sen, to draft the Model Public Libraries Bill for the States. Accordingly the Committee drafted the Model Library Bill and submitted to the Government of India in 1963. The Government of India circulated this draft to the constituent States for consideration. The 14th All India Library Conference held at Patna during 10-15 April 1964, organised a "Seminar on Library Legislation" and discussed the Model Public Libraries Bill of the Government of India, and amendments were recorded. This seminar apprcciated the Government of India's initiative in preparing the Model Bill and the "conference urged the State Governments to take necessary steps to pass library acts before the commencement of the Fourth Five Year Plan. It is also enjoined upon the State Library Associations to press the State legislators to enact library legislation with a provision to levy library cess." The salient features of this Bill are given below:

1. Establishment of State Library Council, which shall advise the Government with regard to the promotion and development of Library Service in the State. Minister in charge of Education shall be the Chairman of the Council.
2. Appointment of State Library Directorate to look into the administrative and technical matters.
3. Treating the employees of the Public Library System as Government employees.
4. Provision of funds by the Government as per the perspective plan prepared by the State Library Committee.
5. No mention about library cess or legal deposit provision of books and newspapers.

The essential item which is missing from the Model Bill is the State Library Authority which has a dominant place in the Model Library Act of Dr. Ranganathan, and the Hyderabad Public Libraries Act, 1955. It is more practical to make one person ultimately responsible for the authority for the effective function of the Act. The provision of the State Library Authority should, therefore, be added and the powers proposed to be vested in the Government should vest in the Minister of Education as State Library Authority.

Model Bill of the Planning Commission

Finding the need of the hour the Planning Commission in their letter dated 15th June, 1964 constituted a "Working Group on Libraries" to advise on the development of libraries during the Fourth Five Year Plan. The Working Group recommended a Library Development Scheme to be implemented in the Fourth Plan period, with a financial commitment of Rs. 309 millions. During the Plan period it was contemplated to establish new libraries and maintain and improve the existing ones. The Working Group submitted its report on 7th September, 1965. The salient features of this Public Libraries Bill are given below:

1. Provision to establish, maintain and develop an integrated and adequate public library service in the State.
2. Provision of State Library Council to advise the Government in the promotion and development of library service.
3. Provision to establish a Directorate of Public Libraries to con-

trol, direct and supervise the libraries.

4. Establishment of a State Central Library as apex library.
5. Provision to establish the District Library Committees.
6. Treatment of all employees as State Government Servants.
7. No library cess and the State Government shall maintain the public library system in the State.

The Working Group of Libraries "has noted the difference of opinion on the question of library cess, and has, therefore, considered it advisable to leave it to the State Governments to take decision on this issue." This bill was circulated to all the States for necessary action. However, on account of various reasons, this was not considered even in a single State.

Model Act of Dr. Venkatappaiah

Indian Library Association which was formed in 1933 has shown keen interest in library legislation. The ILA circulated the Model Public Libraries Act prepared by Dr. S.R. Ranganathan in 1942 to all the Provincial Governments. After Independence, the Eighth All India Library Conference held at Nagpur during 1949 resolved "to request the Government of India to introduce library legislation with a view to establish a national library system, which would co-ordinate the development of libraries in the country". Similarly, the State Governments were urged to introduce library legislation for the establishment and maintenance of Public Library System in their respective States. As mentioned in the earlier chapter, ILA organised its 14th Conference at Patna during 1964, which discussed the Model Public Libraries Bill of the Ministry of Education, Government of India.

In the year 1978, a Seminar on Library Legislation in India was organised during the All India Public Library Convention held at Delhi. This was followed by a panel discussion on "Public Library Services in Delhi – Need for Library Legislation". As followup action of this seminar, a study was made on the working of the Acts in the States, and the States without legislation were urged to enact library legislation.

In 1981 a Seminar on "A Second Look at the Library Legislation in India" was organised at the 28th All India Library Conference held at Hyderabad, and recommended for the enactment of library legislation in all the States and Union Territories of the country. Likewise in most of the All India Library Conferences the ILA passed resolutions on library legislation and passed on to the State Governments and Union Territories for necessary action. The ILA in its Council meeting held on 23rd June, 1989 at New Delhi agreed in principle to hold one-day Seminar in each State on library legislation where there is no Library Act. The ILA Council also resolved to prepare a model Library Act, keeping in view the recent developments and experiences gained from the existing library Acts. Dr. V. Venkatappaiah, the Chairman, Central Sectional Committee: Public Libraries of the ILA, was asked to prepare a Model Library Act. Accordingly Dr. Venkatappaiah drafted the Model Public Libraries Act. This draft was discussed in detail in a National Seminar on Model Public Libraries Act held at New Delhi on 14th February, 1990, organised by ILA in collaboration with RRRLF, in connection with the 9th New Delhi World Book Fair. The Seminar in principle accepted the draft with a few amendments as suggested by the participants. The proceedings of the Seminar form the Chapter 7 of this book. In the light of the proceedings of the Seminar this Model Public Libraries Act was revised and the full text of the revised draft has been given in the Chapter 9 of this book. The revised Model Act appears to be quite comprehensive both in content and size. The salient features of this Model Act are given below:

1. The Model Act starts with a well built up preamble by giving sufficient provision for the access to information including the recognition of RIGHT TO LEARN.
2. Minister for Libraries to be the Head of the State Library Authority.
3. Function of the State Library Council to advise the Government on all matters connected with the Act, with the elected Chairman.
4. Constitution of the Department of Public Libraries, with a professional as Director to direct and control the Public Library System in the State.
5. Establishment of State Public Library and Regional Libraries to serve as reference and research libraries.
6. Constitution of the City/District Library Authorities to render library service in the respective areas.
7. Establishment of the following bodies to carry out the work assigned to them.

1. State Planning Board
2. Staff Welfare Board
3. Board of Library Education
4. State Book Development Council
5. Adult Education Wing

8. Treatment of the Staff working in the Department as Government employees and their recruitment and conditions of service to be governed under the Article 309 of the Constitution.
9. Collection of Library cess on house tax and property tax and on sales tax, vehicle tax and land revenue, and an equal matching grant from the Government.
10. Accountability of the State Library Authority and District Library Authorities.
11. Provision for public enquiry in case of any irregularity or abuse of power.
12. Protecting the rights of the authors by making tne payments to the authors while lending of books from the libraries.

The States and Union Territories, where there is no library legislation, may adopt this Model Act and make modifications to suit the local needs.

Model Union Act of Dr. Ranganathan

In 1948, the Government of India appointed a Committee to suggest the possibilities of establishing a National Central Library at New Delhi. Dr. Ranganathan as a Member of the Committee prepared the "Library Development Plan – Thirty-Year Programme for India with Draft library Bills for the Union and Constituent States". This Development Plan was discussed in the Committee and approved on 7th April, 1948. Sir Maurice Gwyer, the then Vice-Chancellor, University of Delhi was very much pleased with the draft and got it published in a book-form by the University of Delhi. A more refined version of this Union Bill was published in 1957 in the second edition of Dr Ranganathan's famous work "Five Laws of Library Science".

The salient features of the Model Union Library Act are given below:

1. Constitution of a National Library Authority.

2. Establishment of System of National Central Libraries i.e. National Copyright Library, National Dormitory Library, National Service Libraries etc.
3. Constitution of National Library Committee for the purpose of advising the National Library Authority, on all matters arising out of this Act and referred to it.
4. Constitution of the National Library Fund.
5. Amendment to the Delivery of Books and News Papers Act, 1954.

National Central Libraries

Through the Union Library Act, Dr. Ranganathan conceived a grid of three National Central Libraries:

1. National Copyright Library, which consists of all books deposited under the Copyright Act and the Delivery of Books and News Papers Act. These books will not be lent out, to any but for Court of law and be available for consultation after ten years after the year of publication.
2. National Dormitory Library consists of one bound copy of each of the books weeded out from any of the libraries in the country. These books are to be preserved to serve for specialist readers engaged in antiquarian and bibliographical research.
3. National Service Library consists of books of current value and fairly in frequent demand. The system of National Service Libraries shall include the following subject areas:

    1. National Sciences
    2. Agricultural Sciences
    3. Medical Sciences
    4. Humanities and Generation
    5. Social Science, etc.

It is evident that it may not be possible to pass a Union Library Bill without amending the Constitution of India. In the Constitution the subjects of 'libraries' and 'education' were originally included in the State List. In the 42nd Amendment (1976) education was omitted from the State List and added to the Concurrent List. The subject libraries still remains in the State List. So, it is the State Government's responsibility to pass a Library Act. If the Union Government wants to have a library legislation at national level, it has to amend the Constitution. Till such time, it may not be desirable to think about Union Library legislation.

Opinion of the Experts

Shri Gopal Rao Ekbote, former Chief Justice, Andhra Pradesh State, reiterated that as per the Constitution, the Union Government has no jurisdiction over the State in enacting library law and suggested the amendment to the Constitution. Shri G.C. Bansal, in a paper presenting in the National Seminar on Library Legislation held at Aligarh Muslim University during March 1989, emphatically reiterated that "the Government of India, according to the Constitution, could only confer with and advise the State Government in the matter but had no jurisdiction and power to deal with the matter itself since 'Education' was on the 'State List'. To overcome this hindrance and to extend its jurisdiction the amendment known as "Constitution (42nd Amendment) Act, 1976" came in force with effect from 3 January 1977. According to this amendment, the List II: State List and List III: Concurrent List, is shown in Table 4.2.

TABLE 4.2: Ammended Lists of State and Concurrent

	Original		Amended
	List II State List		
"11.	Education, including technical education, medical education and Universities. .	"11.	. . . .omitted"
	List III Concurrent List		
"25.	Vocational and technical training of labour"	"25.	Education, including technical education, medical education and universities . . . . Vocational and technical training of labour"

As a consequence of this amendment 'Education' which was a State subject before the said amendment was brought on to the Concurrent List, as a part of entry number 25, existing already therein. As such, the Government of India also assumed to itself the power to make Acts relating to 'Education' along with the State Governments. However, the Acts thus made by the Union Government would have precedence over the Acts made by the State Governments in such matters.

From the foregoing analysis it is clear that the subject "Libraries" at present constitutes a part of the subjects enumerated in the State List. Therefore, only the State Governments in India have the power to make laws on the subject. The Central Government has no role to play in the matter".

Let us wait till the date of amending the Constitution of India, to see the Union Library Bill on the statute book of India.

For Further Study

F.M. Gardner : *Public Library Legislation — A comparative study.* Paris : UNESCO, 1971, p. 285.

Gopal Rao Ekbote : *Public Library System*, Hyderabad : Ekbote Brothers, 1987, p. 377.

R.L. Mittal : Public Library : An International Survey, Delhi : Metropolitan Book Co. 1971, pp. xvii, 624.

S.R. Ranganathan : *Library Legislation. A Hand-book to Madras Library Act.* Madras Library Association, 1953, p. 312.

V. Venkatappaiah : *Indian Library Legislation.* Vol. I Union Library Bills and Acts, Vol. II *State Library Bills and Acts.* Delhi : Daya Publishing House, 1990, pp. 12, 179; 12, 326.

5

MODEL PUBLIC LIBRARIES ACTS : A Comparetive Study

In the earlier chapter, we traced the history of the Model Public Library Acts/Bills of the past sixty years in this country. Now we will make a comparative study of these Acts/Bills. While studying them we have to take into account the following items in each Act/Bill as the case may be:

1. Coverage of the preamble
2. Governance of the system
3. Advising bodies at State and district levels
4. Administrative bodies at State and district levels
5. Financial resources
6. Audit, Accounts and Accountability
7. Functionality in rendering effective service.

It will be possible to examine the last one when the Model Act comes into operation in any State or Union Territory. However, it should be noted that library and information services will help for the national development and are vital for all the sectors of national activity. Keeping this basic objective in view we will make a comparative study of the four State Model Acts/Bills and one Union Model Act.

Comprehensive Preamble

The preamble of the Act brings into focus the purpose of legislation in a nut shell and declares the reasons and objectives of library legislation. It should be precise and explicit. Whereas the Model Public Libraries Act of Dr. Ranganathan has a simple Preamble "to provide for the establishment and maintenance of a system of public libraries, and for the comprehensive development and organisation of city, rural and other kinds of library service in the State of Granthajagat, the Preamble of the Model Bill of the Ministry of Education refers to the establishment, maintenance and development of libraries in the State of. . . ." The Model Bill of the Planning Commission simply followed the Preamble of the Ministry of Education. This requires modification in view of the latest developments in the library and information system of India. However, an emphatic and precise Preamble was drafted by Dr. Venkatappaiah in his Model Act, keeping all the latest developments in view, and particularly the proposed National Policy on Library and Information System of the Government of India. The Preamble of the Model Act "provides for the establishment and operation of an integrated, comprehensive and efficient rural and urban public library service and access to information including the recognition of RIGHT TO LEARN in the State, for the socio-economic and cultural aspirations of the people, and the matters connected herewith". The Bills under drafting stage may adopt this preamble, which is quite comprehensive in all aspects.

Out of the four Model Acts or Bills of the State so far drafted, the Model Public Libraries Act of Dr. Venkatappaiah has all the components, such as State Library Authority, State Library Council, with a good nomenclature of the libraries, namely State Public Library, District Public Libraries etc. The word "public" has great relevance than the existing State Central Libraries, District Central Libraries etc. without any functional meaning.

The preamble of the Model Union Libraries Act depicts that "it is expedient to provide for the establishment and maintenance of a system of National Central Libraries". Since this Act has not seen the light of the day, one could not find the impact of this Model Act.

State Level Authority

In the very first Model Public Libraries Act (1930) Dr. Ranganathan, insisted that State Library Authority should be the apex body in the system and that the Minister for Education for the State shall be the State Library Authority. It shall be duty of this Authority to provide for the adequate library service in the State. That is why the Ekbote Committee very strongly reiterated the need of a State Library Authority in the Report. In all the Model Acts or Bills drafted so far, the provision for apex bodies are shown in Table 5.1.

TABLE 5.1: The Provision for Apex bodies

S. No.	State and Union	Advisory or with authority
	MODEL ACTS/BILLS (Guidelines)	
1.	Model Act (SRR)	State Library Authority
2.	Model Bill (Ministry of Education)	State Library Authority (Advisory)
3.	Model Bill (Planning Commission)	Committee of Experts
4.	Model Act (V V)	State Library Authority
5.	Model Union Act (SRR)	National Library Authority

In the opinion of the experts, and in the experience of the developed countries there must be State Library Authority, with the Minister for Libraries as its head and a State Library Committee or Council to advise the Government on all matters pertaining to libraries. Both the bodies are necessary in this system.

National Level Authority

Similarly, Dr. Ranganathan introduced the National Library Authority in the Union Libraries Act and stated that the Union Minister for Education shall be the National Library Authority. The Minister shall establish, maintain and manage a system of National Central Libraries and promote and stimulate the establishment in each constituent State of — a state grid of Public Library System, Hospital Library Service and the Prison Library Service. However, the Union Act did not enter in the statute book for various reasons.

Chief Executive at State Level

While implementing various sections of the public libraries Act, and carrying out the programmes of the Government at State and National level a separate Directorate is necessary. The Director or State Librarian or National Librarian will be the Head of the Department. In all the Model Acts, it was stated that the Head of the Department must be professional. Deviation over this will permit the unqualified persons of the other Departments to enter the Department of Public Libraries and settle there and do all possible harm to the profession through their insufficient knowledge about the subject. The professional organisations have taken the issue seriously and have brought to the notice of the higher authorities that unqualified persons should not have any place in the Department. In the five Model Acts so far drafted the position of the Head of the Department is shown in Table 5.2.

TABLE 5.2: Position of the Head of the Department

S. No.	State and Union	Head of the Department
	MODEL ACTS/BILLS (guidelines)	
1.	Model Act (SRR)	State Librarian
2.	Model Bill (Ministry of Education)	Director of Libraries
3.	Model Bill (Planning Commission)	State Library Directorate
4.	Model Act (VV)	Deptt. of Public Libraries
5.	Model Union Act (SRR)	National Libraries

As per the Model Union Libraries Act, the National Librarian "will arrange for carrying out of any cataloguing, *ad hoc* bibliographies, and the linguistic parts of the National Bibliographies assigned to the National Central Libraries by mutual agreement between him and the *State Librarian* and foreign librarians if any". This sub-section of the Act will facilitate the work of streamlining of the compilations and publications of the bibliographies at State level also.

Such duties can be performed by a professional only. That is why Dr. Ranganathan stated that the Union Government shall appoint the National Librarian by rotation, the librarian of one of the National Service Libraries for a period of five years. However, this provision does not permit the Government to appoint any unqualified person to be the National Librarian.

It will not be possible to have a uniform pattern of designation as the subject 'Libraries' is in the State List. But even in the Act itself there must be some provision that a qualified librarian should only be posted as Head of the Department to produce better results from the legislation.

City/District Level Authority

The functions of the district administrative unit is almost same in all the Model Acts or Bill. In principle, the City/District Unit should function as a corporate body, enjoying the autonomy, as in the case of corporate bodies or universities (Table 5.3).

TABLE 5.3: Functions of the District Administrative Unit

S.No.	State and Union	System
	MODEL ACTS/BILLS (guidelines)	
1.	Model Act (SRR)	Local Library Authority
2.	Model Bill (Ministry of Education)	District Library System
3.	Model Bill (Planning Commission)	District Library Committee
4.	Model Act (VV)	City Library Authority/District Library Authority
5.	Model Union Act (SRR)	—

In addition to the District Library Authority some experts argue for the need of the Authorities at Taluk level also for organising and administering public libraries at lower levels efficiently and effectively.

Chairman of the City/District Authority

The Chairman in the District Library Authority will play a dominant role in providing the library service at the village level, following the guidelines of the State Library Authority. He will exercise general control over the District Library Authority. The model of election or nomination or ex-officio position of the Chairman is given in Table 5.4.

TABLE 5.4: Election/Nomination/Ex-officio position of the Chairman

S. No.	State	Head of the District Library Authority
	MODEL ACTS/BILLS (guidelines)	
1.	Model Act (SRR)	1. For cities Mayor of the Municipal Corporation or the President of the Municipal Council or any other Municipal Body of the city, as the case may be, shall be the Chairman of the C L A.

(Contd.)

TABLE 5.4 (*Contd.*)

S. No.	State	Head of the District Library Authority
		2. For districts the Deputy Commissioner or the Collector, as the case may be, of the district shall be the Chairman of the DLA.
2.	Model Bill (Ministry of Education)	Chairman not mentioned
3.	Model Bill (Planning Commission)	Chairman not mentioned
4.	Model Act (VV)	Chairman (elected)
5.	Model Union Act (SRR)	—

There is a provision for Vice-Chairman also in the Model Public Libraries Acts of Dr. Ranganathan and Dr. Venkatappaiah, to preside over the meeting in the absence of Chairman and perform such other duties as the Chairman may delegate from time to time.

Chief Executives at District Level

The City/District Libraries who is also the ex-officio Secretary of the Library Authorities at City/District have to play a key role in implementing the Act. He is the Chief Executive Officer and responsible for the proper control and supervision of the office of the Library Authority. The position of the Executives in the Model Acts is given in Table 5.5.

TABLE 5.5: Position of the Executives in the Model Acts

S. No.	State	Ex-officio Secretary of the Authority
	MODEL ACTS/BILLS (guidelines)	
1.	Model Act (SRR)	Secretary, City/District Library Authority
2.	Model Bill (Ministry of Education)	Not mentioned
3.	Model Bill (Planning Commission)	Not mentioned
4.	Model Act (VV)	Secretary, City/District Library Authority
5.	Model Union Act (SRR)	—

Library Fund

For the maintenance of the library system at the National, State, District and lower levels, the concerned Authorities shall maintain library fund. This fund consists of these levels:

1. National Library Fund
2. State Library Fund
3. City/District Library Fund

The procedure of the constitution of these funds are given below:

National Library Fund

The Model Union Act of Dr. Ranganathan made a provision for the constitution of National Library Fund with the credit of the following funds:

1. The amount provided by the Parliament for the purpose of the Act;
2. Any other amount provided by the Union Government;
3. Amount collected by each of the libraries under the rules of the library;
4. Amount received from endowment if any; and
5. Any contribution from any person or body of persons.

State Library Fund

The Model Act of Dr. Ranganathan mentions that the grants made by the Government at State and the Centre as per the Report of the Finance Commission, from which the State Government may set apart for library purposes, and contributions or gifts to State Library Authority etc. as mentioned below:

1. Grants made by the State Government.
2. The grants which may be provided by the Government of India or Raja Rammohun Roy Library Foundation etc.
3. Funds and other amounts collected by the State Library Authority under the provisions of the Act.
4. Contributions or gifts or donations or deposits etc. made by

public bodies, private bodies or individuals.

5. All interests and profits accruing from any investment or from any transaction in connection with any money belonging to the Authority.

City/District Library Fund

Every City/District Library Authorities shall maintain a fund called City/District Library Fund, from which all expenses under this Act shall be met. In all the Model Acts of the States, the sums credited to the City/District Library Fund are more or less the same as mentioned below:

1. Library cess collected from the local bodies;
2. Contribution made by the State Government;
3. Any special grants given by the State Government;
4. Any grants given by the Government of India to the State Government for development of public libraries; and
5. Any contributions or gifts made by the public for development of public libraries.

At times, this fund may not be sufficient for the maintenance of public library system. In such cases, the Government will consider to increase the rate of library cess or provide special grants to meet the situation.

Library Cess

Dr. Ranganathan, from the very first Model Act of 1930, was pleading for library cess, may be under the influence of British Library Legislation. There is no mention of library cess in the Model Bills of the Ministry of Education and Planning Commission and in the Model Act for the Union. There is also a provision for getting adequate library cess in the Model Act of Dr. Venkatappaiah. The details are given in Table 5.6.

However it is concluded that levying of library cess is necessary for generation of funds perennially, without depending much on the State budget allocation.

TABLE 5.6: Dctails of Library Cess in the Model Act

S. No.	State	Rate
	MODEL BILLS/ACTS (guidelines)	
1.	Model Act (SRR)	A Library cess in a form of surcharge on -- 1. Tax on lands and buildings; 2. Tax on entry goods into the local area for consumption, use or sale therein; 3. Tax on vehicles and; 4. Tax on professions, trades, callings, and employments-- shall be levied at the rate of three paise on a rupee.
2.	Model Bill (Ministry of Education)	No library cess
3.	Model Bill (Planning Commission)	No library cess
4.	Model Act (VV)	Four paise cess per rupee on property tax, house tax, sales tax, vehicle tax, and land revenue.

For Further Study

Report of Advisory Committee for Libraries, 1958. Delhi : Manager of Publications, 1961, 2nd Ed. p. 6,155.

F. M. Gardner. *Public Library Legislation — A comparative study.* Paris : UNESCO, 1971, p. 285.

Gopal Rao Ekbote. *Public Library System.* Hyderabad : Ekbote Brothers, 1987. p. 377

Report of the Committee appointed by the Government of Andhra Pradesh. Hyderabad : Government of Andhra Pradesh, 1978. p. 134

R.L. Mittal. *Public Library : An International Survey.* Delhi : Metropolitan Book Co, 1971.

R.K. Rout (ed). *Library Legislation in India.* New Delhi: Reliance Publishing House, 1986. p. xiv, 376

S.N. Sidhu and B.N. Sharaf. *Public Library Law.* Delhi : Sagar Publication, 1967. pp xvi, 285

S.R. Ranganathan. *Indian Library Manifesto.* New Delhi : A B C Publishing House, 1990. p. 118

S.R. Ranganathan and A Neelameghan (Eds). *Public Library System.* Bangalore : Sarada Ranganathan Endowment for Library Science, 1972. p. 253

V. Venkatappaiah. *Indian Library Legislation,* Vol. I Union Library Acts and Bills Vol.II State Library Acts and Bills. Delhi : Daya Publishing House, 1990, pp 12, 179; 12, 326.

6

MODEL PUBLIC LIBRARIES BILLS : A Review

Introduction

A library legislation is an instrument for the development of public library services of a country or a state in a planned and co-ordinated manner. The need for organising public library services on legislative footing has been recognised by all international and national expert bodies. According to UNESCO Public Library manifesto, public libraries should be "established under the clear mandate of law, so framed as to ensure nationwide provision of public library service". The Advisory Committee for Libraries set up by the Ministry of Education, Government of India in 1957 recommended that State governments should enact comprehensive State Library Law to provide free public library service to the people. The Committee on National Policy on Library and Information System appointed by the Department of Culture, Government of India or D.P. Chattopadhyaya Committee also reaffirmed in 1986 that each State should enact library legislation with a view to developing a network of public libraries extending from the community library of the village through intermediary levels to the district and to the State Central Library. In our country nine States namely, Tamil Nadu, Andhra Pradesh, Karnataka, Maharashtra, West Bengal, Manipur, Kerala, Haryana and Mizoram have so far enacted library laws. Some more States and Union Territories are contemplating to adopt library laws in the coming years. Chattopadhyaya Committee also suggested revision of the Model Public Library Bill in the light of experience gained in recent years.

Model Public Library Bills

There are three model public library bills or acts in existence. The first

Model Public Libraries Act was drafted by Dr. S.R. Ranganathan as early as 1930. On the basis of this Model Act, draft library bills were prepared by Ranganathan for several States before and after Independence. His ideas as reflected in the Model Public Libraries Act have been finally incorporated in the Public Library Acts of Tamil Nadu (1948), Andhra Pradesh (1960) and Karnataka (1965). In the light of operation of these Acts, Ranganathan revised his Model Public Libraries Act in 1972. The second Model Public Libraries Bill was drafted in 1963 by a Committee under the chairmanship of Dr. M.D. Sen, the then Education Secretary to Government of West Bengal, on behalf of the Ministry of Education, Government of India. The draft bill was finally released with certain modifications in 1965. This was followed by another Model Public Libraries Bill prepared by the Library Legislation Sub-Committee of the Planning Commission in 1966.

A Comparative Analysis

It will be useful to make a comparative analysis of the salient features of the three model bills:

1. *Preamble*

While both the Education Ministry and the Planning Commission bills provide for the establishment, maintenance and development of public libraries, the Model Act of Ranganathan provides for the establishment and maintenance of a *system* of public libraries and for the *comprehensive* development and organisation of city, rural and other kinds of library service. Obviously, Ranganathan has laid clear emphasis on public library system for the organisation of a comprehensive public library service.

2. *Definition of Public Library*

Both the Education Ministry and Planning Commission bills define a public library as a library within the public library system of the State which permits members of the public to use its materials without any fees or subscription. Ranganathan widens the definition of the public library as any library, open to public free of charge and maintained and managed by Government or by any local body; an aided library receiving grant-in-aid from the Government according to prescribed rules and any other library notified by the Government as a public library. Thus, even regularly aided subscription libraries have been brought under the scope of the definition of a public library.

3. *State Library Authority*

Ranganathan's concept of State Library Authority underwent an evolution from State Library Committee to *Minister of Education* in course of the years. The Education Ministry Bill provides for the State Library Authority, a body under the chairmanship of the Minister of Education. But the Planning Commission Bill does not mention any person or body as the State Library Authority which shall provide for an adequate library service in the state. But this responsibility is vested in the State Government in both the Model Public Library Bills.

4. *State Library Committee/Council*

In order to advise the State Library Authority or the Minister of Education there shall be a State Library Committee. The similar advisory body is also recommended by the other two bills. The Education Ministry Bill names it State Library Authority and the Planning Commission Bill terms it State Library Council. All these bodies will be headed by the Minister of Education. Despite differences in nomenclature and composition, the function of this central committee is basically the same i.e., to advise the State Authority or the State Government on all matters arising out of the Act or the Bill.

5. *Directorate of Libraries*

The Education Ministry Bill provides that there shall be a State Library Directorate, under the State Education Department, which will constitute the Secretariat of the State Library Authority. This Directorate will be supervised by a Joint/Deputy Director of Education. The Planning Commission Bill does not specify that it will function under the Education Department. Ranganathan's Model Public Libraries Act of 1972 does recommend for the establishment of a Directorate but, according to him, this should be headed by a State Librarian. He also recommends the setting up of a separate Department of Public Libraries. On the other hand, the Model Public Library Bills prescribe that the State Librarian shall be the Librarian of the State Central Library and will function under the supervision of the Director.

6. *Local/District Library Authority*

Library service is rendered locally by an organisation or institution. In any public library system the nature of local library authority needs to be clearly defined. In the United Kingdom Borough Councils and County Councils have been declared as local library authorities. Following the British model Ranganathan has recommended the constitution of a District Library Authority in a district and a City Library Authority in a city having more than one lakh population. An autonomous Local Library Authority having control over local library fund is an important feature of Ranganathan's Model Public Libraries Act. Though autonomous a Local Library Authority is liable to supersession for failure or abuse of power. The Education Ministry's Model Bill has extended the local units to towns and blocks having control over Town Library Fund and Block Library Fund respectively. The Planning Commission Bill further extended the scope of the District Library System and services to Panchayats and villages. There will be a Library Committee under the former Bill, but no such Committee has been specified for Town Libraries, Block Libraries, Panchayat Libraries and Village Libraries under the latter Bill. Ranganathan's Model Act and Planning Commission' Model Bill to some extent emphasised the need for organising District Library System as a means to extend library facilities to larger sections of the people. But the Education Ministry's Model Bill considered a town and a block to be the lowest viable unit of library service instead of a city and a district.

7. *Public Library Finance*

According to the Model Act of Ranganathan, public library service in a state should be financed by funds carried out of (a) library cess, (b) grants from the State Governments, (c) grants from the Central Government, (d) contribution and gifts, and (e) other amounts collected under the Rules of the Act. All such income will be credited to the State Library Fund or the District/City Library Fund as the case may be. The maintenance of State Library Fund and District/City Library Fund is to be provided by rules to be framed under the Act. The Education Ministry's Model Bill, on the other hand, provides for three kinds of library funds, (a) the State Library Fund, (b) the District Library Fund, and (c) the City or Town or Block Library Fund. This is in consonance with its basic proposition that library service should be provided from three levels — the State level, the district level and the city/town or block level. The Planning Commission Bill has remained totally silent on the creation of funds. It recommends that the State Government shall frame the annual budgets of the Directorate of Libraries and the Pubic Library System in the State keeping in view the perspective plan of library development to be prepared by State Library Council.

According to the Model Public Libraries Act of Ranganathan, for a District Library Authority, a library cess in the form of a surcharge on tax on lands and buildings shall be levied, and for a City Library Authority a library cess in the form of a surcharge on (a) tax on buildings, (b) tax on entry of goods, (c) tax on vehicles and (d) tax on professions, trades etc. As regards Model Public Libraries Bill of the Education Ministry, every local body in a district shall levy in its area a library cess in the form of a surcharge on property tax and transfer the collected amount to each City, Town or Block Library Committee according to the area that is within such city, town or block limits. No library cess has been prescribed in the Model Bill of the Planning Commission.

8. *Other Provisions*

The Model Public Libraries Act also includes provision for State Central Library system. The Education Ministry's Model Bill has laid down the functions of the State Central Library and the District Library somewhat in detail. But the most interesting feature of the Bill is a clause recognising the State Library Association as a co-operating institution and ensuring regular grants to it for professional and cultural activities. The Planning Commission Bill, however, drops the latter provision; it gives more emphasis on the detailed definition of the functions of the State Library Directorate, State Central Library and the District Library. Again, according to Ranganathan's Act every member of the State Library Authority or a Local Library Authority and every officer and servant employed under such Authority shall be deemed to be a public servant. The Education Ministry's Bill has not made any provision to that effect. On the other hand, the Planning Commission Bill provides for the creation of a separate cadre of state library employees and the framing of service rules for various categories of library employees within one year after the constitution of the Directorate.

Impact

As stated earlier, the Tamil Nadu, Andhra Pradesh and Karnataka Public Library Acts were based on Ranganathan's ideas. The Model Public Libraries Bill of the Planning Commission seems to have partially influenced the Maharashtra Public Libraries Act enacted in 1967. This Act has not provided for the imposition of Library Cess and consequently no Local Library Fund or Local Library Authority has been created. It has also opted for a State Library Council instead of State Library Authority. The West Bengal Public Libraries Act, 1979, is a mixture of Madras or Tamil Nadu Public Libraries Act, 1948 and Maharashtra Public Libraries Act, 1967, and was thus indirectly influenced by Ranganathan's Model Public Libraries Act and the Planning Commission's Model Public Libraries Bill in so far as the Act has created Local Library Authorities and Local Library Funds but not imposed any library cess. The Manipur Public Libraries Bill, 1988 is more or less influenced by Ranganathan's model except that it has created only one Library Fund i.e. District Library Fund to be administered by the District Library Authority. The Haryana Public Libraries Act, 1989, on the other hand, is prepared on the basis of the Model Public Libraries Bill of the Education Ministry. But the Kerala Public Libraries Act, 1989 is not influenced by any of the Model Public Libraries Bills. It offers a new but not necessarily a better model of Public Libraries Act. This is in brief the review of Model Library Bills and Acts and their impact on the existing library laws of the country.

Critical Comments

The question of a Model Public Libraries Bill or Act arises because in our country the subject "libraries" comes under the State list, and it is the State Government which can enact a library legislation. While the Central Government and the Planning Commission have accepted the expert opinions for developing library services in the States and Union Territories on legislative basis, they have remained silent on Ranganathan's plea for the adoption of a Union Libraries Act.

A Model Act means an ideal Act, and a single model ignores the feasibility of alternative model(s) of library legislation. An Act may be declaratory or permissive, mandatory or obligatory, controlling or regulatory, constitutional or procedural, creative or developmental and so on. The history of library legislation shows that it differs from period to period, state to state and country to country. But the authors of our model bills and Acts could think of only one model for all types of states irrespective of their size, population and socio-economic conditions. There is no reason why there should be a uniform library legislation for a bigger state such as Uttar Pradesh and a smaller state like Mizoram. It is moot point whether some of the smaller states like Sikkim or Meghalaya having only a very small number of public libraries does not need a library legislation. On the other hand, we have the example of Himachal Pradesh which is experimenting with combined public library service and school library service. It is quite possible to adopt a single library law for school libraries and public libraries, particularly in a small state, having one "Department", one "Directorate" and without a "Local Library Authority". The entire state can constitute a viable unit of library service. It is no longer necessary to confine the classification of library legislation as legislation providing for library cess and legislation without library cess. Another vital consideration is whether a library law seeks to promote library service primarily through voluntary organisations or through Government run libraries or through Government sponsored and aided libraries. In short, there can be different models of library law to meet different situations. In a diverse and big federal country like India we cannot talk of framing only one model public library bill. This consideration has guided the Foundation in issuing an appeal to the states which have not yet adopted library legislation to enact a Public Library Act on any model acceptable to them.

One of the important reasons of library legislation is provision for resources for an adequate public library service. According to Ranganathan, "to make away public fund permanently . . . year after year for a particular service should necessarily have legislative sanction. If we leave it to the Executive, we know the ups and downs that library finance will have to undergo. Anything based on legislation is more stable. Therefore, it is that the public library finance should be legislation based." Thus, in order to secure stable finance for public library service Ranganathan recommended imposition of library cess in addition to government grants to a Local Library Authority. But collection of a small fund by means of library cess does not improve resource position substantially. On the other hand, better library service can be provided by a state which has not adopted a library law but made provision for better funding of service out of the state exchequer. What is needed is an awareness to regard public library service as an essential service involving larger allocation of funds. If the government can provide other essential services like education and health without imposing any cess, it is also expected to provide public library service without cess. Viewed from another angle, if the state is unable to insist on library legislation with library cess or funds are to be raised by cess it should be imposed on a wider base like Sales Tax, Excise Duty, Entertainment Tax etc. and not on Property Tax and other minor taxes only. Considering the divergence of views on the imposition of library cess, the Planning Commission's Model Bill, unlike the other two, provides for state financing of public library service through annual budget. Whatever may be the form of a model library bill, the basic issue is finding adequate resources for public library service, and if that condition is satisfied there need not be any controversy over minor details.

An important feature of a good Public Library Act should be provision for organised co-operation among the libraries under the system. In other words, it should provide for the establishment of an efficient and effective administrative machinery which will render optimum service to the people by organising library services on principles of library co-operation and resources-sharing. Ranganathan's Model Act has recognised this principles of library cooperation and resource-sharing. Ranganathan's Model Act has recognised this principle as it provides for the establishment of the State Central Library and the District/City Central Library Systems. But the Education Ministry and the Planning Commission Model Bills seem to give less emphasis on library networking around a viable central library unit. Public libraries under them tend to continue as independent and isolated units. It will have the implication of minimum service with maximum cost. The need for a library legislation is not merely to ensure regular flow of resources but also to make better use of limited resources for optimum service to the public.

Another aspect which needs closer attention is the size of viable unit of public library service. Ranganathan considered a district and a city having more than one lakh population as a viable unit. According to the Model Bill of the Education Ministry, even a Block can be treated as a viable unit. But the Planning Commission's model bill does not seem to have given any indication on the issue; it has merely provided for the establishment of public libraries by the government, from the state headquarters down to the Panchayat level over a period of time. It may be noted that we have small and backward districts in some parts of the country. Cities over one lakh population are growing in number. The present trend in the western countries is for a larger unit or integration of smaller units for better service.

Conclusion

The Model Public Library Act and Bills were drafted about fifteen to twenty years back. In course of the years some of their provisions have become outdated in their essential features. It is an excellent proposition if we can have a library law with provision for raising adequate resources by taxation. It is equally good if adequate resources for public library services can be ensured from the general fund by law. We may have one model of library legislation for bigger states and another model for small states. The Central Government should not recommend only one Model Bill for all the states. A state should be given the option to choose a suitable bill from a variety of Model Public Library Bills. This has become more evident with the amendment of Andhra Pradesh Public Libraries Act and the enactment of Kerala Public Libraries Act in 1989. Andhra Pradesh has substituted the 'State Library Council' with the 'Grandhalaya Parishad', a smaller autonomous body vested with the responsibility of developing public library services all over the state. Kerala, on the other hand, has created bigger State Library Council and District Library Councils with smaller executive committees to support all categories of public libraries existing in the state. These models are not necessarily the ideal models. In the present context what we can and should recommend is that public library services in a state should be organised on legislative basis with a view to establishing an efficient administrative machinery, ensuring adequate provision of funds and building up of a public library system or network in the state for rendering better library and information service to the public.

REFERENCES

UNESCO Public Library manifesto, 1972.

Report of Advisory Committee for Libraries. Ministry of Education. New Delhi :

Manager of Publications, Govt. of India, 1961.

National Policy on Library and Information System : A Presentation. New Delhi, Department of Culture. 1986.

Model Public Libraries Act, 1930 and 1972 by S.R. Ranganathan.

Model Public Libraries Bill (1963) by the Central Ministry of Education (India)

Model Public Libraries Bill (1966), Planning Commission (India), Library Legislation Sub-Committee.

Tamil Nadu (Madras) Public Libraries Act, 1948.

Andhra Pradesh Public Libraries Act, 1960.

Karnataka (Mysore) Public Libraries Act, 1965.

Maharashtra Public Libraries Act, 1967.

West Bengal Public Libraries Act, 1979.

Manipur Public Libraries Act, 1988.

Kerala Public Libraries Act, 1989.

Haryana Public Libraries Act, 1989.

Andhra Pradesh Public Libraries (Amendment) Act, 1989.

Dr. B.P. Barua, Director, Raja Rammohun Roy Library Foundation. Paper presented at the National Seminar on Model Public Libraries Act held at New Delhi on 14 February 1990.

7

PROCEEDINGS OF THE NATIONAL SEMINAR ON MODEL PUBLIC LIBRARIES ACT : A Report*

The Indian Library Association in collaboration with the Raja Rammohun Roy Library Foundation organised a National Seminar on Model Public Libraries Act on 14 February 1990 at TFAI Auditorium, Pragati Maidan, New Delhi, in connection with the 9th New Delhi World Book Fair, organised during 13-18 February, 1990.

Prof. Krishan Kumar, President, Indian Library Association, in welcoming the delegates stated :

Distinguished guests, ladies and gentlemen, it is my proud privilege and a pleasant duty to welcome you all to the 'National Seminar on Model Public Libraries Act' being organised by Indian Library Association and sponsored by Raja Rammohun Roy Library Foundation.

Information is an intangible entity. There is no doubt that information plays a significant role in all human activities, in one form or the other. Efficient and effective use of information will result in greater national development. As a consequence, it will become possible to improve quality of life, which indeed is the goal.

Western society is information rich, which has enabled them to achieve social, economic and technological progress. Information is power, thus information rich countries are in a position to exploit information poor countries such as India. Now the question before us is, how do we make our society information rich. It is here that public libraries can play a significant role. Our country needs to have a net-

---

* Proceedings of the Seminar on Model Public Libraries Act held on February 14, 1990 in New Delhi, prepared by Shri C.P. Vashishth.

work of public libraries. Public libraries can be used as an instrument of social change, leading to economic revolution. Economic revolution can bring improvement in the quality of life of the masses.

In 1981, we had 437 million illiterates in India. The number of illiterates has gone up. All India literacy rate (1981) was 36.23 per cent. In order to eradicate illiteracy, National Literacy Mission (NLM) was launched in 1988. Its primary aim is to initiate a mass movement to mobilize volunteers for literacy work to impart literacy to 30 million illiterates in the age-group of 15—35 years by the year 1990, and additional 80 million by June 1995. In order to institutionalize post-literacy and continuing education, whereby those who have achieved literacy do not lapse into illiteracy, Jana Shikshan Nilayams (JSNs) are being established. A JSN aims to perform a variety of functions including establishment of a library, a reading room and an information window on developmental programmes.

In case, NLM is to succeed in its objectives, then there would be a need for setting up a network of strong public libraries throughout the country. Well-organized public libraries are crucial for the success of any literacy programme. This will save neo-literates from relapsing into illiteracy.

A public library can serve as an information centre for the community, where literates, neo-literates and illiterates can go for information. Our masses need information for their very survival. They may need information about health, agriculture, rules and regulations concerning local bodies etc. A public library should have printed and non-printed materials for this purpose. Video tapes on family planning, agriculture, avoidance of social evils etc., can be acquired for it so that these can be shown to members of the community. It is a wrong notion that a public library is for the literates only. Neo-literates and illiterates can equally benefit from them. Our country has a rich cultural heritage. It had great libraries in the past. We should be proud of its past. But somehow the great traditions in the matter of libraries have not continued. In respect of public libraries, many parts of the country are facing a drought. Do we want our children and young people to be deprived of the facility of world of books due to none of their fault. Remember future generations will not forgive us for our lapse.

The present support to public libraries is inadequate. In this situation, we cannot expect much from public libraries. If they are still surviving, it must be because they have the necessary will to survive under difficult conditions.

There is a need to set up a network of modern public libraries committed to bring social and economic change in the society, involving these in the programmes meant for the uplift of masses. These programmes may be in the area of education (open university correspondence courses), health, family planning, agriculture, industry etc.

In order to achieve a network of public libraries along modern lines, it becomes essential to enact a comprehensive public library legislation in each state. A legislation would have inbuilt provisions for establishing and maintenance of a sound network of public libraries in the State; able to reach every nook and corner; provide for the training of manpower; list duties and privileges of library staff for state library service etc. Already nine states have a library legislation. We can draw lessons from their experience. Model Public Libraries Act drafted by Dr. V. Venkatappaiah shall be discussed at the National Seminar. Hopefully, the Seminar would be able to make fruitful recommendations, which would help in finalising the draft to take shape as an excellent document. A Model Public Libraries Act in the final form shall provide guidelines for revision of existing Acts. Those States, which do not have Public Libraries Act on their statutes can use it as a basis.

Indian Library Association is committed towards enactment of public libraries legislation in each State of the country. Therefore, we shall take suitable steps to publicize Model Public Libraries Act. We would request State library associations to give the highest priority to the development of public libraries. Enactment of public library can serve as an excellent instrument to achieve such a goal.

Dr. V. Venkatappaiah is to be congratulated for preparing an excellent draft in a short time. He has done a commendable job. On behalf of Indian Library Association, I extend him our sincere thanks.

I must thank the members present here for listening to me patiently. I am sure, we shall have fruitful discussion during the deliberations of the Seminar.

Dr. B.P. Barua, Director, Raja Rammohun Roy Library Foundation and the Director of the Seminar presented a document "Model Public Libraries Bills — A Review" to house, and narrated the salient features of various library acts with critical analysis. In his concluding remarks, he said that "We may have one model library legislation for bigger States and another model for smaller States. These models are not necessarily the ideal models. In the present context what we can and should recommend is that public library service in the State be organised on legislative basis with a view to establishing an efficient administrative machinery, ensuring adequate provision for funds and building up a public library system. I am sure that the Model Public Libraries Act, drafted by Dr. V. Venkatappaiah, will help various States in drafting their Bills, for library legislation".

Shri Tripathi, Joint Secretary, Ministry of Human Resource Development, Government of India inaugurated the seminar and said that "public libraries will play a vital role in disseminating information, knowledge and culture. The public library law will ensure a State-wide provision for public library service". On this occasion, Shri Tripathi released the first issue of *Granthana* a new journal of library studies, sponsored by Raja Rammohun Roy Library Foundation, aimed at publishing original contributions, survey reports, short communications pertaining to library studies with a slant towards public libraries.

Prof. K.A. Isaac, Special Officer (Library) M.G. University, Kottayam inaugurating the Seminar, explained the need for library legislation and salient features of the Kerala Public Libraries Act, 1989, which is entirely framed with a different structure, and with a democratic principle.

Prof. Krishan Kumar, President, Indian Library Association, released the book, *Indian Library Manifesto* by Dr. S.R. Ranganathan, which contains the model library acts for the Union and the States. Prof. Kumar said that it is a timely publication and quite useful in drafting the bills by the Union or States.

Shri C.P. Vashishth, General Secretary, Indian Library Association, proposed the vote of thanks.

Business Sessions

Following the inaugural function, the business session started with the working document of Model Public Libraries of Dr. V. Venkatappaiah, the Chairman, Central Sectional Committee: Public Libraries of Indian Library Association. Dr. Venkatappaiah, explained the need and salient features of the Act in brief as mentioned below:

1. Minister of Libraries shall be the Head of the State Library Authority.
2. Elected Chairman for the State Library Council, who advises the Government on the library matters in the State.

3. Separate Department of Public Libraries with a qualified Director.
4. Inter-link between State level to village level libraries and co-ordination between academic and public libraries.
5. State and Regional Public Libraries to maintain as reference libraries. Specific functions to the State, Regional and District Public Libraries.
6. Election of Chairman and Vice-Chairman of City/District Library Authorities (L A) from among the non-official members.
7. Secretary, Library Authority acts as special officer, when the office of the Chairman is vacant.
8. Advisory Committees for Public Libraries at all levels.
9. State Planning Authority.
10. State Institute of Library Education, Training and Research.
11. State Book Development Council.
12. State Welfare Board.
13. All the Staff Members of the Library Authority treated as Government Servants.
14. Systematic release of grants to aided libraries, as in the case of aided schools and colleges.
15. Adult Education Programmes as part of Public Library Organisation.
16. Mobile Library Service in each revenue division, through mobile van.
17. Functioning of Library Authorities with more autonomous powers.
18. Cess collection on sales tax, vehicle tax and land revenue besides house tax, property tax etc. Deduction of cess at source and remittance to Library Authorities.
19. Institution of State and District Library Funds separately
20. Preserving one copy of the book published in the district in the District Public Library for reference.

Lastly, he said that his mission will be successful, if this draft provokes for a new draft for placing before the Assembly.

Later Dr. P.S.G. Kumar, Head, Department of Library and Information Science, Nagpur University gave the following remarks as a resource person.

Though there were Model Bills drafted by Dr. Ranganathan (1950) and Planning Commission (1965), the document prepared by Dr. V. Venkatappaiah has certain special features, which are unique that way. These include, qualified person as 'Director of Libraries', centralised technical services, maintenance of a register of libraries, well laid-out functions of State Central Library, State Library Service, Board of Library Education, Book Development Council, State Library Fund, etc.

Our definition of public libraries should not be idealistic, but pragmatic and realistic. Public Library system failed in India because we are depending more on government than on public. We should also study the public library pattern in the States where there is no library legislation and find out, how far a library law will bring about desired change. We should also study the role of a public library service to be provided, clientele to be served, system to be developed etc., in the context of library legislation. We should also discuss about "Fee based service against free service", library cooperation, amalgamation of small libraries to make them more effective, inter-library membership, role of local bodies, reserve fund, voluntary services, other than book services, etc. There is a need for 'model rules' along with the 'Model Act'.

Prof. G.V.S.L.N. Raju, Department of Library and Information Science, Andhra University, as a resource person stated the defects, in general in the public library legislation. He congratulated Dr. V. Venkatappaiah, for drafting a Model Public Libraries Act. He said that Indian Library Association should take initiative to work out and persue the matter at the Centre and the States for library legislation.

He further said that a State need not wait till the literacy rate reaches to a particular percentage, finally he hoped that the Seminar would be able to arrive at consensus on the broad guidelines to be followed by the States for their legislation.

Shri K.M. Ujlambkar, Retired Director of Libraries, Government of Maharashtra, as a resource person reiterated the need for library legislation. Shri Ujlambkar stated that we did not want leaders, but we want pleaders for advocating the cause of library legislation. Government of India should at least provide a budget of Rs. 2,300 crores, for rendering public library service in the country. Aided libraries and library associations should be supported by State Government under grant-in-aid provision.

Prof. Kishni Navlani of Punjabi University, as a resource person stated that more emphasis should be given to the local needs while preparing the Model Act. The State and the Centre should spend at least 10 per cent of their education budget for public libraries. Public library service shall be integrated with schools and colleges. The public library service must be reviewed at least once in five years. The word "effective" should be added in the preamble.

After comments of the resource persons the following professionals actively participated in the discussions:

1. Shri Arun Roy, Secretary, Bengal Library Association, Calcutta.
2. Prof. B.P. Mangla, Dean, Faculty of Arts and Head, Department of Library and Information Science, Delhi University, Delhi.
3. Prof. K.A. Isaac, Special Officer, M.G. University, Kottayam
4. Shri S.C. Biswas, Director, Central Secretariat Library, New Delhi.
5. Shri M.K. Jain, N A S S D O C - I C S S R, New Delhi.
6. Shri C.V. Subbarao, Senior Librarian, Indian Institute of Defence Studies and Analysis, New Delhi.
7. Shri N.B. Inamdar, Librarian, Osmania University, Hyderabad.
8. Dr. N.K. Sharma, Head, Department of Library and Information Science, Kurukshetra University, Kurukshetra.
9. Dr. Jaktar Singh.
10. Shri Dey of West Bengal.
11. Shri H.J. Upadhay, Director of Libraries, Government of Gujarat.
12. Shri M.N. Chahande, Director of Libraries, Government of Maharashtra.
13. Shri Hajarika of Assam.
14. Shri Nasib Chand, Librarian, State Central Library, Chandigarh.
15. Shri R.K. Prasad, Indian Institute of Mass Communication, New Delhi.
16. Dr. S.F. Rab, A.N.S. Institute of Social Studies, Patna.
17. Shri S.N. Agrawal of Uttar Pradesh Library Association.
18. Shri Singh, General Secretary, Punjab Library Association..
19. and a few more.

At the end Dr. B.P. Barua, Director of the Seminar stated that the suggestions of the resource persons the delegates will be taken care of properly and hoped that some more States and Union Territories shall have a library legislation soon. In this connection he assured that the

Raja Rammohun Roy Library Foundation will give all assistance to Indian Library Association, in persuing the States about library legislation.

Resolutions

1. The National Seminar on Model Public Libraries Act reiterated the need for Public Libraries Act in all the States and Union Territories and request the concerned authorities to take early steps in this regard.
2. The National Seminar on Model Public Libraries Act, request the State Library Associations to organise seminars at State level and send their recommendations to be incorporated in the final draft.
3. The National Seminar on Model Public Libraries Act congratulate Dr. V. Venkatappaiah, for the excellent working document he has prepared keeping all the earlier model bills, draft bills, and acts and the experience gained in recent years.

   This Seminar also request Dr. V. Venkatappaiah, to prepare the Model rules, for easy adoption while implementing the Act by the States and the Union Territories.
4. The National Seminar on Model Public Libraries Act request the U.G.C. to make adequate provision for the refresher courses for college librarians.
5. The National Seminar on Model Public Libraries Act, authorised the President, Indian Library Association to constitute a sub-committee to initiate library legislation where there are no Acts, and improve the Acts, where there are library Acts in the States.
6. The National Seminar on Model Public Libraries Act congratulated the organisers of Indian Library Association and Raja Rammohun Roy Library Foundation for organising the Seminar at a proper time.

8

MODEL PUBLIC LIBRARIES ACT

CHAPTER 1

PRELIMINARIES

1. **Preamble**

An Act to provide for the establishment and operation of an integrated, comprehensive and efficient rural and urban public library service and recognition of *Right to Learn* including the access to information and educational resources in the State for the socio-economic and cultural aspirations of the people, and the matters connected herewith —

BE it enacted by the Legislature of the . . . . State . . . . in the . . . . year of the Republic of India as follows:

2. **Preliminaries**

   1. This Act may be called the . . . . Public Libraries Act, 19 . . . .
   2. It shall extend to the whole of the State of . . . .
   3. It shall apply to all public libraries established, or maintained and administered by Government and City/District Library Authorities (hereafter called as 'Library Authorities').
   4. It shall apply to all public libraries fully or partly financed by the Government and the Library Authorities.
   5. It shall also apply to academic libraries located in Universities, Colleges and Schools in some areas as may be prescribed.

3. **Commencement**

It shall come into force on such date as the Government may, by notification, appoint and they may appoint different dates for different provisions and for different areas.

CHAPTER 2

TERMINOLOGY

4. **Definitions**

In the Act, unless the context otherwise requires:

1. *Academic library* means a library maintained by a Research Institution, University, College or School.
2. *Aided library* means a library declared by the Director to be eligible for aid either from the Government or from the Library Fund in accordance with the rules made under this Act.
3. *Book deposit centre* means a place where few books are kept and returned at certain intervals to the neighbouring library.
4. *Book* includes (1) every volume, part or division of a volume be it a printed book or manuscript or a microforms or a video, audio cassette or a photograph; (2) every sheet of music map, chart or plan separately printed or lithographed; (3) news papers, periodicals and other such materials.
5. *City librarian* means the librarian appointed to be incharge of City Public library and other libraries under the control of City Library Authority.
6. *City library authority* means a Library Authority constituted for a city under Section and sub-divisions.
7. *Competent authority* means any person, officer or any authority authorised by Government by notification to perform the functions of the competent authority under this Act for such area or for such purposes as may be specified in the notification.
8. *Compensatory allowance* means the travelling allowance, the daily allowance or such other allowance which is paid to the members of the State Library Council, Local Library Authorities and their Sub-Committees for the purpose of meeting the personal expenditure incurred by them in attending the meetings or in performing any other functions as such members for the purposes of this Act.
9. *Correspondent* means the Secretary or Executive Officer or Sarpanch as the case may be, of the recognized aided library.

10. *Department* means the Department of Public Libraries as indicated under Section 18.
11. *Director* means the Director of Public Libraries appointed under Section 18.
12. *District Librarian* means the librarian appointed to be incharge of District Public Library and other libraries under the control of Local Library Authorities.
13. *District* means a revenue district excluding the cities in it.
14. *District Library Authority* means a Library Authority constituted for a revenue district.
15. *Division* means revenue division.
16. *Government* means the Government of . . . .
17. *Hamlet* means a population cluster with less than 1000 people.
18. *Library Cess* means the cess levied under Section 86.
19. *Microform* means a generic term indicating any form of micro record such as microfilm, microfiche etc., whether on a flat or roll film, paper etc.
20. *Mobile Library* means a library on a vehicle, covering several service points in a period.
21. *Notification* means a notification published in the . . . official Gazette.
22. *Prescribed* means prescribed by rules made under this Act.
23. *Professional Librarian* means a person qualified by education, training, study and experience of practical library work in a position requiring knowledge of books and of library aims and techniques to that attained through graduation from a library school accredited by an university or Government.
24. *Public Library* means–

    (i) any library established or maintained by City/District Library Authorities including the branches, the mobile libraries, village libraries, and book deposit centres of such a library;
    (ii) any library established, maintained and managed by the Government and declared open to the public;
    (iii) any library established or maintained by a local body or co-operative society or religious endowment or registered body and declared open to the public;
    (iv) any library declared to be eligible for grant-in-aid and receiving aid from the Government or from the Library Fund; or Raja Rammohun Roy Library Foundation; and

(v) any other library notified by the Government as a public library for the purposes of this Act.

25. *Public Library System* means a library system consisting of a State Public Library, Regional Public Libraries, District Public Libraries, Divisional Public Libraries, *Mandal* or Block Libraries, Village Libraries, Book Deposit Centres, Mobile Libraries and other connections and subsidiaries as may grow up in connection with it.
26. *Recognised Library* means a library recognised by the Director in accordance with the Rule made under this Act.
27. *Reference and Research Library* means a library containing reference books, periodical volumes and other reading materials which may not normally lentout and which has research facilities.
28. *Resource Centre* means collection of books or non-book materials of all kinds which are relevant sources of information and instruction in a public or academic library.
29. *Section* means section of the Act.
30. *State* means the State Government or the Union Territory Administration, as the case may be.
31. *State Public Library* means a library established by the Government as the State Public Library under Section 22.
32. *State Librarian* means the State Librarian appointed under Section 23.
33. *State Library Authority* means the Authority under Section 5.
34. *State Library Council* means the committee constituted under Section 8.
35. *State Owned Library* means a library maintained by a Department of the Government, the State Legislature, the High Court, or any other Court or any other Government body.
36. *Regional Public Library* means a library established under Section 26 by the Government as a Regional Public Library.
37. *Town* means a population cluster with 5000 or more people but less than 1,00,000.
38. *Village* means a population cluster with 1,000 or more people but less than 5,000.
39. *Year* means the financial year.

CHAPTER 3

STATE LIBRARY AUTHORITY

5. Minister as State Library Authority

The Minister for libraries shall exercise a general responsibility for the overviewing the function of the public library system in the State. He shall establish, maintain and develop, an integrated comprehensive and efficient library service in the State.

1. The Minister for libraries shall be the State Library Authority charged with the duty of implementing the Act.
2. He shall promote the Public Library Service in the State.
3. He shall sanction the opening of new libraries and also taking over of private libraries.
4. He shall overview the functioning of the libraries under the Act, and act in default, or failure, and to perform any duty by any library authority.
5. He is authorised to make Rules under the Act.
6. He shall develop infrastructural facilities such as buildings, furniture and equipment to all public libraries.
7. He shall also specify, lay down and publish the standards of library service, and see that these standards are strictly observed and that he shall keep the standards under continuous review.
8. He shall arrange the subsidy paid to the authors in respect of books lentout for home reading from the public libraries and exercise control over the Public Lending Right of books and protect the authors from exploitation.
9. He shall organise adult education activities in the State.
10. He shall appoint and control the staff as may be necessary for the efficient performance of duties and functions under the Act and the Rules made thereunder.
11. He shall exercise such other powers and perform such other duties conferred on him by this Act and the Rules made thereunder.

Structure under

MODEL PUBLIC LIBRARIES ACT

State Government

State Library Authority

State Library Council (Advisory)

Directorate of Public Libraries

State Public Library		Directorate of Public Libraries	City	District
1. Administration Wing	Regional/ Public Libraries	1. State Planning Board	City Library Authority	District Library Authority
2. Legal Deposit Wing		2. State Board of Library Education	City Public Library	District Public Library
3. State Library for the Blind		3. Staff Welfare Board		Mobile Library
4. State Bureau of Inter-Library Loan		4. Book Development Council		Block Public Libraries
5. Bureau of Technical Services			Mobile Library	Village Public Library
6. State Institute of Library Education			Public Library	Book Deposit Centre
7 Services, Reference and Research Wing				
8. Adult Educatin Wing				

6. Corporate Body

The State Library Authority shall be a body corporate, having perpetual succession on a common seal with powers subject to the provisions of this Act, and rules made hereunder, to acquire, hold and dispose of property and to enter into contracts and shall by the said name sue and be sued.

7. General Control and Supervision

He shall have general control and supervision of all types of State owned and State assisted libraries in the State.

CHAPTER 4

STATE LIBRARY COUNCIL

8. Constitution of the Council

As soon as may be, after the commencement of this Act, the Government shall, by notification, constitute for the purpose of the Act, a Council called . . . . State Library Council. The Council shall consist of:

1. *Chairman* elected by the Council at its first meeting after its formation from amongst the non-official members of the Council.
2. *Two Members* elected by the Legislative Assembly and one from the Council of the State (if there is a Council).
3. The Secretary to the Government – in the Finance Department.
4. The Secretary to the Government – in the Education Department.
5. *One Person* nominated by Government from amongst the recognized library associations.
6. *One Librarian* nominated by the Government from among the University Libraries in the State.
7. *State Librarian* of the State Public Library.
8. *Two Persons* co-opted by the State Library Council at its meeting for their special knowledge of libraries.
9. *One Person* nominated by the Raja Rammohun Roy Library

Foundation.

10. Director of the Department of Information and Public Relations.
11. *Three* members nominated by Government from among the Chairman of the City/District Library Authorities.
12. *Director of Public Libraries* shall be the Member-Secretary of the Council.

9. **Functions of the Council**

1. It shall exercise leadership in library matters throughout the State.
2. It shall bring administration nearer to the people. It shall shape the library planning and policy and make provision for the specific knowledge and training of staff in those major areas of interest, which are primarily concerned with the success of the movement in the State.
3. It shall be advisory in nature, and a source of expert opinion for the development of library service so as to advise and guide progress of libraries in the State.
4. It shall bring matters of importance on Public Library Service to the notice of the Minister and also advice on any matter referred by the Minister.
5. It shall make recommendations regarding the development, co-operation and co-ordination of library service in the State.
6. It shall initiate any proposal or approve any plan regarding the libraries.
7. It shall guide and direct the improvement of the library services and the implementation of the Act.
8. All the reports required to be placed on the table of the legislature, must be considered first by the Council.
9. It shall report to the Government, every year its findings, regarding the working of the Public Libraries Act and the achievement of standards.

10. **Co-option of Members in Default of Election**

If any of the bodies referred to in Section 8 and its sub-divisions do not, by such period as may be prescribed co-opt a person to be a member of the State Library Council to the vacancy, a person qualified for election thereto and the person so co-opted shall be deemed to be a member of the Council as if he had been duly elected by the said body.

11. **Vacancies**

Any vacancy occurring in the office of a nominated or elected member of the Council before the expiration of his term shall be filled by nomination or election as the case may be, and the person so nominated, or elected shall hold office for the residue of the term of his predecessor.

12. **Term of Office**

1. Every member of the Council other than an ex-officio member, shall hold the office for a period of three years from the date of his election or nomination as the case may be.
2. Provided that such term of a member nominated or elected shall come to an end as soon as the member ceases to be a member of the body from which he was nominated or elected.
3. An outgoing member shall be eligible for re-election or re-nomination, as the case may be, for one more term only.

13. **Disabilities for Continuing as Member**

If any member other than an ex-officio member of the State Library Council, during the period for which he has been nominated or elected:

1. Absents himself without excuse sufficient in the opinion of the Council, from three consecutive meetings of the Council; or
2. In the case of a member elected by any body ceases to be a member of the body concerned, his office in the Council shall become vacant.

14. **Disqualifications**

A person shall be disqualified for being chosen as and for being a member of the State Library Council:

1. if he has been sentenced by a criminal court for an offence involving moral turpitude and punishable with imprisonment for a term exceeding three months, such sentence, not having been subsequently reversed, quashed or remitted unless he has, by order,

which the Government is hereby empowered to make in this behalf, been relieved from the disqualification arising on account of such sentence;

2. if he is an undischarged insolvent; and
3. if he is of unsound mind and stands so declared by a competent court.

15. **Meetings of the Council**

1. The State Library Council shall meet at least four times in an year on dates fixed by the Chairman. One of such meetings shall be the annual meeting.
2. The Chairman may also, whenever he thinks fit, convene a special meeting of the Council for the transaction of urgent business.
3. Subject to prescribed conditions, special meetings shall be convened by the Chairman to discuss matters of urgent importance upon a requisition by members of the Council.
4. One-third of the total number of members of the Council shall be the quorum for a meeting of the State Library Council.
5. The Chairman, if present, shall preside over every meeting of the Council. In the absence of the Chairman, the members present at the meeting shall choose one from among themselves to preside.

16. **Procedure of the Council**

The State Library Council shall transact business in such manner and in accordance with such procedure as may be prescribed.

17. **Act of the Council not to be Invalidated**

No act of the State Library Council shall be deemed to be invalidated by reason only on the existence of any vacancy in or any defect in the Constitution of that Council.

CHAPTER 5

DEPARTMENT OF PUBLIC LIBRARIES

18. Separate Department

1. For the purpose of this Act, a Department of Public Libraries shall be constituted by the State Government with a Director of Public Libraries as its head and other professionals as officers – as the State Government may think fit.
2. The State Government shall appoint officers having the prescribed professional qualifications to practise the library profession.

19. Functions of the Department

1 The Department of Public Libraries under the Director of Public Libraries shall:

1. supervise the State Public Library and Regional Public Libraries and its branches;
2. superintend, direct, control and deal with all matters relating to Local Library Authorities and other Public Libraries;
3. promote the establishment of Public Library service so as to achieve the purpose of this Act;
4. prepare short-term and long-term plans and also supervise the implementation of the approved plan;
5. ensure proper utilisation and control of the Library Fund and also manpower at State and District levels;
6. centralise all impersonal technical work such as acquisition, classification and cataloguing, and co-ordinate the selection, service and maintenance of reading and kindred materials in the Public, Academic, Departmental libraries of the State, according to the agreed conditions;
7. recognise the library associations working in the State;
8. carry out such of the recommendations of the State Library Council as have been approved by the State Government;
9. declare in accordance with the rules made under this Act, what libraries are eligible for aid from the Government;
10. organise National Library Week, seminars, conferences and

book exhibitions etc.;

11. maintain a register of libraries and librarians in the State;
12. fix minimum standards of library service by various libraries under the Department and assist the libraries in maintaining the standards, prepare standard designs for library buildings, equipment, furniture, fittings etc.;
13. fix the boundaries of operation of all Public Libraries and of different libraries in the State;
14. submit to Government every year through the State Library Council, a descriptive and critical report on working of Public Libraries in the State and give publicity for the progress of libraries in the State including the findings of the inspection and audit parties;
15. provide an infrastructure for community information service in all the public libraries in the State;
16. superintend, direct and deal with all matters relating to the Press and Registration of Books Act, 1867 (Central Act 25 of 1867) and maintain and manage the State Copyright Library;
17. assist the State Library Authority and carry on the correspondence and exercise the powers assigned to the Director by it in the discharge of its duties and the exercise of its powers in regard to this Act; and
18. perform such other duties and exercise such other powers as are imposed or conferred by this Act or the Rules made thereunder.

CHAPTER 6

PUBLIC LIBRARY SYSTEM

20. **Pyramidical Structure**

The structural set-up of the State Public Library system shall be as follows:

1. The State Public Library
2. The Regional Public Libraries
3. The City Public Libraries
4. The District Public Libraries
5. The Divisional Public Libraries
6. The Mobile Libraries

7. The Block Public Libraries
8. The Village Public Libraries
9. The Book Deposit Centres

and public libraries located in educational institutions, hospitals and prisons, the libraries under Gram Panchayats, Municipalities, temples, and voluntary organisations and any other library in a village or town or city recognised by the Government as public library.

21. **Maintenance of the Link**

1. An integrated link from the State Public Library to the village libraries shall be maintained for the organisation of the library service in the State.
2. The activities of the libraries in the State shall be co-ordinated.
3. There shall be active co-operation of the libraries in different managements, provided they are State-owned or State-assisted libraries.

CHAPTER 7

STATE PUBLIC LIBRARY

22. **Apex Library**

There shall be a State Public Library located in the State Capital, as a reservoir of books and other materials, for the proper functioning of the State Public Library system.

23. **State Librarian**

1. A wholetime officer having the prescribed professional qualifications to practise the library profession shall be appointed by the State Government as the State Librarian.
2. The State Librarian shall be assisted by technical and non-technical staff in running the library.
3. The status of a State Librarian shall be that of Joint Director of the Department.

24. Functions of the State Public Library

The functions of the State Public Library shall be as follows:

1. to function as a reference and research library;
2. to provide leadership in all activities in the field of libraries;
3. organise a survey and research unit and continuously carry on survey and research on different aspects of the library work;
4. to provide documentation and information services to all and in particular to the Legislative Houses and other Departments of the State Government;
5. to arrange exhibitions and other extension activities on a more meaningful and large scale;
6. to maintain and manage the State Dormitory Library made of atleast one sound copy each of the books weeded out by any library in the State on account of its having become outmoded in content and presentation, in order to meet the demand, at any time from any person engaged in antiquarian or bibliographical research; and
7. to prepare annual report on the functioning of the library.

25. Wings of the State Public Library

The State Public Library should have the following wings:

1. *Administrative Wing*
2. *Legal Deposit Wing*: The State Librarian shall be the officer to discharge the duties and to exercise the powers regarding legal deposit laid down in Parts III and V of the Press and Registration of Books Act of 1867. This wing will also act as Bureau of Bibliographies in the State.
3. *State Library for the Blind*: The State Public Library may maintain a State Library for the Blind for the production, storing and serving of books, sound record of books, and other kindred materials for the blind. The State Library for the blind may collaborate with the National and other State libraries for the blind and undertake such works as may fall to its share by mutual agreement. The carriage of the books for the blind between the State Library for the blind and the blind readers within India shall be done by the Postal Department free of

postal charges.

4. *State Bureau of Inter-Library Loan*: The State Public Library shall maintain a State Bureau of Inter-library Loan. The State Bureau of Inter-Library loan may include in the scheme of inter-library loan the public libraries, and such outlier libraries as are willing to join the scheme on such conditions as may be agreed upon. The State Bureau of Inter-State Library Loan may enter into any scheme of Inter-State library loan as may be agreed upon by the participating States.
5. *State Bureau of Technical Service:* A State Bureau of Technical Service may be maintained by the State Public Library for centralised technical services, such as acquisition, classification, and cataloguing of books for the public libraries and such outlier libraries as are willing to join the scheme on such conditions as may be agreed upon. The Bureau of Technical Service may collaborate with similar bureaus of other States and of the Central Government, and undertake such technical work as may fall to its share by mutual agreement with the participating bureaus.
6. *State Institute of Library Education, Training and Research:* The State Public Library shall maintain the State Institute of Library Education, Training and Research with the following functions:

   (i) to organise inservice training programme for both trained and untrained personnel;
   (ii) to conduct field survey and research;
   (iii) to organise special training programmes;
   (iv) to act as an accrediting and certifying agency for the existing training agencies for the under-graduate level courses; and
   (v) to keep standards in the library training institutions.

   A professional not below the rank of a Deputy-Director shall be kept incharge of each wing mentioned in Section 25.
7. *Services, Reference and Research Wing*

8. *Adult Education Wing*: Ref: Section 81-82.

CHAPTER 8

REGIONAL PUBLIC LIBRARIES

26. Regional Libraries

There shall be Regional Public Libraries in the State, covering different regions in the State. They shall be wholly financed by the State Government.

27. Regional Librarian

1. A whole time officer having the prescribed professional qualifications shall be appointed by Government as Regional Librarian.
2. He shall be assisted by the technical and non-technical staff in running the library.
3. The status of a Regional Librarian shall be that of a Deputy Director.

28. Functions of the Regional Public Library

The Regional Public Library shall have the following functions. It shall:

1. function as reference and research library for the region.
2. organise inter-library co-operation including inter-library loan.
3. participate in the adult education activities.
4. set standards for the Library Authority and their branches, Book Deposit Centres and Mobile Library Services.
5. compile bibliography for the region as well as prepare the Union Catalogue for the region.
6. inspect and supervise Library Authority in the region and provide them technical advice and assistance.
7. serve as an essential link between the State Public Library on the one hand and the Library Authorities in their region on the other.
8. plan the development of library service in the region and implement the same in a phased manner.
9. should act as referral centre of the region.

10. collect manuscripts of the region and transfer them to the State Oriental Manuscripts Library through the Director, and
11. prepare and submit annual report on the working of the library.

CHAPTER 9

CITY/DISTRICT LIBRARY AUTHORITIES

29. Constitution of Library Authorities

1. For the purpose of organising and administering the Public Libraries in the State, there shall be constituted a Library Authority, one for each city and one for each district.
2. Every Library Authority shall by the name of the area for which it is constituted will be a body corporate having perpetual succession and a common seal with power, subject to the provisions of the Act, to acquire, hold and dispose of property and to enter into contracts and shall by the same name sue and be sued.

30. Composition of City Library Authority (CLA)

The City Library Authority (CLA) shall consist of:

1. Two persons from the city nominated by the Government who have rendered eminent service to the cause of public libraries of whom one shall be a lady.
2. Two members elected from among themselves by the presidents of the general bodies of the aided public libraries in the city.
3. Three members elected by the Councillors of the Municipal Corporation from among themselves.
4. One member nominated by the Government from among the members of the recognised library associations working in the city.
5. One librarian of an academic library within the city area nominated by the Government.
6. The District Adult Education Officer.
7. The Deputy Director, Department of Information and Public Relations or Culture.
8. The Executive Engineer, Roads and Buildings.
9. The City Librarian of the City Public Library who shall be the

Member-Secretary of the CLA.

31. **Election of the Chairman and Vice-Chairman**

City Library Authority shall elect one of its members to be its Chairman, and Vice-Chairman in its first meeting from amongst non-official members:

32. **Composition of the District Library Authority (DLA)**

The Library Authority for each district shall consist of the following members.

1. Two Presidents of Panchayat Samitis or equivalent body nominated by Government.
2. One person nominated by the Government from amongst the *sarpanchas* of the Gram Panchayats of each Revenue Division in the District.
3. One person elected by the Council from amongst the Councillors of each Municipal Councils in the District.
4. One Librarian of any Degree College nominated by the Government.
5. District Adult Education Officer or his nominee not below the rank of Gazetted Inspector of the district concerned.
6. One member elected by the presidents of the governing bodies of aided public libraries in the district.
7. Two persons nominated by the Government, who have rendered eminent service to the cause of libraries or adult education.
8. One person nominated by the Government from among the recognised library associations working in the district concerned.
9. The District Public Relations Officer.
10. The District Librarian, District Public Library who shall be the ex-officio Secretary of the Library Authority and of each of the Committees and Sub-committees of the said Authority.

33. **Election of the Chairman and Vice-Chairman**

Every Library Authority shall elect from amongst non-official members one of its members to be its Chairman and another to be Vice

Chairman in the first meeting.

34. Nomination of Members in Default of Election

If any of the bodies referred to in Section 30 or 32 does not, by such periods as may be prescribed, elect or nominate a person to be a member of the City Library Authority or the District Library Authority, as the case may be, the Government shall, by notification nominate to the vacancy a person qualified for election thereto; and the person so nominated shall be deemed to be a member of the Authority as if he has been duly elected by the said body.

35. Vacancies

In the event of a vacancy arising out of death, resignation, disability or otherwise, before the expiry of the term of office of any library authority, other than an ex-officio member, the vacancy shall be filled by election or nomination as the case may be, of another person in the manner provided in Sections 30 and 32 as the case may be and the person so elected or nominated to fill the vacancy shall hold office only so long as the member in whose place he is elected or nominated would have held office if the vacancy had not occurred.

36. Term of Office

1. Save as otherwise provided in this Act the term of office of any member of any Library Authority other than ex-officio members, shall be for a period of five years commencing from the date on which the first meeting was held after the election of Chairman of the Library Authority.
2. An outgoing member of any Library Authority shall be eligible for re-election or re-nomination for not more than one term.

37. Disabilities for Continuing as Member

Any member, other than an *ex-officio* member, of any Library Authority, shall be deemed to have vacated his office during the period for which he has been nominated or elected, if:

1. A member elected by any body referred to in Sections 30 and

32 as the case may be, ceases to be a member of the body concerned, or

2. Absents himself, without excuse sufficient in the opinion of the Library Authority from three consecutive meetings of the Library Authority.
3. When a person ceases to be a member under Sections 30 and 32, the Secretary shall at once intimate the fact in writing to such person and report the same to the Library Authority at its next meeting. Where such person applied for restoration of membership to the Library Authority on or before the date of its next meeting or within fifteen days of the receipt of such intimation, the Library Authority may at the meeting next after the receipt of the application or *suo motu* restore him, as member thereof. Provided that a member shall not be so restored more than twice during his term of office.

38. **Disqualification**

A person shall be disqualified for being chosen as and for being chosen as a member of the Library Authority, if:

1. he has been sentenced by a Criminal Court for an offence involving moral turpitude and punishable with imprisonment for a period of more than three months, for any offence involving moral delinquency, such sentence not having been restored or the offence pardoned and a period of such sentence:

   Provided that the Government may direct that such sentence shall not operate as a disqualification, if he:

   (i) is of unsound mind and stands declared by a competent court;
   (ii) is a deaf, mute or is suffering from leprosy;
   (iii) applied to be adjudicated as an insolvent or is an undischarged insolvent;
   (iv) absents himself from three consecutive meetings without excuse sufficient in the opinion of the Authority to exonerate the absence.

Where a person ceases to be a member under sub-sections mentioned above, the Secretary shall at once intimate the fact in writing to such person and report the same to the authority in the next meeting. Where such person applies for restoration of membership to the authority or before the date of its next meeting or within fifteen days of the receipt by him of such information, the authority may, at the meeting next after the receipt of the application, or *suo motu*, restore him as member thereof:

Provided that a member shall not be so restored more than twice during his term of office.

39. Meetings of the Library Authorities

1. Every Library Authority shall meet at least four times in a year on dates to be fixed by the Chairman of the Library Authority.
2. The Chairman may also, whenever he thinks fit, convene a special meeting of the Library Authority for the transaction of urgent business.
3. Subject to prescribed conditions, special meetings shall be convened by the Chairman to discuss matters of urgent importance upon a requisition by the majority of the members of the Library Authority.
4. A Library Authority shall transact business in such manner and in accordance with such procedure as may be prescribed.

40. Powers and Duties of Chairman and Vice-Chairman

1. The Chairman of a Library Authority shall:

   (i) preside over the meetings of the Library Authority;

   (ii) watch over the financial and executive administration of the Library Authority and exercise general supervision and control.

2. In the absence of the Chairman, the Vice-Chairman present at the meeting shall preside over the said meeting.
3. In the absence of Chairman and Vice-Chairman, the members present at the meeting shall choose one from among themselves, to preside over the said meeting.
4. The Vice-Chairman shall also exercise such powers and per

form such duties of the Chairman as the Chairman, may from time to time as delegate to him.

5. The Chairman and members shall be paid compensatory allowance and provided comforts on par with the Chairman and members of the Zilla Parishad.

41. **Powers and Functions of the Library Authorities**

1. It shall be the duty of every Library Authority to provide library service including access to information to the persons residing in the area within its jurisdiction.
2. It shall establish a City Public Library and other Public Libraries including access to information and in every District establish a City Public Library and at least one Public Library for a population cluster of 5000-25000 and a mobile library for each Revenue division, subject to financial position of the City/District Library Authority.
3. It shall provide such libraries with books, periodicals, newspapers, maps, works and specimen of art and science, films, video, recorders, computers, gramophone records and the like.
4. It shall shift the library from one village to another village or close any Public Library or discontinue any other public library the payment of which is regulated by the rules made under this Act.
5. It shall accept any gift or endowment for any purpose connected with its activities.
6. It shall provide for lectures and conduct other activities connected with public library service including adult education.
7. With the consent of the management and the previous sanction of the Government or an officer authorised by the Government in this behalf, the Library Authority shall acquire any library on such condition as may be approved by the Government or an officer authorised by the Government in this behalf.
8. It should develop community services in the district.
9. Distribute grants for aided public libraries and adult education centres.
10. It shall organise or participate in conference for the discussion of matters relating to the development of public libraries and the library service.

11. With the sanction of the Government it shall do any other thing that may be conducive to the furtherance of the purpose of this Act.
12. It shall exercise such other powers and perform such duties as may be conferred or imposed by or under this Act.

42. **Appointment of the Committees**

1. A Library Authority may appoint a Committee and delegate to such Committee any of its powers or functions under this Act, except the power to levy library cess, to borrow money, to dispose of immovable property and to pass the budget, accounts and the audit and annual reports.
2. A Library Authority may also constitute the following committees:

   (i) The Executive Committee shall be responsible for the executive functions of the Library Authority.

   (ii) The Book Selection Committee for the selection of books and periodicals for the libraries.

   (iii) The Lands and Buildings Committee for examining the proposals for acquisition, sale or gift of land deeds for the library authority and for examining and passing the proposals for the repairs, betterment of the existing buildings or construction of new buildings.

   (iv) The Grant-in-aid Committee for recommending the quantum of grant to be released to aided libraries.

   (v) The Appointment Committee for appointment of the staff required for the Library Authority.

   (vi) The Finance Committee to scrutinise proposals for increase of revenue, examine the receipts and expenditure statements, consider all new propositions affecting finance and to generally supervise the revenue and expenditure of the Library Authority.

   (vii) Staff welfare committee will redress the grievances of the staff working in the Library Authority.

3. The Chairman of the Library Authority shall be the *ex-officio* Chairman of all the committees.
4. The Secretary of the Library Authority shall be the Member

Secretary of all the committees.

5. The members of any committee shall not exceed five including Chairman and Secretary.

43. **Advisory Committees or Reader's Forums**

For the purpose of advising on local requirements relating to library service of each public library shall have the Advisory Committees or Reader's Forums which consist of:

1. the librarian who shall be the *ex-officio* Secretary of the Committee.
2. one member of the Library Authority representing the area which the Public Library services or the Municipal Council or other Municipal Corporation or the Panchayat having jurisdiction over the area, nominated by the Library Authority concerned shall be the President of the Committee.
3. one teacher of educational institutions, and two borrowers of the library will be nominated by the City/District Library authority as the case may be.

44. **Term of Office**

The nominated members of the Library Advisory Committee shall hold office for a period of five years.

45. **Vesting of Properties in Library Authorities**

1. All the property acquired or held in any area by the Library Authority for the purpose of any public library shall vest in the Library Authority of that area.
2. Any immovable property required by the Library Authority shall be deemed to be land needed for a public purpose within the meaning of the Land Acquisition Act, 1894 (Central Act of 1894) and may be acquired under this Act.

46. **Act of the Council not to be Invalidated**

No act of the City/District Library Authority shall be deemed to be invalidated by any reason only on the existence of any vacancy in or any defect in the Constitution of that Authority.

CHAPTER 10

CITY/DISTRICT PUBLIC LIBRARY AND ITS BRANCHES

47. City/District Units

There shall be a City Public Library for each City and District Public Library in each district headquarters, as a reservoir of books and other materials for the public library system under the control of City/District Library Authority as the case may be. It will open the branches wherever possible as per its rules.

48. City/District Librarian

1. A wholetime officer having the prescribed professional qualifications shall be appointed by the State Government as the City/District Librarian.
2. He shall be assisted by the technical and non-technical staff in running the library.
3. The status of a City/District Librarian should be that of Assistant Director.

49. Functions

The functions of a District Public Library shall be as follows:

1. To provide reference and bibliographical service in the district.
2. To give special reference service to the members of the Municipal Council/Corporation of the town/city, in which it is situated.
3. To give special service to student-groups, study circles and other educational groups.
4. To extend library-service in the urban and rural areas by setting up branch libraries, mobile libraries and deposit centres and to extend similar service in the district through the various block libraries and other library units.
5. To feed Block/Libraries with supply of suitable books.
6. To co-operate with and help the subscription libraries in the

district in accordance with the instructions of the Director.

7. To co-operate with other institutions and groups especially the social education institutions and workers, in promoting library mindedness among the people.
8. To arrange conferences, camps and seminars of librarians, and other library workers in the district, and
9. To provide refresher courses for workers in the District Library system.

50. **Sections of the City/District Public Library**

The City/District Public Library shall have the following sections:

1. Lending Section
2. Reference Section and City/District Information Unit
3. News-papers and Periodicals Section
4. Text Book Section
5. Children and Women Section
6. Processing Section
7. Administrative Section
8. Adult Education Section
9. Cultural Activities and Extension Programmes Section

CHAPTER 11

STATE PLANNING BOARD

51. **Purpose of the Board**

For the purpose of advising and guiding the library system in preparing the plans and schemes, the Government shall constitute a State Planning Board.

52. **Head of the Planning**

It will be headed by an officer not below the rank of a Deputy Director.

53. **Norms of Planning**

The State Planning Board shall prepare the norms for the district, region and State plans and they shall be approved by the Government.

54. **Submission of Plans**

1. The City/District Library Authority, at least once in five years wherever, it considers necessary so to do, prepare a scheme for establishing libraries and for spreading library service within its area in such form and manner as may be prescribed. It will submit the plan to the Regional Librarian.
2. The Regional Librarian, adding the plan of his library, consolidate the plan of the region and submit it to the State Librarian.
3. The State Librarian in-turn adding the plan of his library and consolidate the plan of the State and submit it to State Planning Board.
4. Keeping in view of the existing library services provided by all libraries and then making the plan for covering the remaining area by providing library services.
5. The State Planning Board may sanction it with such alteration, if any, as it may think fit after giving the Library Authority or Region an opportunity to make its alterations and thereupon shall give effect to the scheme sanctioned by the said Board.
6. The Board, on application of the Library Authority or region, may modify any scheme sanctioned or replace it by a new scheme.
7. The Board shall conduct constant evaluation of library service to facilitate better planning.
8. The Board shall conduct surveys or sample surveys whenever or wherever necessary.

55. **State Planning Council**

1. The Government shall constitute a State Planning Council, consisting of the following:

    1. Minister for Libraries, who shall be the Chairman.
    2. The Secretary to Government in Education Department.
    3. The Secretary to Government in Planning Department.
    4. The representative of Raja Rammohun Roy Library Foundation.

5. Librarian, State Public Library.
6. Two Chairmen and two Secretaries of the Library Authorities.
7. Director of Public Libraries who shall be the convenor of the Council.

56. **Functions**

It shall be the function of the Council to draw up a plan for library planning for the State and submit it to the Government for consideration and integration with the general economic plan of the State.

57. **Term of Office**

1. The term of office of the members of other than the *ex-officio* members of the Council, shall be two years.
2. The Council shall meet at such times and such places, and shall observe such rules and procedure in regard to the transaction of business at its meetings, as may be prescribed.

CHAPTER 12

STATE LIBRARY SERVICE

58. **Categories of Posts**

1. Notwithstanding any thing in the Act the Government shall, by notification, constitute a State Library Service of appointing the staff in the Department.
2. The State Library Service shall consist of the following categories, namely:
   1. Director
   2. Joint Director
   3. Deputy Director
   4. Assistant Director
   5. Librarians (all cadres)
   6. Card Writers

   and some other categories, as may be notified by Government.
3. The Government by notification may fix the categories in this Department with other Departments.

59. State Library Service

1. All the posts in the Department of Public Libraries whether they exist in State Public Library or Regional Public Libraries or any library working under the Library Authorities shall be filled by appointment of persons belonging to State Library Service.
2. All members of such service shall be Government servants.
3. Their recruitment and conditions of service shall, subject to Article 309 of the Constitution, be regulated by rules, and
4. The salary, allowances, gratuity, pension and other benefits of the members of the State Library Service shall be met from the Consolidated Fund of the State.

CHAPTER 13

STATE WELFARE BOARD

60. Recognition of the Staff Associations

The State Government may grant recognition to the Staff Associations, on such terms and conditions as may be prescribed.

61. Welfare Board

1. The Government may constitute a Staff Welfare Board consisting of the representatives of the:

   (i) Government and Library Authorities,
   (ii) Staff, and
   (iii) Experts from similar organisations to deal with the matters pertaining to the Library Authorities.

2. The term of office and procedure to follow, may be prescribed.
3. It shall meet on such times, and under such rules or procedure in regard to transaction of business, at its meeting as may be prescribed.

62. Welfare Fund

The Government may constitute a Staff Welfare Fund on such terms and conditions as may be prescribed.

CHAPTER 14

STATE BOARD OF LIBRARY EDUCATION

63. Board of Library Education

The State Government shall constitute a Board of Library Education consisting of the following:

1. The Director of Public Libraries who shall be the Chairman of the Board.
2. One University Librarian in the State.
3. The Librarian, State Public Library.
4. One representative from the recognised training institutes (by turns).
5. Two experts in library education nominated by the Director.
6. The Director of State Institute of Library Education and Research shall be the convenor of the Board.

64. Functions of the Board

The Board of Library Education shall have the following functions:

1. To frame regulations and syllabus for the courses;
2. To formulate the standards in library education;
3. To review the position of library education from time to time; and
4. To advise the Government in the matters of library education.

65. Term of Office etc.

1. The term of office other than the *ex-officio* members of the Board shall be three years.
2. It shall meet at least once a year.
3. It shall observe such rules and procedure in regard to transaction of business at its meeting as may be prescribed.

CHAPTER 15

STATE BOOK DEVELOPMENT COUNCIL

66. Constitution of the Council

1. Minister for Libraries, who shall be the Chairman.
2. The Secretary to Government in Education Department.
3. The Director of Printing and Stationery.
4. One representative from Raja Rammohun Roy Library Foundation.
5. One representative from State Academies (by turns).
6. One expert from the book publishing field of the State.
7. The Director of Adult Education.
8. Two representatives from the City/District Library Authorities.
9. The Director of Public Libraries, who shall be the convenor of the Council.

67. Functions

The .... State Book Development Council shall have the following functions. It shall:

1. produce books on functional topics, which contribute to the cultural, social and economic development of the State;
2. produce books on functional literature for neo-literates;
3. produce books for children;
4. produce forms, registers, codes and manuals for the department;
5. promote book industry in the State, by assisting the publishers in rendering expert advice and in designing the books;
6. produce rare books and reference books, needed by libraries which the publishers do not generally venture to publish;
7. distribute the books of the Government and State sponsored Academies to the libraries in the State;
8. serve as a Resource Centre to administer the book acquisition programmes of the department, or any agency commissioned to organise this work;
9. produce non-book materials for the use of libraries;
10. produce brain gain games equipment for the use of children's libraries and children's sections in libraries; and

11. produce publicity material for the department.

68. **Procedure of the Council**

The Council shall meet at such times and such places, and shall observe such rules or procedure in regard to the transaction of business at its meetings, as may be prescribed.

69. **Term of Office**

The term of office of the members other than the Ex-officio members of the Council, shall be two years.

70. **Head of the Council**

An officer not below the rank of a Deputy Director, shall be the head of the Council.

CHAPTER 16

AIDED LIBRARIES

71. **As Part and Parcel of Public Library System**

All the aided libraries in the State shall be treated as part and parcel of Public Library System of the State. They should be given encouragement so as to function as independent units.

1. The Government should minimise the Registration charges for registering the aided libraries under Societies Registration Act.
2. The powers of Registration shall be vested with the Library Authority and recognition with the Director.
3. The Government should formulate the Grant-in-Aid Code, keeping in view of the growing needs and provide grants every year on the lines of grant-in-aid code of the aided schools and colleges.
4. The Library Authorities should provide technical advice and assistance to the aided libraries.
5. They should bring them within the system for the purpose of inter-library co-operation including inter-library loan.

6. The library Authorities should include all these libraries in their developmental schemes and five year plans.
7. The Library Authorities should include the activities of Library Authorities in the Administrative Report along with the critical remarks and appreciation, if any.

72. Absorption of Aided Libraries in the System

All the aided libraries should be absorbed in the State Library System, in course of time, so that the larger units of libraries can serve the people comprehensively and efficiently.

73. Allocation for Grant-in-Aid

The Government shall within the limits of its economic capacity set apart a sum of money annually for being given as Grant-in-Aid (hereafter in this Act referred to as grant) to the aided libraries and adult education centres.

74. Authorities which may Sanction Grant

1. The Government may in such cases as they think fit, by order, sanction grant to any recognised library or adult education centre subject to such conditions as they may impose in that order relating to such grant.
2. Every grant sanctioned under sub-section (2) shall be disbursed by the Director or such other officer subordinate to the Director as the Government may by a general or special order authorise in this behalf in such manner and subject to such conditions as may be prescribed:

   Provided that the institution already in receipt of grant before the commencement of this Act shall continue to receive such grant subject to such conditions as may be prescribed.
3. The correspondent of every recognised institution which is receiving any grant out of State Funds shall be responsible for the fulfilment of all the conditions subject to which such grant has been given.
4. Any money received by way of voluntary donation from donors shall be accepted by the institution and the fact intimated within forty days from the date of such acceptance to the competent authority.

75. Application for Sanction of Grant

1. Every application for the sanction of grant shall be made to the Government through the Director, in such form as may be prescribed and shall contain a declaration signed by the manager of the recognised institution to the effect that the conditions of recognition and of grant are being and shall continue to be fully observed, that all facilities for inspection of that institution, its accounts, registers and other records relating to the grant shall be afforded to the Inspecting staff deputed for the purpose and that all the returns and reports prescribed in this behalf shall be submitted to the competent authority within the time specified by it.
2. The Government, may sanction such grant or for good and sufficient reasons may refuse to sanction such grant.
3. Subject to the other provisions of the Act, any order passed by the Government refusing to sanction the grant shall be final.

76. Power of Government to Withold, Reduce or Withdraw Grant

1. Notwithstanding anything in this chapter the Government may, after such enquiry as they may deem fit, withhold, reduce or withdraw any grant payable to the public library having regard to the funds at the disposal of the Government, the conduct and efficiency and the financial condition of such library after giving an opportunity to the correspondent of the library concerned of making a representation against such withholding, reduction or withdrawal.
2. Without prejudice to the generality of the provisions of sub-Section (1) or any other provision of this Act, the Government may, after such enquiry as they may deem fit, withhold, reduce or withdraw any grant payable to any public library:

   (i) if the correspondent of the institution concerned fails to fulfil all or any of the conditions of Grant;
   (ii) denies admission to any citizen on grounds, only of religion, race, caste, language or any of them;
   (iii) allows any members of the staff employed in the library to take part in any agitation intended to bring or attempt to bring into hatred or contempt or intended to excite or

attempt to excite disaffection towards the Government established by law in India;

(iv) directly or indirectly, encourages any propaganda with the deliberate intention of outraging the religious feelings of any class of citizens of India or insulting the religion or the religious beliefs of that class;

(v) is guilty of falsification of registers, or misuse of funds or otherwise for purposes other than those for which they are collected;

(vi) fails to remedy within such reasonable time as may be specified by the competent authority the defects in the maintenance of accounts pointed out by the auditors; or

(vii) fails to restore within the time specified by the competent authority, an employee whose services have been wrongfully dispensed with or fails to pay him any arrears of salary or other benefits when directed to do so by the competent authority.

77. Utilisation of Funds and Movable Property

1. All the monies collected, grants received and other movable property held by, or on behalf of private libraries shall be utilised for the purpose for which they are intended, and shall be accounted for by the correspondent in such manner as may be prescribed.
2. All the monies received or held by or on behalf of every private library shall be deposited in a bank.
3. The surplus fund of every such library shall be invested in the Government securities or in such other manner as may be prescribed.

78. Management, Handover of Properties, Records etc.

1. In the event of the aided library being closed down or discontinued or its recognition being withdrawn, the management shall hand over or cause to be handed over to the competent authority all the properties, records and accounts of the institution in its possession.
2. Where the competent authority is resisted in, or prevented from, obtaining the possession of properties, records or accounts of

the institution by such management, any magistrate of the first class having jurisdiction, shall, on an application made by the competent authority, by order, after notice to the management, direct delivery of the possession of such properties, records or accounts of the library to the competent authority within the time specified in such order.

3. Where the management fails to deliver possession of the properties, records or accounts within the time specified in the order of the magistrate under clause (1), he shall be punished with imprisonment which may extend to six months or with a fine which may extend to one thousand rupees or with both and the magistrate shall cause the possession of the properties, records or accounts to be delivered to the competent authority taking such police assistance as may be necessary.

79. **Restriction on Alienation of Property of Private Institutions**

1. Notwithstanding anything in any law for the time being in force, no sale, mortgage, lease pledge, charge or transfer of possession in respect of any property of a private library shall be made or created except with the previous permission in writing of the competent authority on an application made in this behalf.
2. No permission applied for under Sub-section (1) shall be refused by the competent authority except where the grant of such permission will, in its opinion, adversely affect the working of the institution.
3. Any person aggrieved by an order refusing permission under sub-section (2) may, in such manner and within such time as may be prescribed, appeal to the prescribed authority.
4. Any transaction made in contravention of sub-section (1) shall be null and void.

80. **Liability of Management to Repay the Debts**

Where any management incurs debts for running a library, it shall be the personal liability of such correspondent to discharge the said debts.

CHAPTER 17

ADULT EDUCATION

81. Programmes of Adult Education

The Government shall constitute a separate agency in the State Public Library to take up activities in the post literacy part of adult education towards the process of life-long education.

The State Librarian is responsible for supervising and carrying out all the adult education activities all over the State. He may delegate the supervising powers to Regional Librarians to watch the progress of adult education.

For promoting adult education in the State the Government shall:

1. involve all the public libraries in programmes of the Total Literacy Mission;
2. raise community awareness about literacy problems.
3. sanction grants to City/District Library Authorities for conducting various adult education programmes in their respective areas;
4. constitute a State Book Development Council for the production of books etc. for adult education and manuals for instructors and learners; and
5. publish books and charts for the post-literacy programmes publicise these programmes.

82. Adult Education in the City Districts

The City/District Library Authorities should take up programmes of adult education. The City/District Librarians are responsible for successfully carrying out the programmes of adult education in the city or district as the case may be. For purposes of conducting adult education activities the Library authorities should:

1. start adult education centres at mandal and village level;
2. appoint branch librarians or teachers or social workers to conduct adult education classes;
3. allot reasonable funds for adult education activities in the annual budget while submitting the budget for approval to the Director of Public Libraries,

4. co-operate with the voluntary organisations engaged in the campaign of removing illiteracy; and
5. stock books, periodicals and non-book materials such as audio visual equipment for that purpose.

CHAPTER 18

CO-ORDINATION AND INTEGRATION

83. **Purpose**

The public libraries should co-ordinate and integrate the activities of various types of libraries, with regard to selection of books, standardisation processing work, inter-library loan and organising of seminars etc.

84. **Guidelines for Co-ordination and Integration**

For purpose of strengthening the bonds of coordination and integration guidelines should be evolved in the following areas of activity:

1. in selection of books and periodicals including the procurement of rare and costly books;
2. in preserving back volumes of periodicals and serials;
3. in standardising the processing work;
4. in implementing the Inter-Library Loan Code;
5. in organising seminars, National Library Weeks, symposia and cultural activities;
6. integrating work of other departments;
7. in co-ordinating with other agencies like:

   (i) Department of Information and Public Relations and Culture;

   (ii) Directorate of Field Publicity, Government of India;

   (iii) State Academies, such as Literary and voluntary organisations; and

   (iv) Professional organisations.

85. Inter-Library Loan and Union Catalogue

An officer not below the rank of an Assistant Director shall act as co-ordinator, who shall also be the Ex-officio head of the State Bureau of Inter-Library Loan. In order to promote library co-operation and inter-library loan the following points are to be born in mind by the authority concerned:

1. A book on the shelf of any library should be made available to any reader whatever be his own service library. To know what books and other materials are available in a particular library, there is need to publish Union Catalogues at the State, regional or district level so that the entire book-resources of the State may be known to all.
2. For standardising all the processing and promoting inter-library loan specific codes and rules have to be formulated.
3. The head of the State Bureau of Inter-Library Loan shall take steps to publish the Inter-Library Loan Code, Union Catalogues, and such codes as may be necessary with the assistance of the State Librarian, Regional Librarians and the Library Authorities.

CHAPTER 19

FINANCE AND ACCOUNTS

86. Library Cess

1. With effect from the date of commencement of this Act, library cess in the form of surcharge at the rate of four paise per rupee on the following taxes be levied and collected by the agencies which collect the taxes and it be remitted to the State Library Fund.

   (i) Sales Tax
   (ii) Vehicle Tax
   (iii) Land Revenue

2. The Library cess collected on property tax and house tax by the Local Bodies shall be remitted to the City/District Library Fund.

87. **Government Grant**

1. The State Government should contribute an amount not less than the total amount of cess collected on the above said three taxes or 6.5 per cent of the education budget which ever is higher. The State Government contribution on the cess collected on sales tax, vehicle tax and land revenue should be credited to the State Library Fund. The grant may be increased as and when new areas are covered by the library service.
2. The Central Government should contribute 6.5 per cent of their Education budget for the development of libraries in the country and distribute the same equitably amongst all the States.
3. The Local Bodies, that is to say, the Municipal Corporation, the Municipalities, Zilla Parishads, Panchayat Samities and Gram Panchayats should contribute an amount not less than 2.5 per cent of their total budget to the City Library Fund or District Library Fund as the case may be.
4. The Government should help the backward districts by evolving suitable criteria in order to ensure equal library service to the people of the State.

88. **Method of Cess Collection**

1. The cess collected on the property tax as well as the land revenue, sales tax and vehicles tax should be deducted by the Government at source and remitted to the Library Funds of City/District or the State, as the case may be.
2. The probable amount of Library Cess due under the preceding year to a Library Authority from each of the local bodies in the district shall be paid by the Government in advances from the grant or other amount payable, by the Government to that local body.
3. If no grant or other amount is payable to a local body by the Government or if the grant amount payable is not sufficient to cover the Library cess due, the whole of the amount of the cess or such portion of it remains unrecovered shall be deemed to be a loan granted by the Government to the local body concerned under the law relating to the grant of loans to local bodies in force from time to time.
4. The Library cess levied on the property tax shall be collected by

the local bodies, and the procedure for the demand, levy and collection of the property tax shall, *mutadis mutandis*, apply to the demand, levy, and collection of the library cess.

5. The local bodies shall reimburse themselves by collecting the library cess along with the property tax. If the tax collected is more or less than the sum mentioned in sub-section (2) of the section, the difference shall be adjusted in the manner prescribed.

89. City/District Library Fund

Every City Library Authority and the District Library Authorities shall maintain a fund called the City Library Fund and the District Library Fund as the case may be, from which all the payments under this Act shall be met. The following sums shall be credited to the City/District Library Fund namely:

1. The cess collected under sub-section (2) of Section 86.
2. The grant under sub-section (3) of the Section 87.
3. Contributions, gifts and income from endowments made to the Library Authorities for benefit of public libraries.
4. Special grants from State Government or Central Government or Raja Rammohun Roy Library Foundation as the case may be.
5. Funds and other amounts collected by the Library Authorities rules or bye-laws made under this Act.

90. State Library Fund

1. The State Library Authority shall maintain a fund called the State Library Fund from which all its payments under this Act shall be met.
2. There shall be credited to the State Library Fund the following sums, namely:

    (i) The grants made by the State Government to the State Library Authority to perform the duties entrusted to it;

    (ii) Grants which the Central Government or Raja Rammohun Roy Library Foundation may make;

    (iii) Contributions and gifts made to the State Library Authority;

(iv) All proceeds of the disposal of the property by or on behalf of the State Library Authority;

(v) Funds and other amounts collected by the State Library Authority under the rules or bye-laws made under this Act;

(vi) All interests and profits arising from any investment or from any transaction in connection with any money belonging to the State Library Authority.

91. Application of Library Fund

1. The moneys in the State Library Fund, the City/District Library Fund shall be utilised by the State Library Authority, the City/District Library Authority for carrying out the purposes of this Act.
2. Without prejudice to the generality of sub-section (1) the moneys in the Library Fund may be utilised to defray expenditure on the following:

(i) Establishment, maintenance and development of public libraries.

(ii) Compensatory allowance payable to the members of State Library Council and Library Authorities and the Committees and Sub-committees appointed by the State Library Council and the Library Authorities.

(iii) Grant-in-Aid to public libraries, library associations, adult education centres received for the purpose by the Government.

(iv) Other necessary expenditures.

92. Accounts

1. An account shall be kept of the receipts and expenses of the State Library Authority and of each City/District Library Authorities.
2. The accounts shall be open to inspection and shall be subject to audit, disallowance and surcharge and shall be dealt with in all other respects in such manner as may be prescribed.

CHAPTER 20

REPORTS, RETURNS AND INSPECTIONS

93. Reports and Returns

Every Library Authority and every person in-charge of public library shall submit such reports and returns and furnish such information to the Director or any person authorised by him in this behalf.

94. Annual Report

The Director shall in respect of each financial year, prepare an annual report of the progress made by the Library Authorities and Government Libraries during the year along with such information and particulars as may be prescribed and submit such report to the State Government through the State Library Council before such date as the State Government may by order specify.

95. Inspection

1. The appropriate Library Authority as mentioned below shall inspect any library under its jurisdiction for verifying whether the provisions of the Act, Rules and Bye-laws made thereunder are duly observed by the libraries.

Authority	*Body*
1. Government	Directorate
2. Director	State Public Library
3. State Librarian	Regional Public Library
4. Regional Librarian	Library Authority and District Public Libraries
5. District Librarian	Divisional and Taluk Libraries
6. Block Librarian	Aided Libraries

An Officer in a superior cadre can always visit a subordinate office, generally or on a specific purpose, as per the rules in vogue.

2. In all the cases, after such inspections are made the inspecting officer shall submit a detailed report of his inspection to the appropriate library authority.
3. The appropriate library authority may consider the report and pass such resolution as it may deem fit. The resolution shall be observed by the library concerned unless it is suspended or cancelled by the Government.
4. For carrying out the provisions of the Act, the State Library Authority shall prepare an Inspection code.

CHAPTER 21

RULES AND BYE-LAWS

96. **Power to Make Rules**

1. The State Government may, after previous publication, by notification make rules to carry out the purposes of this Act.
2. In particular and without prejudice to the generality of the foregoing power, such rules may provide for:

1. *General Rules*

1.1 General Clarifications
1.2 A few definitions
1.3 Rules starts ...
1.4 Publication of Bye-laws

2. *Administrative Authorities*

2.1 Constitution of the State Library Council
2.2 Constitution of the City Library Authority
2.3 Constitution of the District Library Authority
2.4 Activities of the Chairman and Vice-Chairman
2.5 Activities of the Secretary
2.6 Bye-laws for conducting the meetings

3. *Data and Planning*

3.1 Data on the Public Library Management
3.2 Data on the Public Libraries

3.3 Data on the librarians working in the public libraries
3.4 Library development plans
3.5 Annual Report

4. *Development of Assets*

4.1 Opening of new libraries
4.2 Taking-over of the libraries
4.3 Acquisition of immovable properties
4.4 Supply of materials, goods etc.
4.5 Construction and repairs of the buildings

5. *Personnel Management*

5.1 Constitution of the Public Library Service
5.2 Creation of posts
5.3 Control over the staff
5.4 Conduct rules of the employees

6. *Finance and Audit*

6.1 General Rules
6.2 Operation of Library Fund
6.3 Payment of Advances
6.4 Pensionary Benefits to the employees
6.5 Preparation of Annual budget
6.6 Collection of library cess
6.7 Audit and accounts
6.8 Inspection

7. *Grant - in - Aid*

7.1 City/District Library Authority
7.2 Other Public Libraries
7.3 Raja Rammohun Roy Library Foundation
7.4 Professional Organisations and Grant-in-Aid
7.5 General rules of Grant-in-aid

97. Approval of the Rules

Every rule made under this Act shall, as soon as after it is made, be laid before each house of the State Legislature while it is in session for a total period of thirty days, which may be in one session or in two or more sessions and if before the expiry of the session in which it is so laid or the sessions immediately following, both houses agree in making any modification in the rule or both houses agree that the rule should not be made, the rule shall thereafter have effect only in such modified form or be of no effect, as the case may be, so however, that any such modification of amendment shall be without prejudice to the validity of anything previously done under that rule.

98. Powers of the Authorities to make Bye-laws

The State Library Authority or Library Authorities may, subject to the provisions of this Act and the Rules made thereunder and the previous sanction of the Government by notification, make bye-laws generally to carry out the purposes of this Act. In particular and without prejudice to the generality of the foregoing power, such bye-laws may provide for all or any of the following matters namely:

1. The admission of the public to libraries under the control of the State Library Authority and Library Authority in its areas on such conditions it may specify, provided that no fees shall be charged for such admission.
2. The guarantee or security to be furnished by persons desiring to use such libraries against injury or misuse, destruction or loss of the property of such libraries.
3. The manner in which the property of such libraries may be used and the protecting of such property from injury, misuse, destruction or loss.
4. The authority to be exercised by its officers, and servants on the matter or exclusion or removal from any such library of any person who contravenes or does not comply with the provision of this Act or the rules or bye-laws made thereunder.

99. Changes in Bye-laws

The Director may modify or cancel any bye-law made by Library

Authority under Section 96 provided that before modifying or cancelling any bye-law the Director shall give to the Library Authority concerned a reasonable opportunity to make its representation in the matter.

100. **Offences and Penalties**

1. Whoever in a Public Library or other institution maintained under this Act, in any manner is likely to cause annoyance or disturbance to any person using such library or institution, or behaves in a disorderly manner or uses violent or abusive language in any such library or institution; and
2. After due warning persists in remaining therein beyond the hours fixed for closing, shall be liable to be removed from such library or institution and shall also be punishable with fine which may extend to Rupees ten and for a second subsequent offence with a fine which may extend to Rupees fifty.

101. **Public Enquiry**

A competant authority shall hold a public enquiry for the purpose of exercising any other powers or performing any other duties under this Act, in respect of a Library Authority. A copy of the report of any public enquiry shall be furnished to the Library Authority concerned, and representations of such Library Authority, if any, shall be considered before taking any action on the report.

102. **Power of Government to Remove Chairman of the Library Authority**

1. The Government may, by notification, remove any Chairman or Vice-Chairman of the Library Authority who, in their opinion wilfully omits or refuses to carry out or disobeys the provisions of this Act, or the rules, bye-laws or lawful orders made thereunder, or abuses his position or powers vested in him.
2. The Government shall, when they propose to remove a Chairman or Vice-Chairman under sub-Section (1) give the Chairman or Vice-Chairman concerned an opportunity for explanation and the notification issued under the said sub-sections shall contain a statement of the reasons of the Government for the ac-

tion taken.

3. The Government shall have power to review any order of removal published under sub-Section (1) and pending such review to stay such order.
4. Any person removed under sub Section (1) from the office of the Chairman or Vice-Chairman shall not be eligible for re-election to the said office for a period of five years from the date of his removal.

103. **Control of the Library Authority by the Government**

If, at any time, it appears to the Government that, a Library Authority has failed to perform its functions or has exceeded or abused any of the powers conferred upon it by or under this Act, and if the Library Authority omits to remedy such failure, excess or abuse and to give a satisfactory explanation therefore within such time as the Government may fix in this behalf, the Government may suspend, dissolve or supersede the Library Authority and all or any of the powers and functions of such Library Authority to be exercised and performed by the Secretary of the Library Authority.

104. **Secretary as Special Officer**

Where by any reason there is a delay in the constitution of the Library Authority, the Government may appoint the Secretary, Library Authority as *Special Officer* to manage the affairs of the Authority or to perform the functions of the Chairman, as the case may be, for a period not exceeding six months and they may in the like manner from time to time extend such period beyond six months so however, that the aggregate period including the extended period, if any, shall not exceed two years.

105. **Liability of Members for Loss, Waste or Misapplication**

1. Every member of a Library Authority shall be personally liable for the loss, waste or misapplication of any money or other property of the Library Authority to which he has been party, or which has been caused or facilitated by his misconduct or neglect of his duty as a member.
2. If after giving the member or members concerned a reasonable

opportunity for showing cause to the contrary the Director is satisfied that the loss, waste or misapplication of any money or other property of the Library Authority is a direct consequence of a misconduct or neglect on his or their part, the Director shall by order in writing direct such member or members to pay to the Library Authority before a specified date, the amount required to reimburse it for such loss, waste or misapplication.

3. If the amount is not so paid, it shall be recoverable as an arrear of land revenue.
4. An appeal shall lie from the decision of the Director to the Government within such period as may be prescribed and the decision of the Government on such appeal shall be final.

106. **Members and Employees of Library Authority to be the Public Servants**

Every member of the State Library Council or Library Authority and every officer and servant employed under such Library Authority shall be deemed to be a public servant within the meaning of section 21 of the Indian Penal Code.

107. **Provisions relating to Suits etc.**

1. No suit or other legal proceedings shall be instituted against the State Library Authority or a Library Authority or any of its officers or any person acting under its direction until the expiration of two months next after notice, in writing shall have been delivered or left at the office of the authority or at the place of abode of such officer or person; such notice shall state the cause of action, the relief sought, the amount of compensation if any claimed, and the name and place of abode of the intending plaintiff.
2. No suit or other legal proceedings shall be liable against the State Government, the Director, the State Library Authority or a Library Authority, or any member, officer servant or agent of such authority acting under its direction, in respect of anything done or intended to have been done lawfully and in good faith under this Act or any rule, bye-law or order made thereunder.

108. **Power to Remove Difficulties**

If any difficulty arises, in giving effect to the provisions of this Act, the State Government may, by order, do any thing not inconsistent with such provisions which appear to them to be necessary or expedient for the purpose of removing the difficulty provided that no order shall be made under this Section after the expiry of two years from the commencement of this Act.

109. **Orders to be placed before Assembly**

Every order made under the Section shall be laid as soon as may be after it is made, before the Legislative Assembly.

CHAPTER 22

PENALTIES AND PROCEDURE

110. **Penalties for Contravention**

1. If any person wilfully contravenes, or attempts to contravene, or knowingly abets the contravention of, any of the provisions of this Act or any rule made thereunder, he shall be punished with fine which may extend to two hundred rupees and in the case of continuing contravention with an additional fine which may extend to one hundred rupees for every day during which such contravention continues after conviction for the first such contravention.
2. If any person wilfully obstructs any Authority, Officer or persons, from entering any aided library in the exercise of any power conferred on it or him by or under this Act, he shall be punished with fine which may extend to five hundred rupees.

111. **Offence by Companies**

1. Where an offence against any of the provisions of this Act or any rule made thereunder has been committed by a company, every persons who at the time the offence was committed, was incharge of and was responsible, to the company for the conduct of business of the company as well as the company shall be

deemed to be guilty of the offence and shall be liable to be proceeded against and punished accordingly:

Provided that nothing contained in this sub-section shall render any such person liable to any punishment, if he proves that the offence was committed without his knowledge or that he had exercised all due deligence to prevent the commission of such offence.

2. Notwithstanding anything in sub section (1) where any such offence has been committed by a company and it is proved that the offence has been committed with the consent or connivance of, or is attributable to any neglect on the part of any director, manager, secretary or other officer of the company, such director, manager, secretary or other officer, shall be deemed to be guilty of that offence and shall be liable to be proceeded against and punished accordingly.

Explanation— For the purpose of this section:

(a) "Company" means any body corporate and including a firm, a society or other association of individuals, and

(b) "Director" in relation to:

(i) A firm means a partner in the firm.

(ii) Society or other association of individuals means the person who is entrusted under the rules of the society or other respected societies.

CHAPTER 23

APPEALS

112. **Appeals**

Save as otherwise provided in this Act:

1. Any person aggrieved by an order passed by an officer or authority other than the Director under this Act may within thirty days from the date of communication of such order appeal to the Director;
2. Any person aggrieved by an order passed by the Director under

this Act other than or passed by under clause (1) may within thirty days from the date of communication of such order appeal to the Government.

Explanation— For purposes of this section the expression "Director" includes the Joint Director, Dcputy Director, Assistant Director when he exercises the powers of the Director under this Act.

113. **Power of Revision by the Government**

1. The Government may, either *suo motu* or on an application from any person interested either for an examination of the record of public library or of any authority, officer or in respect of any proceedings not being a proceeding in respect of which a reference to arbitrator or an appeal to the High Court satisfy themselves as to the regularity of such proceeding on the legality or propriety of any decision or order passed therein, and if, in any case, it appear to the Government that any such decision or order should be modified, annulled or reversed or remitted for reconsideration, they may pass order accordingly:

   Provided that the Government shall not pass any order adversely affecting any party unless such party has had an opportunity of making a representation.

2. The Government may stay the execution of any such decision or order pending the exercise of powers under sub-section (1) in respect thereof.
3. Every application preferred under sub-section shall be made within such time and in such manner and accompanied by such fees as may be prescribed.

114. **Review**

1. The Government or the Director may *suo motu* at any time or on an application received from any person interested within ninety days of the passing of any order passed by them or him on any provisions of this Act, review any order it was passed by them or him under any mistake whether of fact or of law, or in ignorance of any material fact.

2. The provisions contained in the proviso to the Section (1) and in sub-section (2) and (3) of Section 111 shall apply in respect of any proceeding under this section as they apply to the proceeding under sub-section (1) of that section.

115. Power of Government To Give Direction

1. The Government may, subject to other provision to this Act, by order, direct that Director or any other officer, to make an enquiry or to the appropriate proceedings under this Act in respect of any matter specified in the said order and the Director or the other officer, as the case may be, shall report to the Government in due course the result of the enquiry made or proceedings taken by him.
2. The Government may give direction to any library for giving effect to any of the provision contained in this Act or of any rules or orders made thereunder and the correspondent, as the case may be, of such institution shall comply with every such direction.

116. Delegation of Powers of Government

The Government may, by notification, delegate all or any of their powers under this Act, except those conferred upon them by this section and Sections 107, 108, 109, 110 and 111 to any person or authority subordinate to them subject to such conditions and to such control and revision by such authority as may be specified in the notification, and they may in the like manner withdraw any powers so delegated.

117. Penalty for Obstructing Officer Or Other Person Exercising Powers under this Act

Any person who wilfully obstructs an officer of the Government in the exercise of any power conferred on him, or in the performance of any function entrusted to him, by or under this or any person lawfully assisting such officer in the exercise of such power or in the performance of such function or who fails to comply with any lawful direction made by such officer or person shall be punished with fine which may extend to two hundred and fifty rupees.

CHAPTER 24

PRESS AND REGISTRATION OF BOOKS ACT

118. Amendment to the Press and Registration of Books Act, 1867

The Press and Registration of Books Act, 1867 (Central Act XXV of 1867) shall, in its application to the State of....... be amended as follows:

1. In the first paragraph of Section 9, for clause (a) the following clause shall be substituted, namely:

   (a) In any case, within one calendar month after the day on which any such book shall first be delivered out of the press three copies, and—

2. Any second or subsequent edition of a book in which edition or alternations either in the letter press or in the book prints or other engravings belonging to the book have been made, and three copies of the first of some preceding edition of which books have been delivered under this Act, and—
3. In section II, for the first sentence the following shall be substituted namely:

   "out of three copies delivered pursuant to clause (a) of the first paragraph of Section 9 of this Act the copies shall be distributed to the following institutions:

   1. State Public Library.
   2. District Public Library, in the District where the book is printed.
   3. Central Secretariat Library, New Delhi.

119. Penal Clauses

1. Penal clauses should be added by amendment more strongly, so as to act as deterrent for those who violate the provisions of the Act.
2. The Book Selection Committee of the State should select books

for the public libraries only from the list of books delivered under the Act, and refuse to select any book not so delivered.

120 Heads of Operation

1. An officer not below the rank of an Assistant Director, shall be the Registrar of Books, on the State, who shall also be the Ex-officio head of the State Bibliographical Bureau.
2. The Secretaries of the Library Authorities shall be made Ex-officio Registrars of Books of the City or Districts as the case may be, who are responsible for the collection of books printed in a city or District concerned.
3. The Secretaries should keep one copy of each of these books with City/District Public Library, and should not lend such copy on any case. They should be preserved carefully and made available for reference and research only.

CHAPTER 25

REPEAL AND SAVINGS

121. Savings Clause

All rules, bye-laws and regulations made under the said Acts and in force at the commencement of this Act, shall so far as new rules, bye-laws and regulations are not inconsistent with the provisions of this Act, continue to be in force in respective areas in which they are in force at such commencement and such rules shall be deemed to be rules and such bye-laws and regulations shall be deemed to be bye-laws made under the provisions of this Act until they are superseded or modified by rules and bye-laws made under this Act.

9

MODEL PUBLIC LIBRARIES RULES

1. PRELIMINARIES

1.1 General Clarifications

1. The words LIBRARY AUTHORITY will apply both to the City Library Authority and District Library Authorities.
2. Implementation of the Rules will be notified in the State Government Gazette.
3. The Rules shall be applied to the whole State, unless otherwise stated.
4. The words expressions used but not defined in the Rules, shall have the meaning respectively assigned to them in the Act.

1.2 Definitions

A few definitions, which did not cover in the Act are given below:

1. *Admissible Expenditure* means an expenditure incurred on all or any of the item specified in these rules.
2. *Certificate of Recognition* means a certificate granted to the public library by the Director under rule of Grant-in-aid Rules.
3. *Cooperative Society* means a society registered under the cooperative Societies Act of the State.
4. *Employee* means any person who is borne in the establishment of Library Authority whether he is on duty or under suspension or on leave or on foreign service, either with in or outside the State.
5. *Form* means form appended in the covered rules.
6. *Local Body* means the statutory bodies like Zilla Parishad, Panchayat Samithi, Municipal Corporation, Municipal Council,

Gram Panchayat etc.

7. *Management In Relation To A Public Library* means an association, a body, or persons by whatever designation called having general and financial control over the public library.
8. *Member* means a person who has enrolled himself as a Member in a recognised Public Library in accordance with the rules of that library.
9. *Member of the Family*, includes the spouse, son, daughter, step-son, or step-daughter of an employee, whether residing with the employee or not and any person related to, and residing with the employee and wholly dependent on the employee, but does not include a spouse legally separated from the employee, or a son, daughter, step-son or a step-daughter who is no longer any way dependent upon such employee.

1.3 Rule Starts—

The Rules on a particular subject shall begin in the following manner:

Government of . . . .
G O No: . . . . . . Dated: . . . 19 . . .

In exercise of the powers conferred by sub-section . . . of Section . . . of Public Libraries Act, 19 . . . (Act . . . of 19....). The Governor of . . . . State hereby makes the following rules for the . . . .

2. The Rules shall come into force from the date of publication in the . . . . Gazette.

RULES

1. These Rules shall be called as . . . .

1.4 Publication of Bye-laws

Every bye-law made under Section . . . besides being published in the official Gazette shall also be published,–

(i) in two issues of a daily newspaper of the language of the State circulating throughout the State, in the City or in the District, as the case may be;

(ii) by affixing copies of the bye-law on the notice board of the State Library Authority, or the City/District Library Authority, as the case may be, and by affixing copies of bye-law on the notice Board of the State Public Library and the Public Libraries in the City or District, as the case may be.

2. ADMINISTRATIVE AUTHORITIES

2.1 **Constitution of the State Library Council**

2.1.1 The Director shall address the Government to move the State Legislature for the election of members to be elected by the Legislature to the Committee, in the manner approved by the Speaker of the Legislative Assembly or the Chairman of the Legislative Council, as the case may be.

2.1.2 In respect of the persons to be nominated by the Government under Sections 5, 6 and 12 of the Act, the Director shall address the Government.

2.1.3 Soon after the nominations are completed, the Secretary, Education for the Government or an officer authorised by him shall conduct the election of the Chairman, State Library Council, through secret ballot.

2.1.4 When a vacancy in the committee occurs otherwise than by efflux of time, the Director shall address the appropriate authority with a view to having the vacancy filled up.

When a vacancy in the Committee is due to occur by efflux of time, the Director shall address the appropriate authority one month in advance with a view to having the vacancy filled up as soon as it occurs.

2.1.5. *Meetings of the Committee*

1. The Committee shall meet at least once in six months and at such times and in such places as may be determined by the Chairman.
2. Five members will form quorum.
3. In the absence of the Chairman, the members present at a meeting of the Committee shall elect a Chairman from among themselves, for conducting the proceedings.
4. The Secretary of the Committee shall submit the Minutes of the

meeting within five days to the Chairman, for confirmation, after which the minutes shall be communicated to the members.

2.2 Constitution of the City Library Authority

2.2.1 The Director shall address the Government for nominating two members under Section 30 of the Act.

2.2.2 When an election is due to be held under section 30.2, the Secretary City Library Authority shall convene a meeting of the presidents of the governing bodies of the Public Libraries concerned after giving not less than 15 days notice of the meeting specifying the time and the place at which the meeting will be held for electing members to the City Library Authority. Copies of the notice referred to above shall be served on presidents of the governing bodies either in person or by registered post at the address furnished in the register referred to in the Rule 42.12. The election shall be conducted in the manner indicated in Rule 2.3.2.

2.2.3 The Secretary of the City Library Authority shall address the Commissioner of Municipal Corporation for the election of two members by the Councillors of the Municipal Corporation. The election shall be held at a meeting of the Municipal Corporation presided over by the Mayor.

2.2.4 When a vacancy or vacancies occur owing to efflux of time or for other reasons, the Secretary of the Library Authority shall take immediate action for filling up the vacancy or vacancies in the manner prescribed. He shall also submit reports to the Director from time to time regarding occurrence of the vacancy or vacancies and the action taken for filling them up.

2.3 Constitution of the District Library Authority

2.3.1 The Director shall address the Government for nomination of members under Section 32.1, 32.2, 32.4, 32.7 and 32.8 of the Act.

2.3.2 When elections are due to be held under clause 3 of section 32 of the Act, the following procedure shall be observed:

(a) The Secretary of the District Library Authority shall address the Secretaries of the Municipal Councils in the District, for the election of one member from among themselves by the Councillors of the Council of every Municipality in the District.

(b) Immediately after receipt of the notice from the Secretary of the District Library Authority the Secretary of the Municipality shall place it before the Chairman of the Municipal Council who shall take steps to convene and preside over the meeting of the council in which one member shall be elected from among themselves to the District Library Authority. The name and address of the members so elected shall be reported to the Secretary of the District Library Authority.

Explanation— For purpose of the above rule Aldermen and *ex-officio* Councillors shall be treated as councillors, and are eligible to participate in the election of a member.

2.3.3 When an election is due to be held under Section 32.6 the Secretary, DLA, shall convene a meeting of the presidents of the governing bodies of the Public Libraries concerned after giving not less than 15 days notice of the meeting specifying the time and the place at which the meeting will be held for electing members to the DLA. Copies of the notice referred to above shall be served on presidents of the governing bodies either in person or by registered post to the addresses furnished in the register maintained as per Section 19.11 of the Act.

2.3.4 When a vacancy or vacancies occur under relevant clause 19.11 of the section of the Act, owing to efflux of time or for other reasons, the Secretary of the District Library Authority shall take immediate action for filling up the vacancy or vacancies in the manner provided. He shall also submit reports to the Director from time to time, regarding occurrence of the vacancy or vacancies and the action taken for filling them up.

2.3.5 *Election of Members*

1. The quorum for a meeting convened for the election of a member or members of a District Library Authority shall be one-third of the total number of members whichever less who are eligible to attend the meeting, excluding the President of the Meeting.
2. Every candidate for election shall be proposed by one elector and seconded by another.
3. The name of all the candidates who have been proposed and

seconded at the election and who have not withdrawn their candidature shall be read out by the President of the meeting.

4. If the number of candidates whose names are so read out is equal to the number of vacancies, the President shall declare all such candidates duly elected.
5. If the number of such candidates is less than the number of vacancies the President shall declare all such candidates duly elected and shall either call for fresh nominations or adjourn the election to fill up the remaining vacancy or vacancies at a subsequent meeting.
6. If the number of such candidates exceeds the number of vacancies, the votes of electors present at the meeting shall be taken by ballot.
7. The President shall make adequate arrangements to secure the secrecy of the ballot. He shall not be entitled to vote at the meeting.
8. Every member wishing to vote shall be supplied with a voting paper which shall be stamped with the official stamp of the President of the meeting on which the name of all such candidates shall be typed or legibly written in the following form in English and in any other language considered necessary by the President of the meeting.
9. Each elector shall be entitled to cast as many votes as there are vacancies given not more than one vote to any candidate. He shall then proceed to the place set apart for the purpose and there place a mark on the voting paper against the name of the candidate or the names of the candidates for whom he wishes to vote. He shall then fold up the voting paper and deposit the same in a ballot box placed in the view of the President.
10. The ballot box shall be so constructed that the voting paper may be placed therein but not extracted therefrom without the box being opened.
11. Immediately after the voting is over the President shall open the ballot box and count the votes in the presence of the electors.
12. The candidate who obtains the largest number of votes, or if there is more than one vacancy, as many of the candidates at the top of the poll as there are vacancies to be filled, shall be declared to have been duly elected. If there be an equality of votes between any two or more candidates and the addition of one vote to any one or more of such candidates will entitle him

or them to be declared duly elected, the President shall decide by drawing lots in the presence of the members as to which one or more of such candidates such additional vote shall be deemed to have been given.

13. A voting paper shall be invalid if:

(a) it bears the signature of the voter, or contains any word, sign or visible representation by which he can be identified, or
(b) marks are placed thereon against more names of the candidates than there are vacancies to be filled, or
(c) it is uncertain to which candidate the mark is intended to apply, or
(d) no mark is placed thereon.

14. Immediately after the counting of votes the President shall announce the name of persons elected as members of the District Library Authority.
15. The President shall also draw up a record of the proceedings and sign it, attesting with his initials every correction made therein and also permit any elector present at the meeting to affix his signature if he desires to do so.
16. The President of the meeting shall then make up two separate packets, one containing the voting papers which have been counted and the other containing those which have been rejected, seal such packet and note thereon a description of its contents, the number of the voting papers it contains, the election to which it relates and the date thereof. The packets referred to above shall be kept by the Secretary of the District Library Authority in his own custody for a period of one calendar year and shall, thereafter, unless otherwise directed by the Director, be destroyed. While in the custody of the Secretary they shall not be opened and their contents shall not be inspected by, or produced before any person or authority, except under the orders of the Director or the court.
17. The Secretary of the District Library Authority shall immediately after the election of the members report to the Director the names of the persons elected as members.

2.3.6 *Election of Chairman and Vice-Chairman*

1. (i) The election of the Chairman and the Vice-Chairman of a Library Authority by the members thereof shall be held in the office of the Library Authority at a meeting specially convened for the purpose.

   (ii) Such meeting shall be convened by the District Educational Officer having jurisdiction over the place where the office of the Library Authority is situated as soon as possible after its constitution or the occurrence of a vacancy.

   Note: In the case of election of the Chairman and the Vice-Chairman the District Educational Officer who is the election authority should be furnished with rules and all other information and help necessary to conduct the election. The behaviour of the Secretary should be such that there should not be any room or ground for suspicion or complaint of siding one side or the others. Efforts should be made to fill up the vacancies as far as possible before the election of Chairman and Vice-Chairman. But on this account the election of the Chairman and Vice-Chairman need not be postponed and it can be conducted if there is quorum. A notice of ten clear days specifying the date, hour and place of the meeting should be given to the members. The members who are elected or nominated after the issue of notice are also eligible to participate in the election and it need not be postponed.

   The members nominated or elected under Sections 30 and 32 of the Act are eligible to draw travelling allowance at the prescribed rates from the funds of Library Authority to attend the meeting of the election of the Chairman and Vice-Chairman.

   (iii) Notice of the day and hour of the meeting for the election of the Chairman shall be given to the members of the District Library Authority at least ten (10) clear days before the day of the meeting.

   (iv) Such meeting shall be presided over by the District Educational Office.

2. The quorum for the meeting shall be six members, but if the number of members of the District Library Authority exceeds sixteen, one-third of that number shall be the quorum.

3. A candidate for election to the Office of the Chairman and Vice-Chairman shall be proposed by one of the members of the Library Authority and seconded by another member. The names of all the candidates who have been proposed and seconded at the election and who have not withdrawn their candidature shall be read out at the meeting by the President of the meeting.

4.(i) If there is only one duly nominated candidate, there shall be no ballot and he shall be declared to have been elected.

(ii) If there are two or more such candidates, the votes of the members of the Library Authority present at the meeting shall be taken by ballot.

(iii) The President of the meeting shall make adequate arrangements to secure the secrecy of the ballot. He shall not be entitled to vote at the meeting.

5. Every member entitled and wishing to vote shall be supplied with a voting paper which shall be stamped with the official stamp of the President of the meeting and on which the names of all the candidates shall be printed, typed, cyclostyled or legibly written in the following form in English and in any regional language considered necessary by the President of the meeting. The voter shall then proceed to the place set apart for the purpose and there place a mark on the voting paper against the name of the candidate for whom he wishes to vote. He shall then fold up the voting paper so as to maintain secrecy and deposit the same in a ballot box placed in the view of the President of the meeting, which is so constructed that the voting paper may be placed therein but not extracted therefrom without the box being opened.

6. Immediately after the voting is over the President of the meeting shall open the ballot box and count the votes in the presence of the members and declare the result of the election in accordance with the following instructions:

(i) The candidate who secures the largest number of votes shall be declared to have been duly elected.

(ii) In the event of there being an equality of votes between two or more candidates at the top of poll, the President of the meeting shall cast lots in the presence of the members and the candidate whose name is first drawn shall be declared to have been duly elected.

7. A voting paper shall be invalid if:

(i) it bears the signature of the voter, or contains any word. sign or visible representation by which he can be identified, or
(ii) marks are placed thereon against more than one name, or
(iii) the mark is so placed thereon as to make it doubtful for which one of the two or more candidates the vote was intended to be given, or
(iv) no mark is placed thereon.

8.(i) Immediately after the counting of votes, the President shall announce the names of the persons elected as Chairman of the Library Authority.

(ii) The President shall also record the proceedings in the Minutes Book and sign it, attesting with his initials every correction made therein and also permit any member of the Library Authority present at the meeting to affix his signature in the Minutes Book, if the member desires to do so.

9.(i) The President of the meeting shall then make up into separate packets the voting papers relating to each candidate which have been counted. The voting papers relating to each candidate which have been rejected shall also be made up into separate packets. The President of the meeting shall seal each such packet and note thereon a description of its contents, the number of ballot papers it contains, the election to which it relates and the date thereon.

(ii) The packets referred to above shall be kept by the Secretary of the Library Authority in his own custody for a period of one calendar year and shall thereafter unless otherwise directed by the Director, be destroyed.

10. The election of the Vice-Chairman should be conducted along with the election of the Chairman and the same procedure will be followed without any deviation.
11. The Secretary of the Library Authority shall immediately after the election of the Chairman and Vice-Chairman report to the Director the names of the members elected as Chairman and Vice-Chairman.

2.3.7 *Election Petitions*

1. No election of a member or Chairman or Vice-Chairman of Library Authority held under the provisions of the Act shall be called in question except by an election petition presented in accordance with this rule to the Director by any candidate or elector against the candidate who has been declared to have been duly elected (hereinafter called the returned candidate) or if there are two or more returned candidates, against all or any such candidates.
2. The election petition shall be presented within 15 days of the date of the declaration of the result of the election.
3. The petition shall contain a statement in concise form, of the material facts on which the petitioner relies.
4. Every returned candidate to whose election the petition refers shall be cited as a respondent in the petition.
5. When an election petition has been presented, the Director or any Officer of the Department of Public Libraries authorised by the Director (hereinafter called the enquiry officer) shall proceed to enquire into the petition; provided that the Director shall not authorise any Officer lower in rank than a Deputy Director to enquire into an election petition.
6. The enquiry officer shall serve a copy of the petition along with a notice stating the date, place and time of the enquiry on each respondent, the Secretary of the District Library Authority concerned and election authority. He shall also serve a notice on the petitioner informing him of the date, place and time of the enquiry.

   Explanation— For the purposes of this rule, "Election Authority" means the person presiding over the meeting at which the returned candidate was declared elected.

7. No election petition shall be withdrawn without the permission of the Director.
8. If there are more petitioners than one, no application to withdraw a petition shall be made except with the consent of all the petitioners.
9. An election petition shall abate on the death of a sole petitioner or of the survivor of several petitioners and such abatement

shall be communicated to the Secretary of the Library Authority concerned and the election authority by the Director.

10. On the day of enquiry, and on any other day to which the enquiry may be adjourned, the enquiry officer shall examine the petitioners, the respondents and the witnesses, if any, and shall also consider such evidence as may appear to him relevant to the case.
11. At the conclusion of the enquiry, the enquiry officer shall declare whether the election of the returned candidate or candidates is valid or void.
12. If he declares the election of the returned candidate or candidates void, he shall further pass an order either:

declaring that any other party to the petition who has under these rules claimed the seat has been duly elected; or
directing that a fresh election be held.

13. The order of the enquiry officer shall be final.
14. A copy of every order shall be communicated to the Secretary, Library Authority and the election authority concerned.
15. When an election is declared void and a fresh election is ordered, the seat of the returned candidate or the seats of the returned candidates, as the case may be, shall be deemed to be vacant from the date of the order under sub-rule (11).and the election authority shall forthwith take necessary steps for holding a fresh election. No election of a member or Chairman shall be called in question except by an election petition. Hence even if any material irregularities come to the notice of Secretary or Chairman or other members they should refrain from doing anything which amounts to nullifying the election.
16. *Fresh election of Chairman*: If at any time, the Director of Public Libraries considers that the election of a Chairman of Library Authority was found to be illegal, he may notwithstanding the provisions in Rules 2, 3 and 7 declare such election as void and the election authority shall forthwith take necessary steps for holding a fresh election of the Chairman.
17. *Resignation of Chairman and Members of Library Authority:* The Chairman or any member of the Library Authority may resign his office as Chairman or member by giving notice in writing to the Library Authority except in case, where person

resigning delivers the notice or such resignation personally to the Secretary, Library Authority, the Secretary shall on receipt of such notice of resignation obtain confirmation from the person concerned as to its genuineness. A resignation delivers personally or confirmed as aforesaid shall take effect from the date on which the notice was received.

2.4 Activities of the Chairman and Vice-Chairman

The duties of the Chairman, Library Authority shall be as follows:

1. He shall preside over all the meetings of the Library Authority.
2. He shall appoint the staff of the Library Authority, including the ministerial staff.
3. The Vice-Chairman of a Library Authority shall (a) in the absence of the Chairman, preside over the meetings of the Authority; (b) exercise such powers and perform such duties of the Chairman, as the Chairman may, from time to time, delegate to him.

2.5 Activities of the Secretary

Activities of the Secretary of the Library Authority shall be as follows:

1. He shall convene the meetings of the Library Authority and shall be subordinate to the Chairman.
2. He shall be responsible for the proper control and supervision of the office of the Library Authority and librarians appointed by the Library Authority.
3. He shall submit the recommendations to the Chairman for filling up a vacancy or vacancies in the office of the Library Authority and in Libraries under the control of the Library Authority.
4. He shall post the Chairman with all rules, etc. and up to date information regarding the working of the Libraries in the District.
5. He shall submit to the Director through the Chairman not later than the 30th April every year, a report on the working of the public libraries in the District during the preceding year.
6. He shall be responsible in all administrative matters and for the prompt submission of all replies and returns as when called for

by the Director.

7. He shall be responsible for implementing the resolutions passed by the Library Authority for its sub-committees (and he shall bring to the notice of the Director, for his orders, any resolutions which are not in accordance with the Act and these Rules).
8. He shall draw up the schemes to be submitted by the Library Authority to the Director.
9. He shall correspond with the Director; but in all policy matters, the prior approval of the Chairman shall be obtained.
10. He shall be responsible for proper administration of the Library Fund.
11. He shall be responsible for keeping the Cheque Book under the safe custody.

2.6 Bye-laws for the Conducting the Meetings of the Library Authorities

1. The Library Authority shall ordinarily meet in headquarters of the Authority atleast twice a year, once in January which shall be the annual meeting and once in August/September. The Chairman shall preside over all the meetings of the Authority, and in the absence of Chairman and Vice-Chairman the members present shall elect one of themselves to preside over the meeting.
2. The Secretary, Library Authority shall convene the meeting in consultation with the Chairman, provided that the condition of consulting the Chairman shall not apply when the office of Chairman is vacant.
3. A notice of ten clear days of the meeting shall be given to the members, provided that in case of urgency, the Secretary may convene in consultation with the Chairman a meeting on giving a notice of not less than five clear days.
4. The agenda for the meeting shall be prepared by the Secretary in consultation with the Chairman. The Secretary may include in the agenda any subject which in his opinion should be considered by Authority. He shall also include therein any subject specified by the Chairman or any member. The agenda with a note thereon shall be circulated to the members along with the notice of the meeting. Provided that the condition of consulting the Chairman shall not apply when the office of the Chairman is

vacant.

5. The Secretary, on requisition in writing of not less than one-half of the members then on the Authority, shall convene a meeting of the Authority, provided that requisition shall specify the day, the time and the purpose for which the meeting is to be convened. Provided further that the requisition is delivered at the Authority office during office hours to the Chairman, the Secretary or any other person who may then be incharge of the Authority atleast fifteen clear days in advance of the date proposed for the meeting.
6. On receipt of requisition the Secretary shall convene the meeting giving notice of not-less-than five clear days to the members in consultation with the Chairman. Provided that where Secretary fails to convene the meeting so requisitioned it may be convened by the Chairman on giving five clear days notice to the members. If however, both the Secretary and the Chairman fail to convene the requisitioned meeting, the matter shall be brought to the notice of the Director by any or all thè members who requisitioned the meeting, for such orders or direcctions as he may consider necessary and they shall be final.
7. No business shall be transacted at a meeting unless there be present at least six members and if the number of members then on the Authority exceeds sixteen, atleast one third of that number.
8. If within half-an-hour after the appointed time for a meeting a quorum is not formed, the meeting shall stand adjourned unless all the members present agree to wait longer.
9. A meeting convened on requisition by members in accordance with bye-law No. 5 shall stand cancelled if there is no quorum as prescribed in bye-law No. 7 in half-an-hour after the appointed time for a meeting.
10. An adjourned meeting shall be convened within 30 days from the date of adjournment and a notice of not less than five clear days shall be given to the members of the adjourned meeting.
11. All items which may come before the Authority at any meeting shall be decided by a majority of the members present and voting at the meeting and in the case of equality of votes the presiding member shall have and exercise a second or casting vote. In the case of any resolution not carried unanimously, the names of the members who vote for and against shall be re-

corded with the minute of dissent if demanded by one-fourth of the number of members present at the meeting.

12. No resolution of the Authority shall be modified or cancelled within six months after the passing there of except at a meeting specially convened in that behalf and by a resolution of the Authority supported by not less than 50 per cent of the strength of the Authority.

13. (i) The minutes of the meeting shall be recorded either in English or in the regional language in a book to be maintained for the purpose at the meeting itself and shall be signed by the Chairman or by the presiding member at the end of the meeting.

(ii) The minutes of every meeting shall be communicated to all the members of the Authority and to the Director within ten days of the day of meeting.

(iii) A copy of the minutes should be put up on the notice board of the office of the Authority for information of the public. The copies of the minutes may be supplied by the Secretary to any person who applied for it at a cost of Rs. 10 per meeting. Important resolution may be notified for the information of the public through press note or in such manner as the Authority may decide from time to time without incurring any expenditure on this account.

14. The Secretary shall place before the Authority at every meeting of the monthly statements of accounts for its approval.

15. (i) The Executive Committee appointed under Section 42.2 of the Act, shall consist of the Chairman, Secretary and not more than three other members of the Library Authority. The Secretary shall be the convenor of the Executive Committee. The term of the members of the Executive Committee shall be for a period of two years, from the date of their becoming members of Executive Committee and the membership shall be by rotation.

(ii) The proceedings of the Executive Committee appointed by the *samstha* shall be recorded in writing and submitted to the Library Authority in the next meeting.

16. Other committee appointed by the Library Authority shall consist of not more than five members including the Chairman and the Secretary. The membership of the sub-committee other than of the Chairman and Secretary shall be by rotation.

17. The meetings should generally be held in Headquarters of the Library Authority. If the members so desire for any special reason, the meetings can be held at any place in the district.

3.1 DATA AND PLANNING

3.1 Data on Public Library Managements

1. The Director shall maintain a register of all Public Libraries in the State.
2. The management of every Public Library, other than the libraries managed by Library Authorities shall within thirty days of the establishment of the library, or if the library is already in existence, within thirty days of the coming into force of these Rules, send to the Secretary of the Library Authority, in whose jurisdiction the library is situated, a statement in the following form:

(i) Name of the Library:
(ii) Year of its registration:
(A copy of the Registration certificate should be enclosed)
(iii) Name and address of the President of the Governing body:

(a) Date of his election:
(b) Date by which his term of office will expire:
(a copy of the bye-laws of the library governing the constitution of the governing body and election of its President should be enclosed)

(iv) Reference number and date of order in which the library was declared eligible for aid.
(v) Aid received by the library:
(a) Year:
(b) Amount:
(c) Reference number and date of sanction order:

3. Whenever there is a change in the name and address of the President of the governing body, the management of the library shall report the same to the Secretary of the Library Authority, within a period of ten days.
4. The Secretary of the Library Authority shall record these particulars in a register and maintain it up-to-date.

3.2 Data on Public Libraries

The Secretary, Library Authority should collect the following data from all the public libraries in the district by the end of April every year and submit the same with his analysis to the Director:

1. Serial Number:
2. Name and address of the Librarian:
3. Name of management/Library Authority/Z.P./Municipality/Panchayat/ Grama Sangh/Co-operative Aided:
4. Building – Own, Rented/Rent Free Tiled or Terraced:
5. Furniture – Tables/Chairs/Book Racks, other equipment:
6. Names of members of staff and qualifications:
7. Number of books and periodicals:
8. Number of registered borrowers at the end of year:
9. Total No. of visitors in the year:
10. Number of books consulted during the year:
11. Number of books lent for home reading during the year:
12. Total expenditure in the year:
13. Remarks:

Signature of the
Librarian or correspondent

3.3 Data on Librarians

1. The Secretary, Library Authority should collect the following

data from all the public libraries in the district by the end of April and report the same with his analysis to the Director:

1. Serial Number:
2. Name and address of the Librarian:
3. Name of Library in which employed:
4. Designation and Grade:
5. General Qualifications:
6. Professional Qualifications:
7. Scale of Pay:
8. Present pay including allowance:
9. Age:
10. Total period of service:
11. Professional contributions:
12. Awards, if any:
13. Remarks:

Signature of the
Librarian or correspondent

2. A name entered in Register may be struck off, if a person has not been in library service for a period of three years or if a person has failed to give the Secretary, the Library Authority information about the office held by him.
3. Whenever any change occurs in Libraries and Librarians during the course of the year, the Secretary, Library Authority, shall report the same to the Director.

3.4 Library Development Plans

3.4.1 Each Library Authority shall first prepare and submit to the State Planning Board a tentative outline of the scheme, a picture of the number of main and branch libraries and delivery stations which its area should have ultimately, i.e. when the spread of library service reaches its fulness.

3.4.2 When preparing the tentative scheme, the Library Authority shall consult the local bodies within its jurisdiction regarding the needs of their respective areas and their willingness to fulfil these needs.

3.4.3 A tentative outline scheme shall give the following and any other relevant information:

1. A map of each municipality laying within the positions of the main library and branch libraries and, if any, (existing and proposed), shown by distinctive marks. The basis for the map of each municipality shall be as follows:

   (i) If the population does not exceed 50,000 one main library.
   (ii) If the population exceeds, 50,000 one main library and in addition, a branch library for every 25,000 people in excess of 50,000.

2. The basis for the map of a rural area, i.e. the jurisdiction of the Library Authority excluding the municipalities lying within it, shall be as follows:

   (i) One District Central Library, i.e., the main library of the district headquarters town in all districts.
   (ii) One branch library for each Panchayat with a population of 5000 and above and in exceptional cases, with the permission of the Government, a branch library may be provided for a Panchayat with a population of less than 5000.

   Explanation— In this Rule, the expression population means the population as ascertained at the last preceding census of which the relevant figures have been published.

   (iii) One delivery station for each village or group of villages with a population between 1000 and 5000 and if possible, one delivery station for each village or group of villages, with a population below 1000.

3.4.4 *Preparation of City Library Development Plan*

1. The City Library Development Plan to be prepared by a City Library Authority under sub-section 1 of Section 54 of the Act for establishing libraries and spreading library service within its jurisdiction shall be as in form contained in Annexure I and shall be prepared in the following manner, namely:

   (i) Public Libraries maintained by the Local Body of the City;
   (ii) Other libraries open to the public maintained by other co-

operative agencies;
(iii) School libraries maintained by the Local Body of the City;
(iv) School libraries maintained by other corporate agencies; and
(v) Hospital libraries.

2. The City Library Development Plan to be prepared under sub-rule (1) shall contain the particulars as mentioned below:

Form of the City Library Development Plan

The Development Plan for a city shall furnish the following and any other relevant information about each of the Central and Branch Public Libraries and School and Hospital Libraries to be newly established:

1. The map furnished shall indicate by a distinctive symbol each Public School and Hospital Library to be newly opened, including the Central Library.
2. The division and location therein.
3. The proposed year of establishment.
4. Information about illiteracy; and the kind of library service proposed to be given to the illiterates; and other agencies for the liquidation of illiteracy and the part proposed to be played by the library.
5. The number of adult schools in the division and manner in which the library expects to co-operate with them.
6. The estimated initial cost in regard to:

   (i) Buildings and fittings;
   (ii) Furniture and office equipment;
   (iii) Reading and kindred materials;
   (iv) The number of years over which the expenditure of the initial cost is proposed to be spread;
   (v) The amount which the Government is requested to provide;
   (vi) The other sources from which the rest of the amount is expected to be found;
   (vii) The estimated recurring cost for a year in regard to—

      (a) The staff with details about the number of posts and

grade of salaries;

(b) Furniture and office equipment;

(c) Reading and kindred materials;

(d) Insurance charges;

(e) The amount estimated to be appropriated from the library cess raised,

(f) The amount estimated to be found from other sources with the name of the sources; and

(g) The amount which the Government is requested to provide.

Time-Table of Development

The Development plan for a city shall state the estimated number of years in which full library service will be established and give a summary of the proposals in the form of a tentative yearly time-table giving for each year—

1. The establishment of the City Central Library:
2. The number of Branch Libraries with the proportion of their number of the total population above age 18 and to the number of literates:
3. The number of school libraries:
4. The number of hospital libraries:
5. The strength of the staff required:

(i) Professional:

(ii) Semi-professional:

(iii) Ministerial:

(iv) Unskilled:

(v) The proportion of the professional and semi-professional staff to the total population above age 10 and the literates among them:

(vi) Progressive total of estimated capital expenditure with indication of the amount to be found:

(a) By the Government:
(b) By the Local Body of the City:
(c) From other sources:

(vii) Estimates of annual expenditure with indication of the amount to be found:

(a) By the Government:
(b) By the Local Body of the City:
(c) From the proceeds of the Library cess:
(d) From other sources:

3.4.5 *Preparation of District Library Development Plan*

The District Library Development Plan to be prepared by a District Library Authority under sub-section (1) of Section 54 of the Act for establishing libraries and spreading library service within its jurisdiction shall be as in form contained in Annexure II and shall be prepared in the following manner, namely : 1. Full outline of Plan; 2. Town sub-plan, and 3. Village sub-plan.

The District Library Development Plan to be prepared under sub-rule (1) shall contain the particulars as given below:

Form of the District Library Development Plan

The Development plan of a District Library Authority for establishing libraries and for spreading library service should be submitted in three parts, roughly speaking in the following sequence of priority:

1. Full outline of plan
2. Town sub-plan and
3. Village sub-plan

(1) While executing the plan, it may be expedient to begin with the District Central Library, then implement the Town sub-plan, and thereafter implement the village sub-plan.
(i) Full outline of plan:
(ii) Existing Library Service:

(2) The Development plan of a District Library Authority shall furnish information on the existing Library Service covering the following and any other relevant points: The map of the approved District area in which is shown by distinctive marks the locations of the existing:

(i) Public Libraries maintained by the District Board, if any,
(ii) Public Libraries maintained by Municipal Council or Village Panchayats;
(iii) Other libraries opened to the Public and maintained by other corporate agencies;
(iv) School Libraries maintained by the District Boards, if any;
(v) School Libraries maintained by Municipal Councils or Village Panchayats;
(vi) School Libraries maintained by other corporate agencies;
(viii) Hospital Libraries; and
(viii) Prison Libraries.

(3) Taking over a library :

(i) These Rules are on the analogy of the corresponding Rules for the City Development Plan.
(ii) The number of prisons and the average number of prisoners per day.
(iii) New Libraries to be established.

These Rules are on the analogy of the corresponding Rules for the City Development Plan with the addition of "Prison Libraries" wherever appropriate.

(iv) *Time-table of Development* – These Rules are on the analogy of the corresponding Rules for the City Development Plan and in addition the following:

(a) The number of prisons libraries; and
(b) The total number of libraries.

(4) Town sub-plan –

(i) A Rural Library Development Plan shall furnish a sub-plan for each of the two towns included in the approved rural area, giving details as required for a City Library Plan; and

(ii) In framing the sub-plan for a town, it must be borne in mind that a public library maintained under a town sub-plan will cease to be an independent unit and become a rural branch library as soon as the District Central Library for the approved Rural area of the District within which it lies is established.

(5) *Village sub-plan* – A village sub-plan can be submitted only for the villages and hamlets in an area for which the District Central Library has been established.

(a) A village sub-plan shall furnish the following and any other relevant information about the progressive extension of travelling library service to the villages and hamlets falling within the area of a District Central Library:

1. A map of the area showing the nature of the terrain, the roads to be taken by the travelling library, and the service stations, the ideal to be aimed being one service station for each habitation such that no resident of a habitation has to walk more than a kilometre to reach the service-station.
2. The number of travelling libraries or librachines to be brought with time-table showing the yearly addition and the cumulative total — it being remembered that the ideal to be reached is roughly one librachine for a population of 25,000 or for 10 service stations so that a librachine calls at each service station once in a fortnight
3. The number of travelling staff proposed to be appointed with a time-table showing the yearly addition and cumulative total;
4. The number of social education centres in the range and the manner in which the library expects to co-operate with them;
5. The estimated initial cost with a time-table showing the yearly amount and cumulative total for:

(i) The Librachines and their fittings;
(ii) The garage and servicing place to be added to the rural Central Library Building;
(iii) Furniture and office equipment;

(iv) Reading and kindred materials;

(v) The number of years over which the expenditure of the initial cost is proposed to be spread;

(vi) The amount which the Government is requested to provide; and

(vii) The other sources from which the rest of amount is expected to be found; and

(viii) The estimated recurring cost with a time-table showing the yearly addition in regard to:

1. Staff with details about the number of posts and grades of salaries;
2. Furniture and office equipment;
3. Reading and kindred materials
4. Insurance charges;
5. The amount estimated to be found from library cess.
6. The amount estimated to be found from other sources with the name of the source; and
7. The amount which the Government is requested to provide.

Manner of publication of the salient features of Library Development Plans — The salient features of every City Library Development Plan and District Library Development plan prepared shall be published in the following manner namely, —

(i) By publication in the official Gazette;

(ii) By circulating in the Local papers; and

(iii) The date within which objections have to be forewarded to the District Librarian should be specified in the notice taking into consideration that period to be allowed for sending objection must be a reasonable period after the actual date of publication in the Gazette.

3.5 Annual Report

Every Library Authority shall prepare an Annual Report under Section 94, relating to the progress made during the year and submit the same to the State Government, through the State Library Council, and in the report shall furnish the following information and particulars, namely:

1. Name of the library and address:
2. Year of establishment:
3. Management:
4. Professional staff and their qualifications:
5. Non-professional staff and their qualifications:
6. Other staff:
7. Book stock:

S.No.	Language	Last two years	This year
1			
2			
3			

8. List of newspapers and periodicals and language break-up:
9. Members (Net):

S.No.	Category	Last two years	This year
1	Men		
2	Women		
3	Children		

10. Circulation:

S. No.	Category	Last two years	This year
1	Books lent for reading		
2	Consultation		
3	Home delivery		

11. Binding and repair of books:
12. Stock taking and its results:

13. Finances:

Particulars	Last two years	This year
1		
2		
3		

(i) Library cess collection:
(ii) Grants from Government of India:
(iii) Grants from State Government:
(iv) Grants from RRRLF:
(v) Grants from other sources:

Receipts and charges statement is to be enclosed:

14. Cultural activities statement is to be enclosed:
15. Important visitors to this library during the year:
16. Achievement of the library during the year:-
17. General remarks:

4. DEVELOPMENT OF ASSETS

4.1 Opening of Village/Branch Libraries

The Secretary, Library Authority should submit the proposals about opening of new village or Branch libraries in the under-mentioned pro-forma to the Director, from the list of towns and villages as notified in the City/District Development Plan as approved by the State Planning Board.

4.1.1 *Opening of a Village Branch Library*

1. Name of the District:
2. Name of the Locality where the library is proposed to be opened:
3. Whether Branch Library/Children's Library/village Library:
4. Population of the locality as per latest census report:

5. Library Cess collections in the locality for the past 3 years:
6. Whether there are any libraries existing in the locality or nearby and if so, the details of them:
7. Special reasons for opening a fresh library/village library in the locality:
8. The staff required for the library:
9. The probable expenditure that may be incurred towards the staff, books, furniture and other equipment during the current year:
10. Whether there is budget provision to meet the expenditure during the current year:
11. Remarks:

The resolution of the Library Authority may be obtained and enclosed to the covering letter.

4.2 Takingover of Libraries

The Secretary, Library Authority should submit the proposals about the takingover of old libraries in the undermentioned proforma to the Director, from the list of towns and villages as notified in the City/Development Plan as approved by the State Planning Board:

Takingover of Libraries

1. Name of the District:
2. Name of the management handing over the library:

2(a) Population of locality as per latest census report and; (b) whether there are library facilities around that place:

3. Whether the library is situated in its own building or rent free building or rented:
4. Accommodation available and whether it is sufficient:
5. Details of furniture available and probable cost:
6. Total number of books — language-wise:
7. (i) Staff Employed:

(ii) Qualifications:
(iii) Pay and allowances:

8. Total number of years of service put in by them, their date of birth and present age:
9. Whether the management is willing to transfer their services and if so the post for which they are qualified to work under Library Authority and whether they are willing for the same:
10. Total value of the property to be handedover to the Library Authority:
11. Probable expenditure to be incurred on the staff, books and furniture during the year:
12. Remarks:

Note: The management who is handingover the library shall pass a resolution clearly and specifically in regard to their intention for handing over the library mentioning the movable and immovable properties that are given to the Library Authority. The Library Authority shall also pass a similar resolution for takingover the library. The Secretary shall submit along with the covering letter to the Director both the resolutions and the particulars in the form for permission.

4.3 Acquisition of Immovable Property

4.3.1 Every Library Authority shall before acquiring any immovable property, comply with the following conditions, namely that:

1. the property is approved by the Municipal Health Officer or the District Health Officer, as suitable from a sanitary point of view for the purpose of housing a public library.
2. the property, if intended for the construction or extension of building for public libraries the estimated cost whereof exceeds five thousands rupees, is approved by an officer of the Public Works Department not below the rank of an Executive Engineer as suitable for the purpose.
3. where the property is proposed to be acquired by the Library Authority otherwise than under the Land Acquisition Act, 1894 the previous approval of the Government shall be obtained there for:

(i) Provided that in case of lands, its valuation shall be obtained from the Revenue Department and that no amount in excess of such valuation shall be paid without the previous consent of the Government;

(ii) in the case of buildings, its valuation and a certificate regarding structural stability shall be obtained from the Executive Engineer of the Division, on payment of necessary charges, and that no amount in excess of such valuation shall be paid without the previous consent of the Government; and

(iii) in every case, an encumbrance certificate shall be obtained from the Sub-Registrar's office in respect of the property and examined as to its title by an advocate approved by the Library Authority in this behalf, unless the nature of the transaction is such as will, by law, pass the property free from all encumbrances.

4.3.2 The deed transfer of the immovable property to the Library Authority by sales or by gift shall be in Form I or Form II, as the case may be, appended to these Rules, with such variations as circumstances may require.

4.3.3 All immovable property acquired or held by the Library Authority shall be registered in the name of the Library Authority after meeting the expenditure on stamp duty, if any.

FORM I

Transfer by Sale

This deed of sale made the ________________________ day of ___________19____ between ____________________________ son of ________________ residing at ________________ (hereinafter called the "vendor" which expression shall where the context so admits include his heirs, executors, administrators and legal representatives) of the one part and Library Authority__________________________ of ________________ constituted under the. . . Public Libraries Act, 19. . . (Act No. . . . . . of 19. . .) (hereinafter called the "purchaser" which expression shall where the context so admit, include its successors and assignees) of the other part;

Whereas the vendor is well and sufficiently entitled to the land and premises described in the schedule hereto;

And whereas the purchaser in exercise of its powers has agreed with the vendor to purchase the said land and premises intended to be hereby granted conveyed and assigned, free from encumbrances at the price of rupees ________________ ;

Now this Deed Witnesses that in pursuance of the said agreement and in consideration of the sum of rupees ________________ to the vendor paid by the purchaser on or before the execution of these presents (the receipt thereof the vendor hereby acknowledges) he, the vendor do hereby grant, conveys and assigns to the purchaser all that piece or parcel of land situated in ____________ and more particularly described in the schedule hereunder written and which together with the messuage or tenement erected thereon is commonly called or known as _______________ Together with all buildings, godowns, trees, hedges, ditches, fences, ways waters, water-courses, liberties, privileges, easements, advantages and appurtenances whatsoever to the said piece or parcel of land, messages and premises or any of them in any wise appertaining or heretofore occupied or enjoyed therewith and all the estate, right, title interest, property, claim and demand whatsoever of the vendor into and upon the same premises to have and to hold the said piece or parcel of land, messuage and premises hereby conveyed and assigned to the purchaser forever and the vendor do hereby covenant with the purchaser that he, the vendor, now has good right to grant, convey and assign the premises hereby granted, conveyed and assigned to the purchaser in manner aforesaid that the purchaser shall and may at all times hereafter peacefully and quietly possess and enjoy the said premises free from all encumbrances whatsoever and receive the rents and profits thereof without any lawful eviction, interruption claim or demand whatsoever from or by the vendor or any other person or persons and further that the vendor, and all persons having lawfully or equitably claiming any estate or interest in the said premises or any of them or any part thereof from, under, or in trust for the vendor from or under any of his ancestors shall and will from time to time and at all times hereafter at the request and cost of the purchaser do execute and register or cause to be done, executed and registered all such acts, deeds and things whatsoever for further more perfectly assuring the said premises and every part thereof to the purchaser in manner aforesaid as shall or may be reasonably required.

In witness whereof the vendor has hereto set his hand and seal on the day and year first above written.

SCHEDULE

All the piece or parcel of land and premises situated in the village of ________________ in the registration sub-district of __________ in the registration district of __________ bounded on the north by __________ on the south by __________ on the east by __________ and on the west by __________ bearing re-survey number __________ and old survey No. __________ and containing on the whole by admeasurement __________ (be the same, more or less).

Signed, sealed and delivered by the above named in the presence of:

1.

2.

FORM II

Transfer by gift

This Deed of gift made the day __________ one thousand and nine hundred and __________ between __________ son of __________ residing at __________ (hereinafter called "the donor" which expression shall where the contest so admits include his heirs, executors, administrators and legal representatives) of the one part and the Library Authority of __________ constituted under the . . . Public Libraries Act, 19. . . . (Act No...... of 19....) hereinafter called "the donee" which expression shall where the context admits include his successors and assignees of the other part.

Whereas the donor is well and sufficiently entitled free from encumbrances to the piece or parcel of land and premises hereinafter described and intended to be hereby granted, conveyed and assigned:

And whereas the donor has agreed to transfer the said piece or parcel of land and premises to the donee as a gift subject to the payment by the donee of all existing and future taxes, charges, assessments and ground rent in respect of the same and the donee has agreed to accept the same subject to such conditions.

And whereas the Government of ________ have by an order No. ___________ dated the day of _______________ sanctioned the acceptance of the property.

And whereas the said piece or parcel of land premises is of the value of Rs. ______________ for the purpose of stamp duty;

Now this Deed witnesses that the donor do hereby give, grant, convey and assign to the donee, who hereby accepts the same. All that piece or parcel of land bearing survey No. __________ situated in the village of _______________ in the registration sub-district of ____________ in the registration district of more particularly described in the Schedule hereunder written together with all buildings, trees, commons, liberties, privileges, easements, advantages and appurtenances whatsoever to the said piece or parcel of land, buildings and premises or any of them in any wise apportioning or heretofore occupied or enjoyed therewith and all the estate, right, title, interest, property, claim and demand whatsoever of the donor into and upon the same premises to have and to hold the said piece or parcel of and and premises hereby granted and assigned to the donee forever and the donor do hereby covenant with the donee that the donor now has good right to grant, convey and assign the premises hereby granted, conveyed, and assigned to the donee in manner aforesaid and that the donee shall and may at all times hereafter peacefully and quietly, free from all encumbrances, whatsoever, or by the donor, any person claiming under or in trust for him and further that the donor and all persons having lawfully or equitably claiming any estate or interest in the said premises or any part thereof from, under or in trust for the donor or from or under any of his ancestors shall and will from time to time and at all times hereafter at the request and cost of the donee to execute and register or cause to be done, executed and registered all such acts, deeds and things whatsoever for further and more perfectly assuring the said premises every part thereof to the donee in manner aforesaid or as shall or may be reasonably required.

SCHEDULE

All that piece or parcel of land and premises situated in village of ____________ in the registration sub-district of ____________ in the registration district of ____________ and bounded on the north by ____________ on the south by ____________ on the east by ____________ and on the west by ______________ bearing Re-survey

No. ______________________ and old survey No. ___________ and containing on the whole by admeasurement ____________________ (be the same less or more).

Signed sealed and delivered by the above named in the presence of ____________

Signed, by the Secretary, Library Authority of ____________
in the presence of ______________________________
The common seal of the Library Authority of ____________
was hereto affixed in the presence of ________________

4.4 **Supply Materials, Goods etc.**

4.4.1 Every contract for the supply of materials or goods or for rendering of services to the Library Authority shall be made by calling for tenders, provided that the Library Authority may provide in its bye-laws, the contracts, for supply of materials or goods or for rendering of services, other than those for execution of works, the value whereof does not exceed rupees one thousand in respect of which tenders may be dispensed with.

4.4.2 When tenders are invited they shall be tabulated and scrutinised by the Secretary, Library Authority and placed before the Library Authority Samstha with his recommendations for acceptance.

The lowest tender shall ordinarily be accepted. Where it is considered undesirable to accept the lowest tender, the reasons thereof shall be recorded in writing and made available for the purposes of audit.

4.4.3 *Explanation:* Where the lowest tender is in respect of more than one article, for example, stationery articles, the comparative prices rendered may be considered either individually for each article or conjointly for all the articles or for specified groups of articles, provided that the intention of the Library Authority to accept the lowest tender in any of these ways is made clear in the tender notice. If the tender is considered conjointly for all the articles, or of all the articles in each group, as the case may be, shall be worked out with reference to the rates given in each tender and the lowest tender will be that according to which total cost of the probable requirements of all the articles proposed to be taken together works out to be the lowest.

4.4.4 Where the capacity to supply and the integrity of tenderer are not known or whether they are doubtful, his tender need not necessarily be rejected but such additional security as the Library Authority or the executive committee, authorised by the Library Authority in this behalf considers necessary, shall be taken from the tenderer.

4.4.5 Where the lowest tender is rejected, the next higher tender shall be accepted, unless there are adequate reasons which should be recorded in writing for rejecting that tender also and the records thereto shall be made available for purposes of audit and inspection.

4.4.6 In no case shall a tender be accepted at rates other than those specified in that tender.

4.4.7 There shall be no avoidable delay in the disposal of tenders after they are opened.

4.4.8 (1) Tenders shall be invited by the Secretary, Library Authority in sealed covers in the most open and public manner possible, and invariably:

(a) by a notice in the language or languages of the district posted at the office of the Library Authority and at such other places as the Secretary may deem fit;

(b) by advertisement in atleast one newspaper circulation in the district where the value is expected to exceed Rs. 3,000.

(2) Every notice or advertisement published under sub-rule (1) shall state *inter alia*:

(a) the conditions under which, the officer from whom, and the price, if any, for which, a copy of the Schedule of quantities of the various kinds of articles can be obtained if they cannot be mentioned in detail in the notice or advertisement itself;

(b) the precise form in which the tender shall be made, that is, whether the prices for the various articles are quoted and whether the comparative value of the tender will be examined with reference to each article mentioned in the Schedule of quantities or for all such articles conjointly or for groups of such articles;

(c) the time and place for presenting the tender allowing a period of atleast ten days from the date of publication, of the notice at the office of the Library Authority or of the first advertisement in the newspaper as the case may be;

(d) the time and place for opening the tenders;

(e) the amount of earnest money which should accompany the tender and the amount and the nature of the security which will be required in case the tender is accepted;
(f) the authority competent to accept the tender;
(g) that the authority competent to accept the tender reserves the right to reject any or all of the tender received without assigning reasons; and
(h) that the tenderer who withdraws his tender, without valid reasons (to be decided by the authority competent to accept the tender) shall be liable to have his subsequent tenders summarily rejected.

4.4.9 Nothing contained in these rules shall apply to the purchase of—

(i) stores purchased through the Indian Stores Department or the Stationery Department or through any agency authorised for Government Departments;
(ii) articles from the metal and timber works and factories started by the Government for the re-settlement of ex-service men;
(iii) controlled articles at controlled rates through a permit issued on the orders of Government or their agents;
(iv) petrol from standing firms for its distribution and supply or from their authorised agents at the rates for the time being in forçe;
(v) articles purchased from jails;
(vi) articles obtained from manufacturing units stated by and belonging to the Panchayat Samithis and Zilla Parishads in the State;
(vii) books purchased direct from the authors or the publishers, including cultural organisations; and
(viii) library cards and other stationery articles peculiar to technical work of libraries;

4.4.10 Notwithstanding anything in these rules, the Government may, for sufficient reason, permit the Library Authority to dispense with calling for tenders in any of particular case or class of cases or condone the non-observance of any of the provisions contained in these rules.

4.4.11 Every accepted tender shall be entered into a contract and every such contract shall be made on behalf of the Library Authority by the Secretary of the Library Authority.

4.5 Construction and Repairs of the Buildings

4.5.1 A Library Authority may, at, its discretion entrust any building work to the Public Works Department in accordance with the rules of that Department. For the execution of building work in any other manner, the following procedure shall be followed.

4.5.2 Tenders shall be called for in respect of every work, which is to be executed on contract and the contract amount of which exceeds Rs. 3,000 (Rupees three thousand) in sealed envelopes in an open and public manner as possible, by a notice in the Chief language or languages of the district advertised in one or more newspapers having circulation in the district.

4.5.3 Only Public Works Department registered contractors shall be entitled to tender for the work.

4.5.4 Every notice published under Rule 2 shall state:

(i) When and where the contract documents may be inspected.

(ii) the precise form of tendering, that is, to say, whether it shall be at a specified percentage below or above the estimate rates, or whether definite rates shall be quoted for each item of work included in the Schedule;

(iii) when and where tenders are to be submitted;

(iv) when and where they are to be opened;

(v) the amount of earnest money which shall accompany the tender and the amount and nature of Security required in case the tender is accepted;

(vi) the authority competent to accept the tender; and

(vii) that the authority competent to accept the tender, reserves the right to reject any or all the tenders received without assigning any reasons.

4.5.5 The authority competent to accept the tender shall be either the Chairman or the Secretary or a member of the District Library Authority as may be decided by the District Library Authority in each case.

4.6.6 Before tenders are invited for the execution on a work on contract "contract documents shall be got prepared on payment of charges" if any, by an Engineer of the Public Works Department or Zilla Parishad or any other Engineer approved by the District Library Authority. The "Contract Documents" shall include

(i) a completed set of drawings showing the general dimension of the proposed work, and so far as necessary, details of the various parts;

(ii) A complete specification of the work to be done and of the materials to be used unless reference can be made to some standard specification;

(iii) A schedule of the quantities of the various descriptions of work; and

(iv) A set of "conditions of contract" to be complied with by tenderer in case his tender is accepted.

4.5.7 (i) The precise form of tendering, namely, whether it shall be at specified percentage below or above the estimate rates, or whether definite rates shall be quoted for each item of work included in the Schedule, independently of the rates provided, for the sanctioned estimate shall be decided with the consultation of the Engineer referred to in Rule 6.

(ii) Contractors who are required to tender on percentage basis, may be permitted to examine the estimates but the data statement showing the actual cost of materials shall not be shown to them nor shall it form part of the contract documents.

4.5.8 No tender shall ordinarily be treated as valid unless it is accompanied either by the earnest money specified in the tender notice, or by a treasury receipt in token of the party having remitted the amount of the said earnest money into the treasury.

4.5.9 The amount of earnest money to be deposited shall be sufficiently large as to be security against loss in the case of the contractor failing to furnish the required security within the appointed time after the acceptance of his tender, or until the sums due to him from a sufficient guarantee, as the case may be.

4.5.10 The person authorised by the Library Authority as referred to in Rule 5 shall, at the time and place specified for the purpose, open the sealed envelopes containing the tenders in the presence of such of the tenderers or their authorised agents as may be present. Provided that where the Chairman or a member authorised by the Library Authority in this behalf is not present at the appointed time the Secretary shall open the sealed envelopes and dispose them off.

Until, the sealed envelopes are so opened, they shall be kept in the personal custody of the Secretary, Authority Library. On opening the tenders the person authorised by the Library Authority shall initial the tenders and also at least, with their initials all corrections in each tender, which may have been made by the tenders and attested by him. If there are corrections in the tender unattested by the tenderers a note of such corrections shall be made on the tender itself when it is opened. The Secretary shall enter in a tender register maintained in the office of the Library Authority in the form appended to these rules, the total number of tenders received against each work.

4.5.11 After the tenders are opened, they shall be tabulated and posted in the tender register. The Secretary shall scrutinise the entries in the register and certify that the tabulation is correctly made with reference to the original tenders which shall be preserved and made available for the purpose of audit.

4.5.12(1) The lowest tender shall ordinarily be accepted. Where it is considered undesirable to accept the lowest tender, the reasons shall be recorded in writing by the authority competent to accept the tender and in such a case all the tenders shall be placed in a meeting of the Library Authority for its decision.

(2) Where the capacity for work and the integrity of a tender are not known, his tender need not necessarily be rejected, and such additional security not exceeding 10 per cent of the contract amount as the authority competent to accept the tender considers necessary shall, however, be taken from the tenderer if the circumstances warrant such a course.

(3) Where the lowest tender is rejected by the Library Authority the next lowest tender shall be considered. If it considered undesirable to accept that tender also, the next higher tender shall be considered.

(4) In no case shall a tender be accepted with rates other than those specified in that tender. However, if the Library Authority considers that the rates for certain items in an otherwise lowest tender which is under consideration under sub-rule (1) or sub-rule (3) are pitched too high it may negotiate with the tenderer and secure reasonable rates for those items.

(5) There shall be no avoidable delay in the disposal of tenders after they are opened. In case where the Secretary is himself competent to dispose of tenders, he shall do so ordinarily within a week of the date on which they are opened. In cases where the approval of the Library Authority has to be obtained, the tenders shall be disposed of at its meeting which shall be convened at the earliest opportunity.

5. PERSONNEL MANAGEMENT

5.1 Constitution of the State Library Service

5.1.1 As per sub-section 2 of Section 58 the Government should constitute the State Library Service with the following cadres. The qualifications, authority for appointment etc. are given below:

Sl.No.	Cadre	Qualifications	Appointment authority
1.	Director	1. I or II class M A, M Lib. SC 2. Training in Information technology or computerization 3. 10 Years professional experience	Government
2.	Jt Director/ State Librarian	1. I or II class M A, M Lib SC 2. Training in Information Technology or Computers 3. 5 years professional experience	Government
3.	Dy Director/ Regional Librarian	1. M A, B Lib SC 2. Training in information technology 3. 5 years professional experience	Government
4.	Asst Director/City Librarian/Dt Librarian	1. M A, B Lib SC 2. 5 years professional experience	Director
5.	Senior Librarian	1. B A, B Lib SC 2. 5 years professional experience	Library Authority
6.	Jr Librarian	Intermediate or + 2 C Lib SC	Library Authority

(Contd.)

(Contd.)

Sl.No.	Cadre	Qualifications	Appointment authority
7.	Office Manager/ Superintendent	As prescribed in the State and subordinate service rules	Library Authority
8.	Senior Assistant	As prescribed in the State and Subordinate service Rules	Library Authority
9.	Junior Assistant	As prescribed in the State and Subordinate service Rules	Library Authority
10.	Typist	As prescribed in the State and Subordinate service Rules	Library Authority
11.	Card writer/copiest	As prescribed in the State and Subordinate service Rules	Library Authority
12.	Book Binder	As prescribed in the State and Subordinate service Rules	Library Authority
13.	Record Assistant	As prescribed in the State and Subordinate service Rules	Library Authority
14.	Driver	As prescribed in the State and Subordinate service Rules	Library Authority
15.	Attender/Cleaner	As prescribed in the State and Subordinate service Rules	Library Authority
16.	Attender	As prescribed in the State and Subordinate service Rules	Library Authority
17.	Gardner/Sweeper Watchman	As prescribed in the State and subordinate service Rules	Library Authority

5.1.2 *Method of Appointment:* Following the communal roster and with the directions of the State Government, all the posts should filled up by promotion transfer/direct recruitment only. In case of the Director, the Government may consider to appoint the person from Indian Administrative Service, in some special cases.

5.1.3 Persons dealing with the accounts should pass the Accounts Test for subordinate officers, during the period of probation, failing which they shall not be eligible to draw increments in the time scale of pay applicable to them. Such ineligibility to draw increments shall not have the effect of postponing their future increments after they have so qualified themselves.

5.1.4 All the staff members should pass the language test of the State.

5.1.5 *Age:* No person shall be eligible for appointment to the post by direct recruitment up to Cadre No. 6, if he has completed or will complete the age of 30 years on the 1st of July of the year in which the selection made provided in the case of candidates belonging to any of the aboriginal Tribes in the Agency areas, or scheduled castes and scheduled tribes specified in the State and subordinate services rules of the limit of age shall be thirty five years. For other cadres the rules of the State Government will apply.

5.1.6 *Probation:* Every person appointed to a post shall be on probation.

(a) for a period of one year on duty within a continuous period of two years in case he is appointed by transfer; and

(b) for a total period of two years on duty within a continuous period of three years in case he is appointed by direct recruitment.

5.1.7 *Pay:* They shall be paid monthly pay calculated in the scale of pay as revised by Government from time to time plus usual allowances.

5.1.8 *Savings:* Notwithstanding anything in these rules, a person who is working in the post on the date of issue of these rules shall not be adversely affected solely by reason of his not possessing any of the qualifications prescribed in these rules.

5.2 Creation of Posts

5.2.1 The Government may, either on application by Library Authority or *suo motu,* create the posts, mentioned in the annexure to these rules, for the offices of the District Library Authority and the Public Libraries established or maintained by the District Library Authority on such terms and consideration of the need for the creation of the post and also the financial position of the District Library Authority.

5.2.2 All the charges of the establishment so created shall be met from the Library Fund maintained under Section 80 of the ... Public Libraries Act, 19....

5.2.3 The Director, may either on application by the Library Authority or *suo motu*, abolish or transfer to another library within the jurisdiction of the Library Authority, any of the posts borne on the establishment of the Library Authority.

5.2.4 The posts sanctioned under Rule 5.2.1 may be either permanent or temporary, as may be directed by the Director:

Provided that no post shall ordinarily be retained on a permanent basis unless it has been in existence for a period of not less than three years and the approval of the Director has been obtained.

5.2.5 The Director shall maintain a register showing the number of posts created for the libraries established or maintained by the Library Authorities.

5.3 Control Over the Staff

PART I — GENERAL

5.3.1 These rules may be called the District Library Authority Services (Classification, Control and Appeal) Rules, 19.....

5.3.2 They shall apply to every members appointed in the following categories of posts, whether temporary or permanent:

1. Director
2. Joint Director/State Librarian
3. Dy Director/Regional Librarian

4. Asst Director/City Librarian/District Librarian
5. Senior Librarian
6. Junior Librarian
7. Office Manager/Superintendent
8. Senior Assistant
9. Junior Assistant
10. Typist/Card writer/Copiost
11. Book Binder
12. Record Assistant
13. Driver
14. Attender/Cleaner
15. Gardener/Sweeper/Watchman

5.3.3 If any doubt arises —

1. Whether these rules apply to any persons; or
2. Whether a person to whom these rules apply belongs to a particular service, or as to which of the services, the matter shall be referred to the Director, whose decision shall be final.

PART II — CLASSIFICATION

5.3.4 The various categories of posts under Library Authority shall be classified as follows:

(1) Library Service for the Library Authority in the State consisting of the following categories of posts namely:

1. Director
2. Joint Director/State Librarian
3. Dy Director/Regional Librarian
4. Assistant Director/City Librarian/District Librarian
5. Senior Librarian
6. Junior Librarian

(2) Ministerial Service under the Library Authority consisting of the following categories, namely:

1. Office Manager/Superintendent
2. Senior Assistant

3. Junior Assistant
4. Typist/Card writer/Copiest

(3) Miscellaneous posts under the Library Authority, namely:

1. Book Binder
2. Record Assistant
3. Driver
4. Attender/Cleaner
5. Gardner/Sweeper/Watchman

5.3.5 (1) The following penalties may, for good and sufficient reason, be imposed upon members of the Library Authorities staff, namely:

1. Censure;
2. Fine;
3. Withholding increments or promotions;
4. Reduction to a lower rank in the seniority list or to a lower post, whether in the same service or any other service or to a lower time scale or to a lower stage in a time scale;
5. Recovery from pay of the whole or any part of the pecuniary loss caused to the Library Authority or Government by negligence or breach of orders while working in any Library Authority;
6. Compulsory retirement from Service;
7. Removal from the Service of the Library Authority;
8. Dismissal from the service of Library Authority; and
9. Suspension where a person has already been suspended under Rule 6 to the extent considered necessary.

5.3.5 (2) The Discharge:

1. The discharge of a person appointed temporarily for a fixed period on the expiration of the said period of appointment, does not amount to removal or dismissal within the meaning of this rule.

Explanation — The removal of a person from the service

of the Library Authority shall not disqualify him from future employment.

2. The stoppage or postponement of increments on account of extension of probation does not amount to withholding of increments within the meaning of this rule.
3. The penalty of fine may be imposed only on persons working in the category of peons.

5.3.6 1. A member of a service may be placed under suspension from service pending investigation or enquiry into grave charges where such suspension is necessary in the public interest:

Provided that where a member of a service has been suspended by the competent authority and the investigation has not been completed and the action proposed to be taken in regard to him has not been completed within a period of six months from the date of suspension, the fact shall be reported to the Director if suspended by the Chairman of the Library Authority and to Government, if suspended by the Director for such orders and, that the period of suspension shall not exceed six months without the previous orders of the Director or the Government, as the case may be.

2. A member of a service who is detained in custody, whether on a criminal charge or otherwise for a period exceeding forty eight (48) hours, shall be deemed to have been suspended with effect from the date of detention by an order of the Authority competent to impose the suspension and shall remain under suspension until further orders.
3. A member of the service under suspension shall be entitled to the payment of a subsistence allowance as admissible under Rule 53 of the F.Rs.
4. Where a penalty of dismissal, removal or compulsory retirement from service imposed upon a member of a service who has been placed under suspension is set aside in appeal or on review under these rules and the case is

remitted for further inquiry or action or with any other directions the order of suspension on such member shall be deemed to have continued in force on and from that date of the original order of dismissal, removal or compulsory retirement and shall remain in force until further orders.

5. Where a penalty of dismissal, removal or compulsory retirement from service imposed upon a member of a service is set aside, or rendered void, in consequence of or by a decision of a Court of law, and the Authority competent to impose the penalty, on a consideration of the circumstances of the case decides immediately thereafter to hold a further inquiry against him on the allegation on which the penalty of dismissal, removal or compulsory retirement was originally imposed, the member of service shall be deemed to have been placed under suspension by the authority competent to impose the suspension from the date of original order of dismissal, removal or compulsory retirement and shall continue to remain under suspension until further orders.
6. An order of suspension made or deemed to have been made under this rule may, at any time, be revoked by the authority which made or is deemed to have made the orders or by any authority which made or is deemed to have made the orders or by any authority to which that authority is subordiante.

5.3.7 The authority competent to impose the punishments mentioned in Rule 5.3.6(5) shall be as specified in the Schedule appended to these Rules.

5.3.8 (1) No order imposing on a member of a service penalty in items (i), (ii) and (iii) or item (v) of Rule 5.3.5(1) shall be passed, except after:

(i) the member of the service is informed in writing of the proposal to take action in regard to him, of the allegations on which the action is proposed to be taken and is given an opportunity to make any representation he may wish to make; and

(ii) such representation, if any, is taken into consideration by the authority competent to impose the penalty.

2 (i) In every case where it is proposed to impose on a member of a service any of the penalties specified in items (iv), (vi), (vii) and (viii) of Rule 5.3.5 (1), the authority competent to impose the penalty shall appoint an inquiry officer, who shall be superior in rank to the person on whom it is proposed to impose the penalty or shall itself hold an inquiry. In every such case the grounds on which it is proposed to take action shall be communicated to the person charged, together with a statement of the allegations on which each charge is based and of any other circumstances which it is proposed to take into consideration in passing order in the case. (For detailed instructions see Appendix to these Rules.) He shall be required within a reasonable time, to file a written statement of his defence and to state whether he desires an oral enquiry or to be heard in person or both. The person charged may, for the purpose of preparing his defence, be permitted to inspect and take extracts from, such official records as he may specify, provided that the inquiry officer may, for reasons to be recorded in writing, refuse such permission, if in his opinion such records are not relevant for the purpose or it is against public interest to allow access thereto. On receipt of the statement of defence within the specified time of such further time as may have been an oral inquiry be held if such an inquiry is desired by the person charged or is decided upon by the inquiry officer or is directed by the competent authority. At that inquiry, oral evidence shall be heard as to such of the allegations as are not admitted, and the person charged shall be entitled to cross-examine the witnesses, to give evidence in person to have such witnesses, called as he may wish, provided that the inquiry officer may for special and sufficient reason to be recorded in writing refuse to call a witness. After the oral inquiry is held and the person charged desires to be heard in person, a personal hearing shall be given to him. The proceedings shall con-

tain the charges framed against the person charged along with the grounds, written statement filed in defence, if any, a sufficient record of the evidence adduced during the oral inquiry, a memorandum of the points urged by the person charged during the personal hearing, if any, a statement of the findings of the inquiry officer on the different charges and the grounds therefor.

(ii) Except under very special circumstances to be recorded in writing by the inquiry officer or any officer to whom an appeal may be preferred, no pleader or agent shall be allowed to appear either on behalf of the Library Authority or on behalf of the person charged before the inquiry officer:

Provided that when a request is made by the person charged for engaging counsel on the ground that he is not acquainted with the language in which the inquiry is conducted, the inquiry officer or the officer to whom the appeal has been preferred shall allow the person charged to be represented by a Council.

(iii) After the authority competent to impose the penalty mentioned in clause (a) has arrived at a provisional conclusion in regard to the penalty to be imposed, the person charged shall be supplied with a copy of the report of the inquiry officer and be given a reasonable time not ordinarily exceeding one month, on the penalty proposed. Any representation made in this behalf by the person charged shall be duly taken into consideration by the competent authority before final orders are passed:

Provided that such representation shall be based only on the evidence adduced during the inquiry referred to in clause (a).

(iv) The authority imposing any penalty under these rules shall maintain a record showing:

(a) the allegations upon which action was taken against the person punished;
(b) the charges framed, if any;
(c) the person's representation, if any, and the evidence taken, if any; and
(d) the findings and the grounds thereof, if any.

(v) Every order imposing the penalty shall state the grounds on which it is passed and shall be communicated in writing to the person concerned.

PART IV — APPEALS

5.3.9 Every person who is a member of any of the services specified in Rule 4, shall be entitled to appeal, as hereinafter provided from an order passed by an authority:

1. imposing upon him any of the penalties specified in Rule 5, or
2. placing him under suspensions under Rule 6.

5.3.10 Every member of a service shall be entitled to appeal to the authority competent, specified in the Schedule appended to these Rules from an order passed by the authority:

1. varying to his disadvantage his conditions of service, pay and allowances; and
2. interpreting to his disadvantage the provisions of any rules where by his conditions of service, pay and allowances are regulated.

5.3.11 In case of an appeal, the Appellate Authority shall consider:

1. whether the facts on which the order was based have been established;
2. whether the facts established afford sufficient ground for taking action; and
3. whether the penalty is excessive, adequate or inadequate; and after such consideration, shall pass such order as it thinks proper.

5.3.12 Every person preferring an appeal shall do so separately and in his own name.

5.3.13 Every appeal preferred under these rules shall contain all material statements and arguments relied on by the appellant, but shall not contain any disrespectful or improper language. It shall be self-contained with copies of orders documents. Every such appeal shall be addressed to the authority to whom the appeal is to be preferred and shall be submitted through the Head of the office to which the appellant belonged and through the authority from whose order the appeal is preferred:

Provided that an advance copy of the appeal may be submitted direct to the appellate Samstha simultaneously with the original which is submitted through the usual official channel.

5.3.14 An appeal may be withheld by an authority not lower than the authority from whose order it is preferred if:

1. it is an appeal in case in which, under these rules no appeal lies;
2. it does not comply with all or any of the provisions of Rule 11;
3. it is not preferred within three months from the date on which the appellant was informed of the order appealed against and the sufficient cause is shown for the delay;
4. it is a repetition of a previous appeal and if made to the same appellate authority by which such appeal was decided and no new facts or circumstances are adduced which could afford grounds for a reconsideration of the case; or
5. it is addressed to an authority to which no appeal lies under these Rules:

Provided that in every case in which an appeal is withheld the appellant shall be informed of the fact and the reasons therefor.

5.3.15 When an appeal is withheld at a copy of the order withholding the appeal shall, invariably, be submitted to the authority to whom appeal is addressed.

5.3.16 No appeal shall be allowed or entertained against the withholding of an appeal by a competent authority

5.3.17 Every appeal which is not withheld under these rules shall be forwarded to the appellate authority by the authority from whose order the appeal is preferred with an expression of his opinion.

5.3.18 An appellate authority may call for any appeal admissible under these rules which has been withheld by a subordinate authority and may pass such order thereon as it considers fit.

SCHEDULE

Sl. No.	Name of the post	Authority competent to impose the penalty of			
		Censure	Fine	withholding of increments	withholding of promotion where such stoppage is imposed on the ground of fault or misconduct
1	2	3	4	5	6
1.	Director	Government	Government	Government	Government
2.	Joint Director/State Librarian	Government	Government	Government	Government
3.	Dy Director/Regional Librarian	Government	Government	Government	Government
4.	Assistant Director/City Librarian/District Librarian	Director	Director	Director	Director
5.	Senior Librarian	Director	Director	Director	Director
6.	Junior Librarian	Secretary	Secretary	Secretary	Secretary
7.	Office Manager/Superintendent	Secretary	Secretary	Secretary	Secretary
8.	Senior Librarian	Secretary	Secretary	Secretary	Secretary
9.	Junior Librarian	Secretary	Secretary	Secretary	Secretary
10.	Typist/Card writer/copiest	Secretary	Secretary	Secretary	Secretary
11.	Book Binder	Secretary	Secretary	Secretary	Secretary
12.	Record Assistant	Secretary	Secretary	Secretary	Secretary
13.	Driver	Secretary	Secretary	Secretary	Secretary
14.	Attender/cleaner	Secretary	Secretary	Secretary	Secretary
15.	Gardner/sweeper/watchman	Secretary	Secretary	Secretary	Secretary

Reduction to a Lower rank in the seniority list, or to a lower post or timescale, whether in the same service or in another service	Authority competent to impose the penalty of Recovery from pay of the whole the part of any pecuniary loss cause to DLA or Govt. by negligence or breach of orders	Suspension	Compulsory retirement or dismissal from service	Appellate Authority
7	8	9	10	11
1. Director	Government	Government	Government	Government
2. Joint Director/State Librarian	Government	Government	Government	Government
3. Dy Director/Regional Librarian	Government	Government	Government	Government
4. Assistant Director/City Librarian/District Librarian	Director	Director	Government	Government
5. Senior Librarian	Secretary	Chairman	Government	Government
6. Junior Librarian	Secretary	Chairman	Government	Government
7. Office Manager/Superintendent	Secretary	Chairman	Government	Government
8. Senior Assistant	Secretary	Chairman	Government	Government
9. Junior Assistant	Secretary	Chairman	Government	Government
10. Typist/Card writer/Copiest	Secretary	Chairman	Government	Government
11. Book Binder	Secretary	Secretary	Chairman	Government
12. Record Assistant	Secretary	Secretary	Chairman	Government
13. Driver	Secretary	Secretary	Chairman	Government
14. Attender/cleaner	Secretary	Secretary	Chairman	Government
15. Gardner/Sweeper/Watchman	Secretary	Secretary	Chairman	Government

Instructions for conducting Disciplinary Proceedings

1. Preliminary Enquiry

(a) Before commencing any enquiry against the member of staff of the District Library Authority with regard to a disciplinary matter, it is necessary that there should be sufficient evidence gathered by way of preliminary enquiry.

(b) The authority competent to order the enquiry should be satisfied that there is sufficient *prima facie* evidence to start disciplinary proceedings against an employee of the Library Authority. The preliminary enquiry may be made by an officer under whose administrative control the officer, alleged to be at fault, is working (or was working at the time the acts complained of were committed), but the decision to hold the regular enquiry can only be taken by the authority competent to hold the enquiry.

(c) Any officer can ask for an explanation from a subordinate officer in respect of any matter pertaining to his duties and it will often be advised before directing the holding of an enquiry to obtain the explanation as after obtaining the explanation, the reporting authority may feel that there is no case to initiate disciplinary proceedings at all. The asking of such an explanation is, however, not compulsory and the authority ordering or holding the investigation will have to decide according to the circumstances of each whether such an explanation should be obtained before the issue of a charge sheet or not.

2. Enquiry Officer

It is a fundamental principles of natural justice that the officer selected to make an enquiry should be a person with an open mind and not one who is biased against the delinquent or one who has prejudice against the delinquent.

Without being appointed as enquiry officer or authorised to hold the enquiry by the authority competent to impose the penalty or by a higher authority, one cannot hold the enquiry merely because he is an officer superior to the accused officer. The enquiry can be conducted by the competent authority duly appointed as enquiry officer by the competent authority.

3. Issues of Charge Sheet

(a) The enquiry officer should frame a charge sheet containing:

1. definite charge or charges;
2. under each charge the grounds on which that charge is based;
3. any other circumstances which it is proposed to take into consideration, in passing orders in the case. Each charge should be drawn up clearly and precisely and care should be taken to avoid vagueness; and
4. the charge-sheet should not indicate the punishment to be imposed on the delinquent officer;
5. the charge-sheet should conclude with the following formula:

   "Please show cause why suitable disciplinary action should not be taken against you on the charges mentioned above. You are required herewith, to put written statement you may desire to submit in your defence by . . . . (the date to be specified). Please fill in the questionnaire enclosed and resubmit it. In case you fail to put in your written statement by the above date, the undersigned may proceed with the enquiry on the basis that you have no defence to offer."

4. Written Statement in Defence

The enquiry officer should fix a reasonable time within which the written statement must be filled. In dealing with requests for further time, if any, by the accused employee, the enquiry officer will consider whether the accused is sufficiently active in the preparation of his defence and whether the time asked for is really necessary and justified.

5. Request for an Oral Inquiry and or to be Heard in Person

1. If within the prescribed time, or such further time as the Enquiry Officer may give no written statement in defence is filed and no request in writing is made for oral enquiry for being

heard in person, it is always better that the Enquiry Officer proceeds with the enquiry *ex parte* to satisfy himself about the truth of the charges. An enquiry must necessarily be held when an employee asks for it, or has expressed a desire to be heard in person, or having regard to the written statement in defence, or the statement in defence, or the statement made by the employee himself, when he is heard in person, a further enquiry is necessary to decide the truth of the charge.

2. The enquiry officer shall examine the delinquent orally, if he desires to be heard in person. The delinquent should not be compelled to be a witness against himself.

Recording of Evidence

1. At the oral enquiry, evidence should be heard on charges which are not admitted. The enquiry, however, should not extend to matters not mentioned in the charge sheet.
2. The evidence should be recorded first and the accused servant given an opportunity to cross-examine the witness.
3. The evidence of each witness should be recorded in the form of narrative and when the evidence is completed, it should be read over to the witness and if necessary, explained to him in the language in which it was given. If the witness denies the correctness of any part of the evidence when it is read over to him the enquiry officer may either carry out the correction or instead of correcting the evidence make a memorandum of the objection taken and add such remarks as he thinks necessary. Then the statement shall be signed by the enquiry officer. Copies of such evidence as are required by accused servants should be supplied to him free of cost.

7. **Inspecting of Documents by the Accused**

The enquiry officer should give every reasonable facility to the accused to inspect any documents or records necessary for the purpose of preparing his defence. Such inspection should be arranged in the presence of a responsible officer to ensure that the records are not tampered with in any manner.

8. Enquiry Officer's Responsibility

It is the enquiry officer's responsibility to arrive at the truth or falsity of the charges against the accused. For this purpose, it is his responsibility to put whatever questions as may be necessary both to the witnesses examined in support of the charge and to the witnesses produced by the accused.

9. Submission by the Accused Officer of Another Written Statement

After the entire evidence has been heard, the person charged shall, if he so desires, put in a further written statement in his defence and also explain his defence orally to the enquiry officer.

10. Drawing up of the Findings by the Enquiry Officer

1. On completion of the enquiry, including the personal examination of the accused, if any, the enquiry officer shall record his findings in respect of each charge, with reasons therefor and forward the proceedings to the authority appointing him. The enquiry officer should not rely on any document or material which the delinquent had no opportunity to explain.
2. The proceedings forwarded shall contain:
    1. the charges framed against the accused along with the grounds of charges;
    2. written statement filed in defence, if any;
    3. record of the evidence given during the oral enquiry;
    4. a memorandum of the points urged by the accused during the personal hearing if any;
    5. a statement of the findings of the enquiry officer on the different charges and the grounds therefor.

11. Provisional Conclusion

The authority competent to impose punishment on perusal of the proceedings shall come to a provisional conclusion in regard to the penalty to be imposed.

12. Giving of a Second or Further Opportunity to Person Charged

If the penalty proposed is any of the major penalties, namely, reduction to a lower rank in the seniority list or to a lower post or time scale, compulsory retirement, removal or dismissal from service, the person charged should be supplied with a copy of the report of the inquiry authority and be called upon to show cause within a reasonable time, not ordinarily less than one week, or exceeding one month, against the particular penalty proposed to be inflicted. Any representation in this behalf submitted by the person charged shall be duly taking into consideration before final orders are passed.

13. Drawing up of the Final Order

The final order containing the decision of the authority competent to impose the penalty should be self-contained order. The order should set out briefly the relevant facts and findings. Copy of this order should be supplied to the accused officer.

14. Cases in which Procedure detailed above need not be followed

The procedure laid down in a Rule 8 (2) of these rules need not be followed in a case when a person is punished on the ground of conduct which has led to his conviction on a criminal charge by a competent judicial authority.

15. Procedure to be followed in Cases of Minor Punishments

It is not necessary to follow the elaborate procedure detailed above in respect of minor penalties, namely:

1. Censure;
2. Fines;
3. withholding of increments of promotion; and
4. recovery from any of the whole or part of any pecuniary loss caused to the Library Authority or Government by negligence or breach of orders.

But before imposing any such punishment, the accused should be given an opportunity to make a representation against the particular penalty proposed to be imposed. In such case there is no need to hold any elaborate enquiry and in the first instance itself, the delinquent officer can be asked to show cause against the particular penalty proposed to be imposed and orders passed after taking account the explanation given by him.

16. **Suspension**

The authority competent to suspend the employee while issuing the orders of suspension should invariably mention in the said order that the suspension is made in the public interest and also indicate the subsistence allowance which should be paid to the accused. The order of suspension cannot be given retrospective effect and it should take effect only from the date of service of that order on the delinquent.

Whenever the proceedings are not completed within six months and it is necessary to keep the officer under suspension further, the matter should be reported to the competent authority, (Director or Government, as the case may be) giving full details leading to delay with particulars of the date of enquiry, whether the enquiry was conducted on the dates, on which the case was posted; if not the reason therefor, etc., and the need to keep the officer under suspension beyond the period of suspension and the orders of the competent authority should be obtained.

When an employee is suspended, he is free to go wherever he likes, but he must leave his address with the Head of his office or if he is himself the Head of the office, with his immediate officer. He must obey all orders to attend any inquiry into his conduct, and if he fails to do so, the inquiry may be held in his absence.

17. The employee of the Library Authority cannot insist as a matter of right to be represented by a lawyer in disciplinary proceedings against him. When he makes a request for engaging a counsel in any such disciplinary proceeding the enquiry officer should take into account all the circumstances and decide whether the denial of professional help will prejudice the accused employee in his defence and if so the enquiry officer must allow him to be represented by a council. When the request for engaging a counsel is on the ground that the accused employee is not acquainted with the language in which the proceedings are conducted, the enquiry officer must allow him to be represented by counsel.

FORM I

1. Have you any objection to the form of any of the charges?
2. In addition to the written statement of your defence which you are now required to submit, you are entitled to continue your defence, by either of the following methods:

   (1) an oral enquiry in your presence:
   (2) to be held in person without an oral enquiry:

Please state in columns opposite whether you require either method to be adopted.

(*Note:* If you choose method (a), the following witnesses will be called to prove the charges.)

Witnesses examined in your presence at the preliminary enquiry:

1 ....
2 ....
3 ....
4 ....

Witnesses not yet examined in your presence:

1 ....
2 ....
3 ....
4 ....

The evidence recorded from (1) above at the preliminary enquiry will be read out at the regular enquiry and you will be given an opportunity to cross-examine the witnesses again. Any evidence recorded from (2) above at the preliminary enquiry will also be read out at the regular enquiry unless you prefer that any of the witnesses to be examined in the brief before you instead. Whichever course you choose you will be given an opportunity to cross-examine them.

3. (1) Do you wish to give evidence yourself?
   (2) If so, on what points?

4. (1) Do you wish to have any witness examined on your behalf?
   (2) If so state their names and note briefly the matters to which they are called to depose.

Note: After the completion of the enquiry you may, if you so desire, put in further written statement of your defence.

5.4 Conduct Rules of the Employees

1. *Short Title, Application and Commencement*

These rules may be called the .... Library Authority Employees (Conduct) Rules, 19..... They shall apply to every person who is borne on the establishment of the Library Authority or holds any post under the Library Authority:

Provided that nothing in these Rules shall apply to:

(i) persons who are not full-time employees but are engaged to do any work without prejudice to the regular practice by such persons of their professional in other respects:
(ii) persons paid from contingencies.

2. *General*

1. Every employees shall be devoted to his duty and shall maintain absolute integrity, discipline, impartiality and a sense of propriety.
2. No employee shall behave in a manner which is unbecoming of such employee or derogatory to the prestige of Library Authority.
3. No employee shall act in a manner which will place his official position under any kind of embarrassment.

3. *Joining of Associations by Employees*

No employee shall join, or continue to be a member of an association, the objects or activities of which are prejudicial to the interests of the sovereignty and integrity of India or public order.

4. *Strikes*

No employees shall participate in any strike or similar activities or incitement thereto.

Explanation: The expression "similar activities" shall be deemed to include:

1. absence from duty or work without permission;
2. neglect of duty with the object of compelling any superior officer or the Library Authority to take or omit to take any official action;
3. any demonstrative fast, like hunger-strike with the object mentioned in item (ii), or
4. concerted, or organised refusal on the part of the employees to receive their pay.
5. demonstrations: No employee shall participate in any demonstration which is against the interests of public order.
6. gift, services, entertainments, addresses and other forms of felicitations:

(i) No employee shall accept, or permit any member of his family to accept, from any person any gift, the receipt of which, or any service the performance of which, will place such employee under any kind of official obligation or embarrassment in relation to any person. If however, the offer of a gift cannot be refused without giving undue offence to the donor, it may be accepted and the matter reported to the Secretary, Library Authority for decision as to its disposal, or receive any address or accept any felicitation or entertainment held in his honour:

Provided that nothing in this sub-rule shall apply to the gifts of flowers or fruits of trifling value; or gifts of a value, reasonable in all circumstances of the case, from relations, and gifts of value less than fifty rupees from personal friends presented to any member of his family on ceremonial occasions such as weddings; the performance of an occasional service of trifling character, the sitting for a group photo with the officers and members of the staff of his office.

(ii) If any question arises whether the receipt of a gift or the performance of a service places the employee under any kind of official obligation or embarrassment, the decision of the Director shall be final.

(iii) No employee shall receive any key, scissors, or other similar articles offered to him in connection with any ceremonial function such as the laying of foundation stone or the opening of a building.

7. *Subscriptions*

No employee shall, except with the previous sanction of the Director, ask for, or accept, or in any way participate in the raising of any subscriptions, or other pecuniary assistance in pursuance of any object, whatsoever.

8. Lending, borrowing and insolvence:

No employee shall:

(1) engage, either by himself or through others, in the business of money-lending, or lend or borrow money, either by himself or through others, in a manner which will place him under any kind of official obligation to any person or cause official embarrassment to him.

(2) The prohibition in sub-rule shall not apply to

(i) any transaction of an employee with a co-operative society registered or deemed to have been registered under the law relating to co-operative societies for the time being in force in the State;

(ii) an employee who lends money while acting as an executor, administrator or a trustee without profit or advantage to himself; and

(iii) an employee who belongs to a joint Hindu Family carrying on the business of money lending as an ancestral profession: Provided that he takes no active share in that business and it is not employed in the district in which the said business of the family is carried on.

9. Acquiring or disposing of immovable or movable property:

(1) employee shall, except after previous intimation to the Library Authority, acquire or dispose of, or permit any member of his family to acquire or dispose of, any immovable property by exchange, purchase, sale, gift or otherwise, either by himself or through others:

Provided that any such transaction conducted otherwise than through a regular or reputed dealer shall be with the previous sanction of the Chairman, Library Authority.

(2) An employee who enters into any transaction concerning any movable property exceeding rupees one thousand in value, whether by way of purchase, sale or otherwise, shall forthwith report such transaction to the Chairman, Library Authority:

Provided that any such transaction conducted otherwise than through a regular or reputed dealer shall be with the previous sanction of the Chairman, Library Authority.

(3) Nothing in sub-rule (2) shall apply to any purchase made by an employee for the performance of weddings, religious or social functions.

(4) No employee shall engage in any transaction which is of a speculative character relating to the purchase, sale or exchange of any immovable or movable property.

(5) The provisions of sub-rule (1) and (2) shall not apply to —

(i) the acquisition or possession of any property as trusted executor or administrator, or

(ii) any land belonging to the Library Authority or the Government which is sold or granted on lease to any employee in accordance with the provisions of the Act or any other law or rules or bye-laws made thereunder or any other rules in force.

(6) Every employee, other than a member belonging to the last grade service, and an attender under Library Authority service shall, on first appointment in the Library Authority service, and thereafter before the 15th January, each year submit to the Library Authority through the proper channel a declaration in the form given in the Annexure to these Rules, of all immovable property owned, acquired or inherited by him or held by him on lease or mortgage, either in his own name or in the name of any member of his family or in the name of any other person. The declaration shall contain such further information as the Library Authority may, by a general or special order, require. If in any year, a Library Authority employee has not acquired or disposed of any immovable property or any interest therein, he shall submit a declaration to that effect.

(7) The Library Authority or any authority empowered by it may, at any time by general or special order, require an employee to submit within a specified period, a full and complete statement of all immovable property and movable property, of the specified value held or acquired by him or by any member of his family. Such statement shall, if so required by the Secretary, include particulars of the means by which, or the sources from which, such property was acquired.

(8) If an employee is under orders of transfer to a place in which he possesses or has an interest in any immovable property, he shall forthwith report the fact to his immediate superior officer.

10. Private Trade, business and investments:

(1) No employee shall engage himself directly or indirectly in any trade or business save in the course of his immediate official duties.

(2) No employee shall speculate any investment.

(3) No employee shall make, or permit any member of his family to make any investments likely to embarass or influence him in the discharge of his official duties.

(4) The decision of the Director shall be final in respect of any question arising under this rule.

11. Promotion and management of companies in private capacity:

No employee shall, in his private capacity, except with the previous sanction of the Director, take part in the promotion, registration or management of any bank or other company registered under the relevant law for the time being in force:

Provided that an employee may, in accordance with the provisions of any general or specific order of the Director, take part in the promotion, registration or management of a co-operative society registered under any law relating to co-operative societies for the time being in force in the State.

12. Private employment:

No employee shall, except with the previous sanction of the Director, undertake any employment or work other than that connected with his official duties:

Provided that an employee may, without such sanction, undertake honorary work of a special or charitable nature or an occasional work of a literary, artistic or scientific character subject to the condition that such work does not interfere with his official duties, but he shall not undertake or shall discontinue such work, if so directed by the Director.

13. Communication of official documents or information:

No employee shall, except in accordance with the provisions of the Act or the Rules and bye-laws made thereunder or any general or special order of the Secretary, Library Authority, communicate directly or indirectly any official document or any of its contents, or any official information to any other employee not authorised to receive the same or to any non-official person or the press:

Provided that an employee may contribute an article of a scientific or technical character to a non-government publication with the previous permission of the Director. While applying such permission, he shall submit to the Director a manuscript copy of the article.

14. Connection with Press:

No employee shall, except with the previous sanction of the Director, own wholly, or in part, or conduct or participate in the editing or the management of, any newspaper or non-government publication.

15. Participation in radio broadcast and contribution to newspaper and periodicals:

(1) No employee shall, except with the previous sanction of the Director or any authority empowered by him or in the course of discharge of his official duties, participate in a radio broadcast, or contribute any article or write any letter either in his own name or anonymously, pseudonymously or in the name of any other person, to any newspaper or periodical:

Provided that no such sanction is necessary if such broadcast, article or letter is of a purely literacy, artistic or scientific character, or if such broadcast relates to a talk arranged under the general or special order of the Director and the employee may accept the remuneration prescribed for such broadcasts, articles or letters.

(2) For the purpose of sub-rule (1) the Chairman, Library Authority may exercise the power of Director in respect of employees working under his Library Authority and may refer any case to the Director for orders if he considers such a course desirable.

16. Criticism of the policy or action of the Library Authority, Government or any other State Government or Central Government:

(1) No employee shall, by any utterance, written or otherwise, criticise any policy or action of the Library Authority or Government or any other State Government or the Central Government nor shall he participate in any such criticism:

Provided that nothing in this rule shall be deemed to prohibit any employee from participating in discussions, at any private meeting solely of Library Authority or of any association of Library Authority Employees, of matters which effect the interest of such employees individually or generally.

(2) No employee shall, in any writing published by him, or in any communication made by him to the press, or in any public utterance delivered by him, make any statement of fact or opinion which is likely to embarrass:

(i) The relations between the Central Government, or the Government of any State and the people of India or any section thereof; and
(ii) The relations between the Central Government and the Government of any Foreign State.

(3) An employee, who intends to publish any document or make any communication to the press or deliver any public utterance containing statement in respect of which any doubt as to the application of the restrictions imposed by sub-rule (2) arises shall submit to the Director the draft of such document, communication or utterance and shall, thereafter, act in accordance with such orders, as may be passed by the Director.

17. Evidence before any committee, commission or other authority:

(1) No employee shall give evidence in connection with any enquiry conducted by any committee, commission or other authority.
(i) In India, except with the previous permission of the Director, and
(ii) Outside India, except with the previous sanction of the Central Government.

(2) Where any sanction is accorded under sub-rule (1), no employee giving such evidence shall criticise the policy of the Central Government or of a State Government.
(3) Nothing in sub-rule (1) shall apply to:

(i) evidence given before a statutory committee, commission or other authority which has power to compel attendance and the giving of answers; and

(ii) evidence given at any departmental inquiry ordered by the Government, Director or Chairman.

18. Taking part in politics and elections:

(1) No employee shall be a member of, or be otherwise associated with any political party or any organisation which takes part in politics, or shall he participate in, subscribe in aid of, or assist in any other manner, any political movement or activity.

(2) It shall be the duty of every employee to endeavour to prevent any member of his family from taking part in, subscribing in aid of, or assisting in any manner, any movement or activity which is or tends directly to be subversive of the Central Government or of a State Government being prejudicial to national security; and where an employee is unable to prevent a member of his family from taking part in or subscribing in aid of, or assisting in any other manner, any such movement or activity, he shall make a report to that effect to the Director.

(3) Nothing in sub-rule (2) shall apply in respect of any member of the family of an employee standing for an election to Parliament or any House of State Legislature or Library Authority or body or canvassing for other candidates in any such election.

(4) If any question arises as to whether any movement or activity falls within the scope of this rule, the Chairman shall refer the matter to the Director whose decision thereon shall be final.

(5) No employee shall canvas or otherwise interfere or use his influence in connection with or take part in, an election to Parliament or any house of a State Legislature or any Library Authority or any Body.

Provided that —

(i) an employee qualified to vote at such election may cast his vote, but where he does so, he shall give no indication of the manner in which he proposes to vote or has voted.

(ii) an employee shall not be deemed to have contravened the provisions of this rule by reason only that he has assisted in the conduct of an election in the due performance of a duty imposed on him by or under any law for the time being in force.

(6) The display by an employee on his person, vehicle, residence or any of his property, of any election symbol shall amount to using his influence in connection with an election within the meaning of sub-rule (5).

(7) The provisions of sub-rules (5) and (6) shall not apply to an employee required or permitted by or under any law or order of Government to be a candidate at an election to a Library Authority or body.

19. Address while under suspension:

When an employee is under suspension, he is free to go anywhere he likes, but he shall leave his address with the head of his office, or if he is himself the head of the office with the Chairman. He shall also leave his address with the officer, if any holding an enquiry into his conduct.

20. Vindication of acts and character of an employee as such:

(1) No employee shall, except with the previous sanction of the Director, have resource to the press or any court for the vindication of his official act which has been the subject matter of adverse criticism or an attack of a defamatory character in public.

(2) Nothing in sub-rule (1) shall be deemed to prohibit an employee from vindicating his private character, or an act done by him in his private capacity.

(3) No employee shall, except with the previous sanction of the Director, accept from any person or body compensation of any kind for malicious prosecution or defamatory attack in respect of his official act, unless such compensation has been awarded by a competent court of law.

21. Working with or under, near relatives in Library Authority Service:

Every member borne on the establishment of the Library Authority shall inform his immediate official superior in writing if another member of the establishment of the Library Authority who is near relative, is to work or working in the said Library Authority in any capacity.

22. Employment of a member of the family in a private firm:

Whenever a member of the family of an employee who is solely dependent on him wishes to accept employment under any person, or with any firm or company, having official connection with such Library Authority, shall obtain the prior sanction of the Director.

23. No employee shall deal, in his official capacity, with any matter which directly or indirectly concerns himself or any of his relatives or dependents.

24. Influencing authorities for furtherance of interests:

(1) No employee shall bring or attempt to bring any extraneous influence to bear upon any authority for the furtherance of his interests. The penalty for contravention of this rule shall be withholding of promotion for him either permanently or for such period as the competent authority may determine.

(2) An employee causing his own case to be made the subject of an interpellation, or discussion in either the general body of the Library Authority or in the sub-committee constituted under the provisions of the Act, or of discussion in either House of the State Legislature or Regional Committee shall be deemed to have contravened the provisions of sub-rule (1).

(3) It will be improper for an employee who makes any representation to the higher authority through the proper channel, to brother the higher authority with advance copies thereof:

Provided that an employee may send a copy of any representation made to the competent authority through the proper channel, direct to the higher authorities if the representation is made after exhausting such of the statutory remedies as were open to him and after receiving intimation that his representation has been withheld.

25. Bigamous Marriages:

No employee who has a wife living shall contract another marriage notwithstanding that such subsequent marriage is permissible under the personal law for the time being applicable to him. No female employee shall marry any person who has a wife living.

26. Application for private employment:

(1) No employee shall apply for private employment or signify his willingness to accept such employment without having previously obtained the permission in writing of the appointing authority in respect of the post which he is applying.

(2) (a) Permission to apply for, or accept private employment shall normally be granted to a person who is on leave preparatory to retirement, unless the employment is in a trading concern in India. Permission to apply for or accept private employment in a trading concern in India will be granted only in very exceptional cases and may be subject to the condition of immediate retirement.

(b) Even in the case of other employees, subject to consideration of public interest, forwarding of application should be the rule rather than the exception. Ordinarily, every employee shall be permitted to apply for an outside post even though he may be holding a permanent post, but this should not be done more than once a year.

(3) If a person who is refused permission to apply for or accept private employment wishes to resign his appointment under the Library Authority such resignation shall ordinarily be accepted.

(4) Where a person, who is not on leave preparatory to retirement, is permitted to apply for or accept private employment, he shall resign his appointment under the Library Authority immediately on accepting such employment:

Provided that resignation tendered by a Library Authority employee under sub-rules (3) and (4) shall not be accepted by the appointing authority until it has been ascertained that there are no demands outstanding against him. A certificate to this effect signed by the Secretary or Chairman, Library Authority under whom the employee is working shall be attached to the connected file.

27. Interpretation:

If any question arises relating to the interpretation of these rules, the decision of the Director shall be final.

ANNEXURE

Statement of immovable property and interests in immovable property possessed, acquired or transferred by during the year ending the 31st December, 19........

[Sub-rule (6) of Rule 10]

Note: Property in which the employee had acquired an interest before the year for which the return is submitted and in which he retained an interest during that year should be shown first, then those properties regarding which transactions took place during that year.

1. Name of the employee:
2. Office held:
3. Date of entering Library Authority:
4. Nature of property i.e., (1) house (Stating whether they are with or without gardens) and the uses to which they are put; (2) Lands whether used for purposes of agriculture or as gardens or for any other purposes:
5. Whether acquired before or during 19......
6. Whether relinquished during 19......
7. Situation of land or other property:

(1) Village:

(2) Taluk:

(3) District:

(4) Survey number:

8. Extent and assessment of lands:

   (1) Dry:
   (2) Wet:

9. Extent:
10. Assessment:
11. Sircar or Inam:
12. From whom acquired or in whose favour relinquished:
13. In whose name registered after acquisition/or before relinquishment:
14. By what means and for what purpose acquired:
15. Year, month and day of deed:
16. Rights possessed in the land:
17. Price paid or obtained for the land:
18. If acquisition sanctioned by the Library Authority, number and date of Library Authority order in which sanction was accorded:
19. Remarks:

I, ... do solemnly declared that I do not at this time possess either in my name or in that if any other person, and that I have not, during the year 19....... acquired in my own name or in that of any other person, or parted with any immovable property or any beneficial or other interest in immovable property other than what is entered in this return.

Station Signature
Date Office

Note:

(1) The statement must be submitted punctually on the 15th January of the year.
(2) New acquisitions during the year to which the return relates

should be entered in red ink. Particulars of any immovable property of which the Library Authority employee may dispose during the year should also be entered in the annual return.

6. FINANCE AND AUDIT

6.1 General Finance Rules

6.1.1 The Library Fund of a Library Authority maintained under section of the Act shall be deposited in the following banks.

(1) State Bank of India
(2) District Cooperative Central Bank
(3) Post Office Savings Bank

Note: The Library Authority can invest any sums not required for immediate use after obtaining the resolution of the Authority. The Secretary shall submit an application specifying the details along with the resolution of Authority to the Director. According to the existing orders the amount shall be invested in the District Cooperative Central Bank only.

The Director may sanction permanent advance to the Office of the Library Authority and the libraries under its control.

6.1.2 All payments out of Library Fund of every Library Authority in respect of the bills presented to the Library Authority shall be made only after the bills are passed by the Secretary of the Library Authority.

6.1.3 Except in the case of petty contingent expenditure, permanent advance payments shall be made by cheques drawn on the bank in which the Library Fund of Library Authority is lodged.

6.1.4 The Bank in which the Library Fund is deposited shall, so far as the Fund to the credit of the Library Authority admits, pay all orders or cheques against the Fund which are so signed.

6.1.5 All orders of cheques against the Library Fund shall be signed by the Secretary of the Library Authority.

The responsibility for any illegal, irregular, unauthorised or over payment shall rest with the Secretary who shall be required to make good the same. In cases, however where the Chairman issues orders authorising expenditure contrary to rules and against the advice of the Secretary, responsibility for the illegal, irregular, unauthorised or over payment shall rest with the Chairman who shall be required to make good the same.

6.2 **Operation of Library Fund**

6.2.1 These rules may be called the Library Fund Rules.

6.2.2 The purposes for which the Library Fund may be applied include all objects expressly declared obligatory or discretion by the relevant laws or rules made thereunder and in general expenditure incidental to the administration of the Library Authority and the fund shall be applied with in the District subject to these rules and such further rules or special orders as the Government may issue in this behalf from time to time and shall also be applied to such purposes outside the district if the expenditure is authorised by the Act or specially sanctioned by the Government or Director of Public Libraries.

6.2.3 The objects of expenditure incidental to the administration include:

(1) The provision and maintenance of the office of the Library Authority, District Public Libraries and other branch libraries and Book Deposit Centres and Record Room and of other offices including cost of apparatus, fittings and insurance; purchase of books, periodicals, newspapers, manuscripts, maps and specimens of Art and Science, Lantern slides, Cinema Projectors, Recorders, Radios, and the like;

(2) Salaries, allowances, liveries, contributions to the pension and provident fund, gratuities and pensions, the cost of maintenance of the vehicles of the Library Authority and all expenditure incidental thereto. Expenditure in connection with the deputation of candidates to the CLSc, and BLISC Course;

(3) Stationery, printing and all office and advertising expenses including the cost of reporting, the proceedings at the meeting of the Library Authority;

(4) Law charges except in case of appeals against surcharge certificate issued by the auditor;

(5) Election expenses;

(6) Library Authority's library surveys, the preparation of maps of the District and of extension of the library building;

(7) The preparation and maintenance of record of rights of immovable property owned or possessed by the Library Authority;

(8) The acquisition of lands and buildings for all or any of the purposes of the Act and the maintenance of the buildings; and
(9) Organisation of seminars, conferences, book exhibitions etc.

6.2.4 The Library Fund may be applied for contributing to the funds of any aided libraries in the district under Rules, Public Libraries Rules, 19.......

6.2.5 The payment of any sum of the library fund may be made or authorised by the Secretary of the Library Authority in the absence of budget provision in the case of:

(1) Refund of taxes, and surcharge fees under the Act or any law;
(2) Repayments of moneys belonging to contractors or other persons and held in deposit and of moneys collected or credited to the library fund by mistake;
(3) Sums payable under a decree or order of a Civil Court passed against the Library Authority;
(4) Any sum which the Secretary of the Library Authority is required under any law to pay by way of compensation or expenses; and
(5) Expenses lawfully incurred in anticipation of recoupment from a person liable under any provision of law:

Provided that the Secretary of the Library Authority shall forthwith communicate the circumstances under which the payment was made or with audit to the Director of Public Libraries who shall take such action as may, in the circumstances, be necessary or expedient to cover any expenditure not covered by a budget provision.

6.2.6 The Secretary of the Library Authority shall not overdraw from the library fund.

6.2.7 When the Secretary of a Library Authority makes over charge of his office either temporarily or permanently, he shall send a specimen signature of the relieving Secretary together with a certificate in the form given below to the Treasury Officer or any Bank in which the moneys of the Library Authority are lodged.

FORM OF CERTIFICATE
[*See* Rule 8]

To

....
....
....

I have this day .... handed over charge of the office of the Secretary, Library Authority to Shri .... whose specimen signature is given below:

....
Relieving Officer Relieved Officer

6.2.8(1) Cheque books shall be kept in the personal custody of the Secretary of the Library Authority and when a transfer of charge takes place, a note shall be recorded in the Cash Book over the signature of both the relieved and the relieving Secretaries showing the unused cheques, and cheque books made over and received by them respectively.

(2) Every person having any claim against the library fund shall present a bill at the Library Authority office. Whenever possible such bill shall be in the form prescribed for the purpose and the claimant shall duly date and sign the same and stamp it wherever necessary.

(3) Whenever possible printed forms shall be used in preparing bills.

(4) Where a claimant presents a bill in a form different from the one prescribed for the purpose a separate bill in the proper form shall be prepared by the officer incurring the expenditure and the claimants' bill shall be attached thereto as a sub-voucher.

(5) Every bill shall be presented to the Secretary of the Library Authority who shall make it over to the person in charge of accounts. The latter shall enter it in the Register of bills and check and examine the bills as regards its admissibility with reference to sanction or other documents, the propriety of the claim and the arithmetical corrections. If on such check

and examination, the bill is found to be correct and in order, it shall be placed before the Secretary of the Library Authority for signing the payment order in the bill which shall run as follows:

"Pay by cheque Rupees .... only (amount in words and figures) and debit to .... (Major, Minor or detailed heads). Where payments have to be made in cash, cheques shall be drawn in favour of the Secretary of the Library Authority himself. All such sums shall be noted, in a cash book maintained by the person in charge of accounts.

6.2.9(1) Separate acknowledgments (stamped wherever necessary) shall be taken where disbursements are made in the Library Authority Office in the last column of the bill and in other cases in the acquittance register from each officer, or servant to whom any salary or allowances is paid except when the drawer of the bill is the sole payee and has already furnished a receipt (stamped wherever necessary) on the bill itself.

(2) Where the Secretary of the Library Authority makes any payment from a sum drawn by him from the treasury or any bank in which the moneys of the Library Authority are lodged, he shall, unless a receipt (Stamped wherever necessary) has been furnished on the bill itself, obtain and attach to the bill a separate receipt (stamped wherever necessary).

6.2.10(1) Whenever any item of expenditure requires the sanction of any authority higher than the officer or servant drawing the bill, such sanction shall be obtained and the terms thereof shall be quoted on the bill. (A copy of the order of the sanction shall also be communicated to the auditor who audits the accounts of the Library Authority under Rule 20 of the Public Libraries Rules, 19....).

(2) No item of expenditures shall be sanctioned by the Secretary of the District Library Authority unless a certificate in the following form has been furnished in respect thereof:

FORM OF CERTIFICATE

"The amount may be met from the budget allotment of .... The amount spent under this head up to date is................................ The amount sanctioned up to date but not spent is.. The balance remaining will be ....

(3) If there is no budget provision under the head concerned and the Library Authority decides to find the amount by reappropriation from another head, the words "by reappropriation" shall be added after the word "met" in the form of certificate mentioned in sub-rule (2).

(4) The certificate shall be entered in the agenda circulated before the meeting and if accepted by the Library Authority, it need not be written again as part of the resolution in the minutes book. If, however, the Library Authority makes any alteration either in the account of expenditure or in the head from which the expenditure is to be met, then certificate as amended shall form part of the resolution of the Library Authority and be entered as such in the minutes book.

(5) As sanction of any fresh charge which has not been acted upon for a year shall be held to have lapsed unless it is specifically renewed:

Provided that this sub-rule shall not apply to a case where an allowance sanctioned to a post or posts has not been drawn by the particular incumbent or incumbents appointed to the said post or posts; additions made gradually from year to year to a permanent establishment under a general scheme which has been sanctioned by the proper authority; and expenditure on works which shall be governed by the provision laid down in sub-rule (6).

(6) The sanction to an ordinary annual maintenance estimate shall lapse on the last day of the financial year to which it relates. If, however any inconvenience is likely to cause in any exceptional case from stoppage of the work on that date, the repairs may be carried onto completion, and the expendi-

ture incurred after that date shall be treated as expenditure against a fresh repair estimate for the next year; estimates for special repairs shall remain current till the completion of the repairs in the same manner as estimates for original works and the approval or sanction to an estimate for any building work other than annual maintenance shall, unless such work has been commenced, cease to operate after a period of three years from the date on which it was accorded.

6.2.11 An order directing the payment of any claim made in a bill shall be valid only for a period of six months and shall be renewed, if payment is to be made thereafter.

6.2.12 No claim against the Library Authority (other than one relating to any officer or servant of the District Library Authority which will be governed by Rules separately framed in that behalf) shall be admitted for payment.

1. Where a bill is presented after a period of more than six months, but not more than one year, from the date on which the claim became due, without the order of the Secretary, Library Authority.
2. Where a bill is presented after a period of more than one year, from the date on which the claim became due, without the order of the Chairman of the Library Authority.

6.2.13 1. Any deficiency, loss or unprofitable outlay occasioned by the negligence or misconduct of any person shall be reported immediately after the discovery to the Examiner of Local Fund and Panchayat Raj Accounts and the Director of Public Libraries. A further and complete report shall also be forwarded to the same officers, as soon as the matter is fully enquired into, setting forth the nature and extent of the defaulcation or loss, the errors or omissions in following the rules by which a such defaulcation or loss was rendered possible, and the prospects of effecting a recovery.

2. Loss by theft or otherwise of other property shall also be reported to the Examiner of Local Fund or Panchayat Raj Accounts and the Director of Public Libraries, if the value

of the property lost exceeds ten rupees.

3. The submission of the reports prescribed by sub-rules (1) and (2) shall not debar the Secretary of the Library Authority from taking such further action as may be considered necessary.

ESTABLISHMENT BILL

6.2.14 Pay bills shall be prepared in prescribed form (as may be laid down by the Government from time to time).

6.2.15 The monthly pay bill of the establishment of the Library Authority shall be supported either by an absentees statement in such form as may be laid down by the Government from time to time or by a certificate in the bill that no leave has been granted to any member of the establishment.

6.2.16 To the first pay bill in which a periodical increment is drawn by the Government from time to time shall be attached.

6.2.17 1. The pay of an officer or employee lent by the Government or transferred from any other Library Authority shall be drawn only after the receipt of a last pay certificate which shall be in such form as may be laid down by the Government from time to time, granted by the Head of his former office. Such certificate shall be attached to the first pay bill drawn after such loan or transfer.

2. The pay and allowance in respect of such employee shall be claimed and paid by the former Library Authority only up to the date of his relief from that Library Authority. His transit pay and transfer T.A. shall be borne by the Library Authority to which he is transferred.

3. The leave applied for by an employee other than a Secretary, Grade-I Librarian after getting relief from the former Library Authority and before joining the new post shall be sanctioned by the competent authority in the Library Authority to which he is transferred. The leave salary of such employee shall be borne by the former provided there is sufficient leave to his credit.

6.2.18 Pay, leave salary allowances may be drawn for the day of an employee's death; the hour at which the death takes place shall not affect the claim.

6.2.19 Payments due to a deceased officer or servant of the Library Authority shall not be made except on the production of an authority of the nature specified in sub-clauses (i), (ii), (iii), (iv) and (v) clause (b) of subsection (1) of section 214 of the Indian Succession Act, 1925, (General Act XXXIV of 1925):

1. to the extent of Rs. 1,000 (one thousand rupees only) under the orders of the Secretary, Library Authority responsible for the payment, if he is satisfied after such enquiry as he may consider sufficient about the right and title of the claimant; and
2. to the extent of above five hundred rupees, under the orders of the Chairman of the Library Authority on the execution of an indemnity bond with such surety or sureties as he may require, if he is satisfied, after such enquiry as he may consider sufficient, about the right and title of the claimant and considers that undue delay and hardship would be caused by insisting on the production of such authority.

6.2.20 The last payment of an employee's pay and allowances or in case he is finally quitting the service of the Library Authority at the end of any leave granted to him, the last payment of his leave salary shall not be made, until it has been ascertained that there are no demands outstanding against him. A certificate to this effect signed by the Secretary of the Library Authority shall be attached to the bill in which such pay and allowances or leave salary is claimed.

6.2.21 Arrears of pay shall be drawn not in the monthly bill but in a separate bill which shall quote the bill from which the claim was omitted or withheld or on which it was refunded by deduction. Pay bills shall be signed by the officers incharge of the establishment or institution concerned and shall be passed by the Secretary of the Library Authority.

6.2.22 Cheques in respect of payments of salary and fixed allowances shall not be issued before the first working day of the month following that to which the payment relates:

Provided that when an officer or employee is finally quitting the service of the Library Authority or being transferred to the service of another local authority or the Government, cheques may be issued on the date of such event;

Provided further that when the first three days of a month are public holidays on which payments are not made at the Treasury or Bank in which the moneys of the Library Authority are lodged, cheques may be issued on the last working day before the holidays; Provided also that when the Government sanctions payment of salaries to Government servants at an earlier date on any occasion, cheques may be issued for payment of salaries on the date so notified by the Government.

6.2.23 The Secretary of the Library Authority drawing a bill for salary and allowances shall be personally responsible for the amount so drawn until it has been disbursed to the proper person or persons and their acquittances (stamped wherever necessary) have been obtained. If the payee does not present himself within thirty days from the date of the drawal of money, the amount drawn for him shall be refunded by short drawal in the next bill. The amount or salary and allowances drawn shall not in any circumstances be placed under deposit.

6.2.24 In order to facilitate the check of the monthly bill for recurring charges, such as establishment, house rent and fixed travelling and conveyance allowances an audit establishment register in the prescribed form shall be maintained in the office of the Library Authority.

6.2.25
1. Travelling allowance other than fixed travelling allowance shall be drawn in a separate bill in the prescribed form.
2. When a conveyance, for which a conveyance allowance is drawn is temporarily out of use, the conveyance allowance may continue to be drawn up to maximum period of 10 days. In such a case, the officer or employee claiming the conveyance allowance shall furnish the certificate as to the actual number of days on which the conveyance was not in use during the month.

6.2.26 Fixed travelling and conveyance allowance shall be drawn in the pay bill of the officer or employee concerned and not on travelling allowance bills. To every bill for conveyance allowance, a certificate shall be attached that the conveyance was actually maintained in good condition and used by the officer concerned during the month.

6.2.27 The Library Authority shall not without the previous sanction of the Director of Public Libraries divert even temporarily any of the following earmarked funds for purposes other than those for which they are collected or allotted:

1. Funds collected for the opening and maintenance of libraries;
2. Special State grants sanctioned for specific purposes;
3. Receipts derived from the sale of capital asset;
4. Funds relating to institutions and works transferred by the Government;
5. Donations and contributions received from the public in any form for the specific purpose; and
6. Loan funds:

Provided that the previous sanction of the Government should be obtained for diversion of the special grants sanctioned by them for any specific purposes.

6.2.28 Any claim of a member of the Staff of Library Authority for arrears of pay, allowances or increment of pay which have been allowed to remain in abeyance shall, before payment, be investigated by the Secretary of the Library Authority:

1. with the sanction of the Library Authority, in case of claim relating to a period not exceeding six months; and
2. with the sanction of the Director of Public Libraries, in the case of claim relating to a period exceeding six months.

6.2.29 The payment of arrear claim ordered under clause (i) of rule, shall not exceed the amount found to be actually due under the claim in respect of a period of one year immediately preceding the date of detection of the under payment. If, in any particular case, it is considered that for special reasons a large concession should be granted, the Secretary, Library Authority shall consult the Examiner of Local Fund Accounts, in the first instance, and then obtain, if the Examiner of Local Fund Accounts so advises, the sanction of the Director of Public Libraries, for payment of arrears for a period exceeding one year:

Provided that such consultation with the Examiner of Local Fund Accounts shall not be necessary in respect of any arrear claim involving a sum not exceeding rupees twenty-five in each case.

6.2.30 No claim for travelling allowance will be entertained if it is made after three months from the date of completion of the journey to which it relates.

Explanation— For the purpose of this rule, the date of detection of an under payment will be the date on which the under payment is detected by or brought to the notice of the Secretary, Library Authority, or if it is first detected in audit, the date of detection by the Audit Department. An arrear claim resulting from an order issued with retrospective effect does not arise until the order is issued and shall not, therefore, be treated as a claim allowed to remain in abeyance during the period prior to the date of the order. An order passed with retrospective effect shall, for the purposes of this rule be deemed to be one which, in the circumstances of the case could not have been passed earlier or which was deliberately held over pending consideration. The power conferred on the Library Authority under clause (i) of rule (1) shall not be delegated by the Library Authority.

6.3 **Payment of Advances**

6.3.1 No advances shall be granted by the Library Authorities to its officers or employees for any purpose except for the following, namely that of:

1. Purchasing conveyances;
2. Journeys on tour or transfer;
3. Purchasing mosquito nets, if the officers or employees reside or work in areas included in the list of areas where there is a risk of malaria drawn by the Director of Medical Services;
4. Advances on the eve of important festivals.

Provided that the Director may, in special cases, permit the grant of advances for purposes other than those specified above, subject to the availability of funds with the Library Authority after meeting all items of expenditure.

Note: The festival advances shall be sanctioned during the financial year to full time staff. It shall be recovered in ten equal instalments.

2. The rules issued by Government from time to time in regard to sanction of similar advances to Government employees shall be observed by the Library Authority subject to the condition that sufficient funds are available with the Library Authority after meeting all items of expenditure without asking any additional

grant from the Government in this behalf.

3. The Chairman, Library Authority, in respect of the Secretary, and the Secretary, Library Authority in respect of the other employees shall be the sanctioning authorities of the above advances.
4. The Secretary, Library Authority shall be responsible for proper recovery of the advances sanctioned to the employees.

Advances for Purchasing Conveyances

6.3.2 A Library Authority may, at its discretion, grant an advance to any of its permanent officers or employees for the purchase of motor car/motor cycle or bicycle, subject to the following conditions, namely:

1. The advance shall be granted only when the Library Authority considers that in the interest of the service of the Library Authority the officer or employee should use a motor cycle or bicycle for the discharge of his official duties;
2. The Motor Cycle Advance shall be sanctioned only to those officers or employees drawing a basic pay of Rs......... and above and the amount sanctioned shall be recovered in 50 equal instalments.
3. If the amount of such advance is for the purchase of Motor Cycle, it shall not exceed Rs.......... or fifteen months pay or the anticipated price of the Motor Cycle, whichever is less. If the amount of advance is for the purchase of a bicycle it shall not exceed four months pay of the employee of Rs......... or the estimated prices of the bicycle, whichever is less;
4. The principal of the advance shall be recovered in not more than the instalments specified in Rule 7, and after the principal is completely recovered, the interest shall be recovered in two instalments;
5. If the actual price paid for the motor cycle or the bicycle is less than the advance taken the balance shall forthwith be refunded to the Library Authority;
6. The advance for the purchase of conveyance shall not be granted under the rule to the employees paid from contingencies.

6.3.3 The Library Authority shall at the time of payment of the advance for the purchase of a motor cycle, obtain from the officer or employee concerned, an agreement in the form prescribed in the First

Schedule to this order.

6.3.4 The officer or employee shall:

1. execute at his expenses Mortgage bond in the form prescribed in the Second Schedule to pledge the motor cycle to the Library Authority as security for the advance;
2. produce for audit, the accounts connected with transaction; and
3. keep the motor cycle, duly insured. He shall be responsible for the payment of the insurance premia until the advance is fully repaid. The Library Authority shall furnish intimation to the Insurance Company in the form prescribed in Third Schedule.

6.3.5 The Library Authority shall, when granting an advance for the purchase of a bicycle, take sufficient security for the repayment of advance. Such security shall be exclusive of the bicycle purchased.

6.3.6 The officer or employee who has been granted the advance for the purchase of a bicycle shall within a month from the date of drawal of the advance purchase bicycle and produce to the Library Authority, the accounts connected with the transaction, failing which the amount of the advance shall be recovered in full from his pay.

6.3.7 1. Every advance made under Rule 2 shall be repayable in equal monthly instalments not exceeding fifty if the advance is for the purchase of a motor cycle or for the purchase of a bicycle:

Provided that if in any case, where the amount of advance divided by the number of instalments involved a fraction of a rupee, the amount of each instalment except the last shall be rounded off to the next higher whole rupee, the necessary reduction being made in the amount of the last instalment.

2. The recovery of the instalment of the advance shall be effected regularly from the monthly pay bill of the officer or employee concerned and shall be watched through the register of advances recoverable, to be maintained in the Office of the Library Authority;
3. Simple interest shall be charged on the advance at the rate fixed by the Government for their employees from time to time and shall be calculated on the balance outstanding on the last day of each month. The interest thus charged shall

be recovered in one or more instalments, each such instalment being not appreciably greater than the instalment by which the principal was recovered. The recovery of interest shall commence from the month following the month when the whole of the principal has been repaid;

4. In case of death of the officer or employee of the Library Authority of termination of his service, the balance of the advance, if any, with interest thereon shall be recovered immediately in one lump sum.

Journeys on Tour or Transfer

6.3.8 1. Where an advance is made to an officer or employee for journeys on tour, the amount of such advance shall not exceed the travelling allowance admissible under the rules and should also not exceed the amount likely to be required to meet the officers or employees' personal travelling expenses for a month or for the probable duration of the tour, whichever is shorter;

2. The advance shall be recovered in full from the travelling allowance bill relating to the journey in respect of which the advance is drawn;

3. When the officer or employee has drawn an advance of this kind, he should not be granted a second advance of the same kind until the first one has been fully adjusted. The adjustment of the advance shall be watched through the register of tour advance maintained in the office of the Library Authority.

6.3.9 1. Advance may be made to an officer or employee under orders of transfer up to an amount not exceeding one month's substantive pay plus the travelling allowance to which he may be entitled under the rules in consequence of the transfer;

2. Such advance shall be recorded to the officers' or employees' last pay certificate;

3. The advance of pay shall be recovered from the pay of the officer or employee in three equal monthly instalments beginning with the month in which a full month's pay is drawn after the transfer. The just two instalments should

be fixed in whole rupees and the remaining balance including any fraction of a rupee shall be recovered as the third instalment;

4. The advance of travelling allowance shall be recovered in full on the submission of the officer' or employees' travelling allowance bill;
5. The adjustment of the above advance shall be watched through the Register of Advances recoverable.

Advance for the Purchase of Mosquito Nets

6.3.10 1. An advance made to an officer or employee for the purchase of mosquito nets shall be limited to the amount actually required for the purchase of mosquito nets for his use and for the use of the members of his family subject to a maximum of a month's pay of the officer or employee concerned including dearness allowance or Rs.... whichever is less;

2. The advance shall be free of interest;
3. The advance shall be repayable in equal monthly instalments not exceeding twelve;
4. The recovery of instalment of advance shall be made regularly from the monthly pay bill of the officer or employee and watched through the Register of Advances. In case of death of the officer or employee or termination of his service, the balance of advance if any, shall be recovered in one lump sum.

Festival Advance

6.3.11 1. A Library Authority may grant festival advance to its officers and employees including the workers paid from contingencies at the rate applicable to Government employees of similar status;

2. Casual employees shall not be eligible for the advance;
3. Before these advances are sanctioned to temporary staff; sureties, from permanent officers or employees or any other form of security considered adequate by the Library Authority shall be obtained. The Library Authority may at its discretion dispense with those requirements in the case

of temporary staff who have completed three years of continuous service and are likely to continue in service till the adjustment of the advance;

4. The advance shall be admissible on the eve of any festival mentioned in the list of holidays notified by the Government every year irrespective of the community to which the applicant may belong and also irrespective of whether a general holiday or optional holiday has been declared for the festival in question;
5. Only one advance shall be sanctioned to an individual in a financial year;
6. No further advance shall be granted until the arrears of the previous advances, if any, have been completely recovered;
7. The advance is admissible only to those on duty or on earned leave on full pay at the time the advance is drawn;
8. The advance shall be paid not earlier than two weeks immediately preceding the festival;
9. The advance shall be recovered in not more than six equal monthly instalments by deduction from the pay bill, the first instalment being recovered from the pay following the month in which the advance was made. The amount of each instalment shall be rounded off to the nearest rupee, any balance being recovered in the last instalment;
10. The recoveries of the advance shall be watched through the Register of Festival Advances maintained in the office of the Library Authority.

6.3.12 1. Whenever the advance is not completely recovered before the transfer of an employee from the Library Authority to another Library Authority the details of the dues should be shown in the last pay certificate and sent to the office to which the employee is transferred;

2. On receipt of the last pay certificate, the Library Authority to which the employee is transferred should immediately reimburse the amounts of advances of pay, travelling allowance and other advances detailed in the last pay certificate in lump sum to the office which originally paid the advances and take action to recover the balance of amounts due from the employee as detailed in the last pay

certificate;

3. In the case of transfer of a Government employee to the service of the Library Authority on foreign service terms, the foreign employer should reimburse the amount of advance of pay and travelling allowance in lumpsum to Government on reversion from foreign service, the competent authority in Government will reimburse the amount of advance of pay in lump sum to the foreign employer.

SCHEDULE I

[*See* Rule 3]

An Agreement made on ____________________day of____________ One thousand nine hundred and _____________________between __________________ (hereinafter referred to as the Borrower which expression shall include his heirs, executors administrators, legal representatives and assignees) of the one part and the Library Authority of the other part;

Whereas the Borrower has purchased/agreed to purchase the motor cycle/bicycle described in the schedule hereunder;

And whereas, the Borrower has under the provision of the .... Financial Rules (hereinafter referred to as the said rules) applied for Library Authority for a loan of Rs. ________________________ for purchase of a Motor Cycle/Bicycle;

And whereas, the Library Authority have agreed to lend the said amount to the Borrower on the terms and conditions hereinafter contained;

Now it is hereby agreed between the parties hereto that in consideration of the sum of Rs. ___________ to be paid by the Library Authority to the Borrower, the Borrower hereby agrees:

1. To repay to the Library Authority, the said amount with interest calculated according to the said rules by monthly deductions from his salary as provided in the said rules and hereby authorises the Library Authority to make such deductions; and
2. Within one month from the date of drawal of the advance to expend the full amount of the said loan in the repayment of any loan obtained by him from a private party the ________ (Bank) for the purchase of the said motor cycle or if the actual

price paid is less than the loan to repay the difference to the Library Authority forthwith and ____________________;

3 To execute a document hypothecating the said motor cycle/bicycle to the Library Authority as security for the amount to be lent to the Borrower as aforesaid and interest in the form provided by the said Rules ____________________;

And it is hereby agreed and declared that if the motor cycle/bicycle is not purchased and hypthecated as aforesaid within the one month from the date of drawal of the advance or if the Borrower fails to repay the amount of the loan obtained by him from a private party/__________ (Bank) for the express purpose of purchasing the said motor cycle/bicycle within one month from the date of drawal of the advance of if the Borrower within that period becomes insolvent or quits service of the Library Authority or dies, the whole amount of the loan and interest accrued thereon shall immediately become due and payable.

SCHEDULE

1. Description of motor cycle/bicycle:
2. Maker's name:
3. Description:
4. No. of Cylinders:
5. Engine Number:
6. Chasis Number:
7. Cost Price:

In witness whereof the Borrower and ____________________ for and on behalf of and by the order and direction the Library Authority have hereunto set their hands the day and year first above written.

____

____

(Signature and Designation of the Borrower).

*Signed by the said in the Presence of —

1__________________________

2__________________________

(Signature of the Witnesses).
Signed by (name and designation)

____

for and on behalf of the Library Authority in the presence of —

1__________________________

2__________________________

(Signature of the witnesses).

____

____

(Signature and Designation of the Officer)

*Name and designation of the Borrower.

SCHEDULE II

[*See* Rule 4 (1)]

Form of Mortgage Bond for a Motor Cycle/Bicycle on Account of which a Servant has drawn an Advance

This Indenture made this ____________ day of one thousand and nine hundred and ____________________ between (hereinafter called the Borrower, which expression shall include his heirs, administrators, executors and legal representatives) of the one part and the Library Authority of the other part;

Whereas the Borrower has applied for and has been granted an advance of Rupees _______________ to purchase a motor cycle/bicycle on the terms of Article of the Financial Code (hereinafter referred to as the said Code which expression shall include any amounts thereof or additions thereto for the time being in force);

And whereas one of the conditions upon which the said advance has been granted to the Borrower is that the Borrower will hypothecate the said motor cycle/bicycle to the Library Authority (hereinafter called the Government as a security for the amount lent to the Borrower and whereas the Borrower has purchased with or partly with the amount so advanced as aforesaid the motor cycle/bicycle particulars whereof are set out in the Schedule hereunder written;

Now this indenture witnesseth that in pursuance of the said agreement and for the consideration aforesaid the Borrower doth hereby covenant to pay to the Library Authority the sum of Rs ______________ aforesaid or the balance thereof remaining unpaid at the date the Library Authority may put to sale and out of motor cycle/bicycle either by public auction or private contact of the sale moneys retain the balance of the said advance then remaining unpaid and any interest due thereon calculated as aforesaid, and all costs, charges, expenses and payments properly incurred or made in maintaining, defending or realizing their rights hereunder and shall pay over the surplus, if any, to the Borrower, his executors, administrators or personal representatives. Provided further that the aforesaid power of taking possession or selling of the said motor cycle/bicycle shall not prejudice the right of the Library Authority to sue the Borrower or his personal representatives for the said balance remaining due and interest or in the case of the motor cycle/bicycle being sold the amount by which the net sale proceeds fall short of the amount owing and the Borrower hereby further agrees that so long as any moneys are remaining due and owing to the Library Authority he the Borrower, will insure and keep insured the said motor cycle/bicycle against loss or damage by fire, theft or accident with an insurance company to be approved by the Accountant General, and will produce evidence to the satisfaction of the Accountant General, that the motor insurance company with whom the said motor cycle/bicycle is insured have received notice that the Library Authority are interested in the Policy and the Borrower hereby further agrees that he will not permit or suffer the said motor cycle/bicycle to be destroyed or injured or to deteriorate in a greater degree than it would deteriorate by reasonable wear and tear thereof and further that in the event of any damage or accident happening to the said motor cycle/bicycle the Borrower will forthwith have the same repaired and made good.

SCHEDULE

1. Description of motor cycle/bicycle:
2. Maker's name:
3. Description:
4. No. of Cylinders:
5. Engine Number:
6. Chasis Number:
7. Cost Price:

In witness whereof the aforesaid ______________________ (Borrowers name) and ______________________ for and on behalf of the Library Authority, have hereunto set their respective hands.

*Signed by the said in the Presence of —

1. ______________________
2. ______________________

(Signature of Witness).
(Signature and Designation of the Borrower)

Signed by (name and designation)

for and on behalf of the Library Authority in the presence of —

1. ______________________
2. ______________________

(Signature of the Witnesses)
(Signature and Designation of the Officer)

*Name and designation of the Borrower.

SCHEDULE III

[*See* Rule iii]

Form of Letter intimating to the Insurance Company, The Library Authorities Interest in a Motor Cycle/Bicycle Insurance Policy

From:

____

____

To:

____

____

Through the Accountant General,

Dear Sir,

I am to inform you that the Library Authority are interested in the motor cycle/bicycle insurance Policy No. ________________ secured in your company and to request that you will kindly insert a clause to the following effect in the policy.

Form of clause to be inserted in the insurance policy:

1. It is hereby declared and agreed that Shri ___________________ (the owner of the motor cycle/bicycle, hereinafter referred to as the insured in the schedule to this policy) has hypothecate the motor cycle/bicycle to Library Authority ..... security for an advance for the purchase of the motor cycle/bicycle and it is further declared and agreed that Library Authority ______________________ are interested in any moneys which but for this endorsement be payable to the said Sri ____________ (the insured under this policy) in respect of the loss or damage to the said motor cycle/bicycle (which loss or damage is not made good by repair, reinstatement or replacement) and such moneys

shall be paid to the Library Authority as long as he is the mortgagee of the motor cycle/bicycle and his receipt shall be full and final discharge to the Company in respect of such loss or damage.

2. Save as by this endorsement expressly agreed, nothing herein shall modify or effect the rights or liabilities of the insured or the company, respectively, under or in connection with this policy or any term, provision or condition thereof.

Application form for Bicycle Advance

1. Name of the applicant:
2. Office in which serving:
3. Post held at present:
4. Age and length of service:
5. Whether the appointment is temporary or permanent:
6. Date of compulsory or optimal retirement from service:
7. Basic pay exclusive of allowances:
8. Whether applicant owns at present any bicycle:
9. Prior to this, was any bicycle loan sanctioned?
10. Whether a new or second hand bicycle will be purchased and in either case, state the probable price:
11. Amount of advance applied for:
12. Number of instalments in which the amount will be repaid:
13. Signature of the applicant:
14. Recommendations of the Head of the Office:

Form of Application by a Library Authority Employee for an Advance for the Purchase of a Motor Cycle

1. Name:
2. Designation:
3. Address:
4. Pay:

1. Substantive pay: Rs.
2. Officiating pay or drawn in a temporary post, if the employer holds no substantive post:

5. Date of superannuation or retirement:
6. Amount of advance applied for: Rs.
7. 1. If the employee is on leave, date of expiry of leave:
   2. If the employee is about to proceed on leave:

      1. Date of Commencement of leave
      2. Date of expiry of leave

8. 1. where is the Motor Cycle/Bicycle to be purchased:
   2. If so, anticipated price of Motor Cycle/Bicycle:

9. 1. If the old moto cycle/bicycle was traced in which the employee went on leave and a new car/cycle has been delivered to him on return from leave:
   A. Price of the New Motor Cycle/ Bicycle: Rs.
   B. Amount deducted in respect of the old motor car/cycle:
   2. Whether the Officer is or was in possession of a Motor Cycle/ Bicycle and:
   3. If the answer to (2) above is a affirmation, amount or the anticipated amount of the sale proceeds of the Motor Cycle/ Bicycle:
10. Are any negotiations or preliminary

enquiries being made so that delivery may be taken of the Motor Cycle/ Bicycle within one month from the date of drawal of the Advance:

(a) Certified that the Information given above is complete and true.

(b) Certified that I have not/taken delivery of the Motor Cycle/ Bicycle on account of which I apply for the advance, that I shall complete the payment for the taking possession of the Motor Cycle/Bicycle before the expiry of one month from the date of drawal of the advance, and that I shall insure it within one month from the date of taking delivery of it.

OR

Certified that I have not taken delivery of the Motor Cycle/Bicycle on account of which I pay for the advance, that I shall not take delivery of it until I received the advance a week before the expiry of my leave and pay for it, and that I shall insure it within one week from the date of taking delivery of it.

Date: Signature :

Designation :

6.4 **Pension-cum-Gratuity Fund**

SCHEDULE II

Rules relating to the Library Authority Pension-cum-Gratuity Fund to be constituted in each Library Authority :

6.4.1 These Rules may be called the Library Authority Pension-cum-Gratuity Fund Rules, 19......

6.4.2 These Rules shall apply to the Library Authorities in the State.

6.4.3 Every Library Authority shall establish and maintain a Pension-cum-Gratuity Fund called the Library Authority Pension-cum-Gratuity Fund for the benefit of the employees of the Library Authority who are eligible for the Liberalised Pension Scheme sanctioned in G.O. No.—Finance, dated—. This fund shall form part of the Library Authority Fund as an earmarked fund. The fund shall be formed out of and maintained by every Library Authority out of the grants released by the Government for this purpose.

6.4.4 The grants-in-aid to be sanctioned by Government for each year towards meeting the expenditure on pension in respect of each employee of Library Authority shall be claimed by each Library Authority in advance. The expenditure on pensions incurred by Library Authority in excess of the grants sanctioned by Government in a year shall be claimed by Library Authority by way of additional grants in the first quarter of the succeeding year.

6.4.5 The Funds shall be administered by the Secretary, Library Authority. The Secretary, Library Authority shall maintain cash book, Nomination Register, a register of investments and pension payment audit register in the forms appended to these Rules. He shall also maintain such other Registers as may be prescribed by Government. All charges incurred during the year for establishment created for the maintenance of fund shall be initially met from salary grant of each Library Authority.

6.4.6 The Register referred to in Rule 7 shall be maintained in accordance with such instructions as will be issued by the Director of Local Fund Audit from time to time for carrying out the purposes of the Fund.

6.4.7 Any doubts arising in administering the fund shall be referred to Government for clarification.

6.5 **Preparation of Annual Budget**

6.5.1 These rules shall be called the Library Authority Budget Rules, 19...........

6.5.2 The Secretary, Library Authority shall prepare every year a budget in Form 'A' showing the probable receipts and expenditure of the Library Authority for the succeeding year.

6.5.3 The working balance to be provided for in the budget shall be at least 5 per cent of the estimated receipts excluding State grants and debt heads of the estimated receipts.

6.5.4 The budget in the language of the Library Authority shall be circulated every year to the members of the Library Authority at least one week before 31st December so that the members may have adequate time of examining the same, before the meeting of Library Authority held for its approval.

6.5.5 The budget and explanatory note thereon with the suggestions if any, of the members shall be placed by the Secretary before the Meeting of the Library Authority held for its approval not later than 25th January, every year.

6.5.6 After approval by the Library Authority the Secretary shall submit the budget to the Director for approval by 1st February every year.

6.5.7 The Director shall sanction the budget with modifications if any, after satisfying himself on the following points, namely:

1. The estimate of receipts is exhaustive and cautious and provides for the collection of the entire outstanding cess and the cess falling due during the budget year;
2. The recommendations, if any, of the Government or the Director have been duly taken into consideration while framing the budget;
3. Provision has been made for all obligatory charges for efficient running of the Library Authority and carrying out development activities prescribed by the Government and the Director from time to time;
4. Provision has been made for discharge of all liabilities in respect of loans contracted by the Library Authority and all other commitments;
5. Variations between the figures of the budget year and those of the previous year have been properly explained;
6. The working balance is not less than the minimum specified in Rule 4; and
7. The Secretary, Library Authority shall forward a copy of the budget approved by the Director to the auditor.

6.5.8 The sanctioning of the budget shall not, by itself, be deemed to authorise the Library Authority to incur all the expenditure provided for therein. The orders of the competent authority for the sanction of any item included in the budget should invariably be obtained before expenditure is incurred on that item.

6.5.9 No Library Authority shall authorise any item of expenditure not included in the budget or in excess of the budget allotment, without indicating the source from which the money required for the proposed expenditure is to be found. Whenever, the sanction of any authority is required for any proposed expenditure, such sanction shall be obtained before or after the Library Authority considers the proposal according to the instructions by the Director in the matter.

6.5.10 All allocations made in the budget shall lapse at the end of the year for which the budget relates and no part of any allocation remaining unexpended at the end of the year shall be reserved or appropriated by transfer to the deposits of any other head or drawn in order to avoid lapse and for disbursement after the end of the year.

6.5.11 All expenditure incurred during the course of the year shall be regulated strictly in accordance with allocations made in the budget for the year as approved by the Director. Where an allocation under any head of account is subsequently found necessary a revised or supplementary budget may be framed by reappropriation from other heads, subject to the conditions and limitations in Rule 14.

6.5.12 (i) All applications for reappropriation shall be made in Form 'B' and shall be submitted to the Library Authority by the Secretary and after its approval, such of the applications which require the approval of Director shall be sent in time for his approval, before the end of the year, according to instructions in this behalf issued by the Director.

(ii) The Secretary, Library Authority shall within a week from the date on which the Director of Public Libraries or the Library Authority as the case may be, sanctions any such applications forward a copy thereof to the auditor.

6.5.13 Where it is found necessary to find allocation from working balances or any other sources in the case of Library Authority it may be sanctioned subject to the following conditions and limitations:

(i) The working balance shall not be reduced below the minimum specified in Rule 4;

(ii) Applications for allotments or additional allotments shall be made in Form 'C' and submitted to the Library Authority by the Secretary. Such applications shall be submitted to the Director in time to admit the passing orders on them by the Director before the end of the year; and

(iii) The Secretary, Library Authority shall, within a week from the date on which the Director of Public Libraries sanctions any such applications, forward a copy thereof to the auditor.

6.5.14 To facilitate preparation of the detailed budget on correct lines, the following instructions are to be followed:

(i) That the statement in the Form 'D' shall be appended to the budget estimate;

(ii) For all capital expenditure such as purchase of land and buildings detailed reasons necessitating the purchase shall be stated;

(iii) In respect of loans contracted and outstanding at the time of preparation of budget, a statement of outstanding loans in the Form 'E' shall be enclosed to the budget estimate.

(iv) Form 'A' Column (2) shall give figures of actuals for the year previous to the one shown in Column (3). Column (3) shall give budget estimate figures of the year previous to the one for which budget estimates are prepared. Column (4) shall give revised estimate figures of the year previous to the one for which budget estimates are prepared. Column (5) shall show the estimates for the year for which the budget estimates are prepared.

Example: If the budget is prepared for the year 1991-92, the Column (2) should give actuals for 1989-90, Column (4) should give revised estimates 1990-91, Column (5) should show the estimates for the year 1991-92, i.e., the year for which the budgets are prepared.

6.5.15 *Annual Account* – The annual account shall be prepared by the Library Authority under the same heads of account as that of budget proforma and in Form 'F'.

FORM A

Budget of............................ for..........................

Head of Account	Actuals 1989-90	Budget Estimates 1990-91	Revised Estimates 1990-91	Budget Estimates 1991-92	Explanation for Variation
1	2	3	4	5	6

TOTAL OPENING BALANCE

(I) (A) *Receipts —Ordinary*

(i) Library cess
(ii) Contributions
(iii) Gifts
(iv) Fines
(v) Income from endowments
(vi) (a) Government grant under Section ... of the Public Libraries Act, 19 ...
(b) Grants for specific purposes
(1) Social Activities and Seminars
(2) Opening of Branch Libraries
(3) ... ...
(4) ... ...
(c) General Grants
(vii) Funds and other amounts collected by the Library Authority not covered by the above item.
(viii) Amount realised by sale of condemned articles, books, newspapers and magazines, etc.
(ix) Interest on investments
(x) Miscellaneous receipts

Total (i to x)

(B) Deduction
(i) Refunds (Details to be specified)
(ii) Amount transferred to capital

Total deduction (i+ii)
Total ordinary (A-B) Rs.

II. *Receipts — Capital*

(i) Government Grants
(a) Equipment and furniture Grant
(b) Books
(c) Miscellaneous
ii) Loans
(iii) Endowments and contributions
(iv) Investments realised
(v) Amount transferred from ordinary receipts
(vi) Cost of Books recovered

Total (i to vii) Rs.

III.*Deposits and Advances*

(i) Deposits

(ii) Advance recovered

(iii) Refund of permanent advance

Total ordinary and Capital (I+II+III)

Grant total including Opening Balance

I. *Expenditure — Ordinary*

A. Staff

(i) Pay and other allowances

(ii) Contributions to Provident Fund (by management)

(iii) Pension

(iv) Gratuity

B. Travelling Allowances

(i) Chairman

(ii) Members

(iii) Establishment

C. Contingencies

(i) Rents and Taxes

(ii) Postage

(iii) Stationery

(iv) Printing

D. Other items of equipment (Recurring nature):

(i) Periodicals

(ii) Repairs

(a) Buildings

(b) Furniture, etc.,

(iii) Contributions

(iv) Interest on and repayment of loans

(v) Lectures and classes

Total Ordinary (A+B+C+D)

II. *Expenditure — Capital*

(i) Lands and buildings

(ii) Investments

(iii) Purchase of Books

(iv) Furniture

(v) Other equipment of capital nature

Total (i to v)

III. *Deposits and Advances*

(i) Deposits

(ii) Advances

(iii) Permanent Advance

Total (I to III)
Total capital (II+III)
Total Ordinary and capital (I+II+III)
Total closing balance
Grand Total including Closing balance

FORM B

Application for Allotment or Additional Allotment of Funds by Reappropriation Required by the Library Authority

Particulars of work or purpose	Head of account name of work, etc., for which additional allotment is required	Amount provided for the work or purpose in the budget	Amount subsequently allotted or transferred	Amount spent up to date
1	2	3	4	5

Amount required to meet probable expr. up to the end of year	Total Columns (5) and (6)	Amount now required to be transferred (i.e. column (7) *minus* column (3) *plus* column (4)	Reasons for exceeding the original allotment	Head of account or source from which transfer is applied for	Anticipated savings from which funds may be allotted
6	7	8	9	10	11

Sanctioned .... subject to the modifications.

FORM C

Application for Allotment of Additional Funds from the Balance Required by the Library Authority

Particulars of work or purpose	Head of account in which or name of work for which allotment is required	Amount provided for the work or purpose in the budget	Amount subsequently allotted or transferred	Amount spent up to date	Amount now required to meet pro-expr. up to the end of the year
1	2	3	4	5	6

Amount now required by transfer from the balance	Reasons for exceeding the original allotment	Reference to previous correspondence and the No. and date of the sanction order	Amount of closing balance provided in the budget revised with reference to the actual opening balance of the year
7	8	9	10

Total of allotments made from such balance including those not applied for	Net balance available	Percentage of estimated receipts	Remarks
11	12	13	14

Note: It should be explained in the remarks column how the difference between columns (6) and (7) is proposed to be met.

Sanctioned in .... Subject to the modification.

FORM 'D' (I)

Office (Temporary Establishment)

Number of the officers and designation, class or category of establishment	Details of appointment in each class or category	Scale of Pay	No. of persons at oach rate of pay
1	2	3	4

Pay that will be drawn on 1—4	No. of vacant posts	Provision that will be made in the budget estimates for 19..... -19.... on account of class or category of officers or subordinates	Authority charge in the strength or scale of pay or compared with the current year's estimates
5	6	7	8

FORM 'D' (II)

Number Statement

(Allowances)

Name of the officer and designation of appointment	Station	Pay of appointment	Nature of allowance attached (whether local house rent, conveyance and fixed allowances)
1	2	3	4

Amount of fixed allow-ances for each kind	Provision to be made in the budget estimates of the ensuing financial year for each class or category or officers or subordinates	Authority for charge in the number of amounts as compared with the current year's budget estimates (Co. No and Date)
5	6	7

FORM 'E'

Loan Statement for the Year (to which the Budget Estimates Relates to)

Heads	Total loan taken	Years in which taken	Order granting the loan	Terms of repayment and the annual instalment
1	2	3	4	5

Amount outstanding at the beginning of the year	Amount repaid during the year		
	Principal	Interest	(Balance loan outstanding at the close of the year)
6	7	8	9

FORM 'F'

Head of account	Actuals for 1969-70	Budget Estimates for 1970-71	Actuals for current year 1969-70	Budget preparation current year 1971-72
1	2	3	4	5

TOTAL OPENING BALANCE

I (A) *Receipts–Ordinary*

(i) Library cess
(ii) Contributions
(iii) Gifts
(iv) Fines
(v) Income from Endowments
(vi) Government grant under section .... of the .... Public Libraries Act, 19 ....
(vii) Amount realised by sale of condemned stores (including newspaper etc.)
(viii) Other receipts
Total (i to viii) Rs.

(B) **Deduct**

(i) Refunds
(ii) Amount transferred to capital
Total deduction (i + ii)
Total ordinary (A - B)

II *Receipts–Capital*

(i) Government grants
(ii) Loans
(iii) Endowments and contributions
(iv) Investments realised
(v) Amount transferred from ordinary
(vi) Cost of books recovered
(vii) Other receipts
Total (i to vii) Rs.

III *Deposits and Advances*

(i) Deposits
(ii) Advance recovered
(iii) Refund of permanent advance
Total ordinary and capital (I+II+III)

1. *Expenditure–Ordinary*

A. Staff
(i) Pay and allowances
(ii) Contributions to Provident Fund (by Management)
(iii) Pension
(iv) Gratuity

B. Travelling Allowances:
- (i) Chairman
- (ii) Members
- (iii) Establishment

C. Contingencies
- (i) Rents and Taxes
- (ii) Postage
- (iii) Stationery
- (iv) Printing
- (v) Other items

D. Other items of equipment (of Recurring nature):
- (i) Periodicals
- (ii) Repairs to buildings
- (iii) Contributions
- (iv) Interest on and repayment of loans
- (v) Lectures and classes

Total Ordinary (A+B+C+D)

2. *Expenditure — Capital*

- (i) Lands and buildings
- (ii) Investments
- (iii) Purchase of Books
- (iv) Furniture
- (v) Other equipment of capital nature

Total (i to v) Rs.

3. *Deposits and Advances*

- (i) Deposits
- (ii) Advances
- (iii) Permanent Advance

Total (i to iii)
Total Capital (2+3)
Total Ordinary and capital (1+2+3)
Total closing balance
Grand Total including
Closing balance

6.6 Collections of Library Cess

6.6.1 Cess shall be collected promptly by the local bodies mentioned in Section 86 of the Act and 75 per cent of the cess collections so made in a particular year be remitted by the said local Authorities to the Treasury Account of the Library Authority concerned immediately after the close of the financial year and the balance of 25 per cent be remitted after the audited figures become available.

6.6.2 The Secretary of a Library Authority shall report to the Director the failure of a local Authority to collect cess and the Director shall bring it to the notice of the Director of Municipal Administration in the case of a Municipal Committee or Municipal Corporation or the Collector, in the case of any other Local Body.

6.6.3 The Director of Municipal Administration and the Collector shall take disciplinary action against the person or persons responsible for the delay in the remittance of the cess to the Library Authority.

Note: The Director shall issue instructions from time to time on the steps to be taken regarding the realisation of cess. The Secretaries are requested to contact District Panchayat Officers, Secretaries of Municipalities, and the District Collector and discuss with them about Cess Collections and also request them to cooperate with the Authority and render all possible assistance so as to provide better library facilities in the District. The monthly return prescribed on Cess Collections by the Director should be submitted regularly. All efforts should be made in this direction. The D.C.B. register shall be maintained properly and the same may be watched promptly.

The cheques received from Panchayats may carefully be entered in the register and sent to the concerned Bank for realisation. If there is any difficulty, the Secretary may contact concerned persons in this regard and see that such difficulties are overcome. No cheque should be lost or remain un-cashed by the end of the year. The cooperation of members of Authority, the staff and Chairman may be fully utilised for Cess Collections. When the procedure for the Cess Collections is changed in course of time, many of the hardships will be mitigated.

6.7 **Audit and Accounts**

6.7.1 The accounts of each Library Authority shall be audited annually by the Examiner of Local Fund Accounts and his departmental staff or by the departmental auditors authorised by the Director. The Library Authority shall submit all their accounts to the auditors as required by them.

6.7.2 The auditors may:

(1) in writing require the production of any book, deed, contract, account, voucher, receipt or other documents, the persual or examination of which they consider necessary.
(2) in writing require any person who has the custody or control of any such document or who is accountable for it to appear in person before them.
(3) require any person so appearing to make and sign a declaration with respect to such document or to answer any question or to prepare and furnish any statement relating thereto.

6.7.3 The auditors shall:

(1) report to the Library Authority any material impropriety or irregularity which they may have observe in the expenditure or recovery of moneys due to the Library Authority or in the accounts;
(2) furnish to the Library Authority such information as it may require concerning the progress of their audit;
(3) report to the Library Authority any loss or waste of money or other property owned by or vested in the District Library Authority caused by neglect or misconduct, with the names of persons directly or indirectly responsible for such loss or waste and;
(4) submit to the Library Authority a final statement of the audit and a copy thereof to the Director on or before 30th June of every year or within such period as the Government may from time to time notify.

6.7.4 The Secretary to the Library Authority shall submit replies to the audit reports to the Director and a copy thereof shall be submitted to the examiner of Local Fund Accounts. The Director shall review the replies with reference to the remarks of the Examiner of Local Fund Accounts, if any, and issue necessary instructions to the Library Authority.

6.7.5 The Director shall submit to Government for their information within one month of the receipt of the reports referred to above a consolidated review of these reports with special reference to the irregularities and special features, if any, noticed in Audit and the action taken to remedy them.

6.7.6 The auditors may disallow every item contrary to law and surcharge the same on the person making or authorising any person to make such payment and may charge against any person to make such payment and may charge against any person responsible therefor the amount of any deficiency, loss or unprofitable outlay incurred by the negligence or misconduct of that person or of any sum which ought to have been, but is not brought into account by that person and shall in every such case, certify the amount due from such person.

6.7.7 The auditors shall state in writing the reasons for their decision in respect of every disallowance, surcharge or charge.

6.7.8 Every sum certified to be due from any person by the auditors under the Act, shall be paid by such person to the Library Authority within 14 days, from the date of intimation by the Chairman of the said *Samstha* or by the Director of Public Libraries to such person of the decision of the auditors unless within that time he has appealed to the Government against the decisions and such sum if not so paid or such sum as the Government shall on appeal, declare to be due shall be recoverable by the Library Authority.

6.7.9 Notwithstanding anything contained in these Rules, the Government may at any time direct that the recovery of the whole or any part of the amount certified to be due from any person by auditors under the Act shall be waived, if in their opinion such a course is necessary considering all the circumstances of the case.

6.7.10 At the request of the Department Auditors are taking up the audit work from the middle of April. Before the audit takes place all the registers and records shall be brought up to date. It is desirable to make a review of all the accounts registers etc. so as to rectify the defects noticed before they are pointed out by audit.

6.7.11 After the receipt of audit report recoveries ordered in the audit report should be effected promptly. The persons concerned should be served with notices for refunding the amounts to be certified by the auditors. Recovery of small sums towards excess T.A. etc.

should be made from the pay bill of the concerned employee.

6.7.12 Wherever orders of Director of Public Libraries or Government have to be obtained, proposals should be submitted immediately. The replies to the audit report shall be placed before Library Authority at its meeting.

6.7.13 The Secretaries should review the pending audit objections and initiate action for their earliest settlement. The quarterly progress report of audit objections pending may be submitted to the Director promptly.

6.8 **Inspection and Reports**

6.8.1 The Directorate shall be inspected by the Government once in an year.

6.8.2 *Inspection and Reports*: The District Central Libraries and the offices of District Library Authority shall be inspected by the Director of Public Libraries or an Officer deputed by him once a year.

6.8.3 The Branch Libraries shall be inspected by the Secretary of the Library Authority concerned once a year.

6.8.4 The Secretaries of the Library Authority shall submit copies of the reports of the Inspections conducted by them to the Director within 15 days from the date of the Inspection.

7. GRANT-IN-AID

7.1 **City/District Library Authority**

1. The Library Authorities, which are not financially sound due to a meagre library cess collections should approach the Government for grant-in-aid. The Government may release the grants considering the merits of the case.
2. However, the Government should release special grants for the development of undeveloped pockets and the agency areas.

7.2 **Grant-in-Aid to other Public Libraries**

1. These rules are called Grant-in-aid Rules of the Department of Public Libraries of the Government of . . . and shall apply to all the public libraries managed by the Local Bodies, Religious Endowments, Co-operative Societies, Voluntary Organisations

etc.

2. *Preamble*: A sum of money is annually set apart with this Department and with the Library Authority of the District, to be expended under these rules as Grant-in-Aid to recognised libraries, under private managements, Corporate Bodies and Local Bodies, whose purpose is to contribute towards the general spread of knowledge and education, through the Public Libraries. Such grants will be given subject to the condition, hereinafter specified and with due consideration of the requirements of such locality and of each library and of the funds available.
3. *Object of Grants*: The grants may be given to aided libraries for the following purposes:

A. *Normal Grants*

1. Books and periodicals
2. Salary of the Staff
3. Rents, Rates, Taxes
4. Book Binding, mending and preservation

B. *Special Grants*

5. Building Construction and repairs
6. Library Furniture and fittings

C. *Additional Grants*

7. Adult Education Programmes
8. Text Book Section
9. Children's Section

4. *Interpretation of Rules*: The interpretation of any rule in these rules shall in the first instance rest with the Director. The right of final interpretation and the right to change or modify the rules are fully reserved by the Government.
5. *Eligibility*: Annual grant of any kind shall be sanctioned to the Aided Libraries under the following management:

1. Municipalities and Municipal Corporations

2. Zilla Parishads, Panchayat Samithies and Panchayats
3. Co-operative Societies and Religious Endowments
4. Voluntary organisations, such as Gram Sanghams, Mahila Mandals, Balanda Kendrams etc.

6. *Registration:* The management of the library which needs grant-in-aid should be registered under Societies Registration Act. Government may permit the libraries at a concessional rate of Rs. 5 as in the case of Youth Clubs and Mahila Mandal.

7. *Recognition:*

1. An institution which seeks aid should be recognised by the Director. Application for recognition shall be made in a prescribed form (Annexure I) to the Secretary. Libraries of less than one year standing are not eligible for recognition. A certificate of recognition is appended in the Annexure II.
2. *Refusal of Recognition* – If the recognisation applied for is refused, a copy of the order shall be sent by registered post to the management stating the reasons for which recognition is refused:

   Provided that the management may within thirty days from the date of the receipt of the Order submit an appeal to the State Government whose decision shall be final. Any appeal received after the period of thirty days shall not be entertained unless management shows good and sufficient cause for not submitting the appeal in time;

   Provided further that nothing in these Rules shall be deemed to prevent the management from making a fresh application for recognition under these Rules.
3. *Withdrawal of Recognition* – If the Director is satisfied that the management of a Public Library has committed breach of any of the conditions of recognition, or has failed to observe any of the conditions specified in the Certificate of Recognition, he may for reasons to be recorded in writing and after giving the management an opportunity of being heard withdraw the recognition, which order shall be communicated to the management by the registered post and the Certificate of Recognition granted to management in respect of such Public Library shall be

deemed to be cancelled:

Provided that the management may within thirty days from the date of the receipt of the order submit an appeal to the State Government whose decision shall be final. Any appeal received after the period of thirty days shall not be entertained unless management shows good and sufficient cause for not submitting the appeal in time;

Provided further that nothing in these rules shall be deemed to prevent the management from making a fresh application for recognition under these rules.

8. *Access*: The Library shall be kept open to the public for consultation, loaning of reading and kindred materials within the premises, and without any restriction on the basis of caste, creed religion or sex and free of charge, except those relating to proper behaviour and public health.

9. *Maintenance*: Every library on behalf of which aid is sought shall be under the management of a body which is recognised by the Director and who in the capacity of proprietors of trustees or of members of a Committee, or Association by which the library is maintained, shall undertake to be answerable for the maintenance of the library and its branches and of the fulfilment of such rules of discipline as are prescribed from time to time. The management may, with the approval of Secretary, Library Authority appoint a person as Correspondent to transact the current business of the library with the Department.

10. *Library Service*

1. A Library, Reading room or club should have been organising service for a minimum period of 2 years immediately preceding the date of registration to enable to gain eligibility for the grant and or franchise in the election for the membership of Library Authority.
2. It should be opened at least 3 hours in a day.
3. It should have a minimum of 500 books and be subscribing to at least 2 dailies and 5 other periodicals.
4. If it is a reading room or club, it should subscribe at least 2 dailies and 8 other periodicals and such reading room or club should within period of 2 years from the date of registration ac-

quire or strengthen their existing book stock to a minimum of 500 books.

5. It should provide a space for at least 20 readers to sit and study.

11. *Withdrawal of Grants*: Grants will ordinarily be withdrawn from any library if any of the members of the Governing Body of a library, or any member of its staff inculcates opinions tending to excite feelings of disloyality and dissatisfaction among the public, or there is falsification of registers, misuse of funds, or other proved fraud, or irregularity, or there is failure to remedy the defects in the organisation of the library.

12. *Audit*: Payments of all grants will be subject to audit by a Registered Auditor or Chartered Accountant. The management concerned may be called upon to refund the amount paid or such portion of it as the Director may decide. Such refund may be made either by adjustment in any other grant payable to the Library or in such other manner as the Director may deem fit.

13. *Defunct Libraries:* The regulations of a library may contain provisions concerning its field of activity as well as the composition of its management. If the aided library ceases to exist, its property shall be taken over by the Library Authority of the District Concerned.

14. *Sanction of Grant*: Grants under this chapter may be sanctioned annually for the maintenance of the libraries at the rates fixed by Government from time to time. The annual grant paid to a library shall be considered as having been paid in respect of the previous years working of the library.

15. *Sanctioning Authority*: Except in cases where a reference to Government is required or where authorities subordinate to the Director have been permitted to sanction grants all grants paid from provincial funds are sanctioned by the Director. Grants under Library Fund are sanctioned by the Library Authority of the District.

16. *Changes*: Information about change of management or Byelaws of libraries should be sent to the Secretary, Library Authority, by Regd. Post, within 15 days from the date of change.

17. *Minimum Grant*: There should be a minimum grant for every library/reading-room/club. Such a grant should not be less than Rs. . . . . so as to enable it to run its day-to-day service. It should, however, be eligible to special/additional grants for books, furniture, equipment etc.

18. *Application for Grant*: Application for admission to aid shall be

made in the prescribed form (Annexure III) each year to the Director through the Secretary, not later than the end of 1st July of each year. The application shall be accompanied by a report and accounts of the library for the previous year and such other returns as the Director may prescribe from time to time with a view to ascertain the financial position of the library and its eligibility for aid.

In the matter of fixing up quantum of grant for these libraries/ reading-rooms/ clubs some weightage will have to be given to units belonging to backward and tribal regions.

19. *Inspection*

1. Libraries with a book stock of 15,000 and above shall be inspected by the Director of Public Libraries or an officer authorised by him.
2. Libraries having a book stock of above 5,000 and below 15,000 shall be inspected by the Librarian, District Central Library or a Grade : I Librarian authorised by him.
3. Libraries having book stock of below 5,000 shall be inspected by any librarian of the Branch Library, authorised by the Librarian, District Central Library.

   The Inspection report in the prescribed form (Annexure-III) should be submitted through the Secretary, Library Authority to the Director of Public Libraries not later than 31st July of every year.

20. *Accounts and Records:* The Accounts, records and the statistics prescribed by the Director of Public Libraries should be open for inspection by the Director of Public Libraries or any librarian deputed by him. The accounts of the library should be audited by an agency recognised by the Government.

21. *Aid*: The Director shall determine which libraries shall be admitted to aid after taking into account the character, efficiency and the financial condition of the library, the needs of the locality and the funds at his disposal.

22. *Adjustment of Grants*: The grants will be adjusted to the Library Authority of the concerned District. The Secretary shall draw the amounts as per the orders of the Director and pay the amounts to the managements or withdraw by the Authorities empowered to sanction such grant at a time before payment and shall not be deemed to be a

debit enforceable by suit or by any other legal process.

BOOKS AND PERIODICALS

23. *Type of Books*: Books to be purchased should conform to the following rules—

1. They should be of general interest and cultural value.
2. The books, if they are fiction, must be of standard authors and must not be of doubtful taste.
3. Books abusing one community or religion should not be purchased.
4. The industries, agriculture and trades of the locality shall be taken into consideration at the time of purchasing books, provided that the State Library Council shall be entitled to prohibit or proscribe the purchase of any Magazine, Newspaper, periodical or book which in its opinion does not stand the above-mentioned tests.

24. *Rate of Grant*: In normal areas for purchase of books and periodicals the management share will be 1/3 and the Government grant will be 2/3. The entire expenditure on books and periodicals is admissible for assessment of the grant and grant would be worked out on the basis of 1:2.

25. *Payment of Grant*: The grant shall be paid only on submission, before the date specified in the order sanctioning the grant, of vouchers duly receipted. It shall be drawn on a bill by the Secretary and paid to the management by way of demand draft.

26. *Ceasing of Property*: If a library which has received aid under this chapter has within five years from the date on which a grant under this chapter is drawn, been closed or diverted to other purposes, the Library Authority shall be at liberty to cease the books, towards the supply of which the grant was given.

27. *Valuation*: When the Government purchases the articles at the valuation so fixed, the amount to be paid to the management shall be only the excess of the valuation over the amount already given as grant towards their original purchase. Alternatively, the Government may direct the articles to be sold in auction in which case the proceeds shall be credited into the "Library Fund" provided that if the proceeds exceed the amount of grant already paid towards the purchase of the

articles, the difference shall be payable to the management of the Library.

SITES AND BUILDINGS

28. *Grants for Sites and Buildings:* Besides the annual maintenance grants, special grants may be sanctioned for any of the following purposes:

1. Acquiring land for the location of library
2. Purchasing, erecting, enlarging or improving the buildings
3. Executing extensive alterations and major repairs to buildings.

The purchase of land, or new buildings, or extensions or alterations to the existing buildings may be done in consultation with the Director or with a person, authorised by him.

29. *Grant*: The quantum of grant regarding the building construction work in a normal areas is 40 per cent management share and 60 per cent Government grant, and in Backward, drought-affected, slum and tribal areas the management share is 10 per cent and the Government grant is 90 per cent.

If the Director considers the scheme in general as essential and suitable, subject to availability of funds, the correspondent shall then submit to him in duplicate detailed plans, specifications and estimates, (which may include architects and Engineer's fees), prepared by a recognised professional Engineer or Architect. No building operations shall commence until the issue of favourable orders on the suitability of the design and the reasonableness of the estimate. In respect of cases, where a grant is supplied for and proposed to be considered, the Director shall call for a valuation of the work done from the Executive Engineer, Public Works Department or Panchayat Raj Department.

30. *List of Works*: The Director will maintain a list of works approved by him. But the inclusion of a work in the list referred to implies no liability on the part of Government, legal or moral, for making a grant, though managements will not be precluded thereby from applying for a grant after buildings are completed. The Director will each year recommend for the consideration of Government such new schemes out of the list as considers deserving of grant and will authorise payment of grant under specific sanction of the Government in each case out of the funds placed at his disposal for the purpose.

supply of which the grant was given at a valuation to be made by an officer to be deputed by the Government for the purpose.

42. *Valuation*: When the Government purchases the articles at the valuation so fixed, the amount to be paid to the management shall be only the excess of the valuation over the amount already given as grant towards their purchase. Alternatively, the Government may direct that the articles shall be sold in auction in which case the proceeds shall be credited to the "Library Fund" provided that if the proceeds exceed the amount of grant already paid towards the purchase of the articles the difference shall be payable to the management of the institution.

43. *Staff*: The management should appoint the required staff to manage the libraries. The appointments should be made as per the guidelines of the Library Authority.

If they appoint qualified staff, the salaries should be paid on par with the staff of Library Authority. The management should follow the service conditions, as fixed by the Department from time to time.

ADDITIONAL GRANTS

44. *Additional Grants*: In addition to these the libraries should be given special grants for taking up work in the following areas also:

1. *Adult Education Programme*: For stocking reading material useful for neo-literates and extending assistance in this programme, an amount of Rs. . . . per annum may be provided (remuneration for teacher as already provided in the National Adult Education programme of the Government of India).
2. *Text Books*: In the villages and other non-urban areas a quiet place for young students to sit and study is generally not available because of large size of an average family and the little space and lighting facility available at home. It is, therefore, necessary that libraries should take the responsibility for providing such special accommodation. The centre should be open for at least 4 hours in a day and should provide accommodation for at least 6 students. A special grant of Rs. . . . per annum for first 3 years and Rs. . . . per annum thereafter may be provided for this activity after due inspection and verification.
3. *Children's Section*: These libraries should be given special grants for organising special cells for children. The grant may be Rs. . . . per annum for the first 2 years and Rs. . . . per annum

thereafter. Every one of these libraries should be required to provide special accommodation and facilities for women, farm and factory workers and attend to their conveniences.

45. *Payment of Grant*: The grant shall be paid only on the submission, before the date specified in the order sanctioning the grant, of vouchers duly receipted. It shall be drawn on a bill prepared in the prescribed form of the Government Grant.

46. *Ceasing the Property*: If a library which has received aid under this chapter has within five years from the date on which a grant under this chapter is drawn, been closed or diverted to other purpose, the Library Authority shall be at a liberty to cease the articles towards the supply of which the grant was given at a valuation to be made by an Officer to be deputed by the Government for the purposes.

47. *Valuation*: When the Government purchases the articles at the valuation so fixed, the amount to be paid to the management shall be only the excess of the valuation over the amount already given as grant towards their purchase.

Alternatively, the Government may direct that the articles shall be sold in auction in which case the proceeds shall be credited to the "Library Fund" provided that if the proceeds exceed the amount of grant already paid towards the purchase of the articles the difference shall be payable to the management of the institution.

48. *Utilisation of the Grant*

1. *Books* – Seventy five per cent of the grant received by the library should be utilised for the purchase of new books for the library.
2. *Other than books* – The remaining twenty five per cent of the grant received by the library may be utilised for other library purposes, if necessary, with the previous approval of the Secretary of the Library Authority concerned.
3. *Submission of Vouchers* – A copy of each bill paid out of the grant with the certificate of payment written on it and signed by the Chairman of the Managing Committee or the Executive Officer of the approved corporate body and the receipt of the party receiving the money, should be sent to the Librarian of the Library Authority concerned at the end of each month, along with a statement of the utilisation of the grant in the form prescribed by the Director.

4. *Physical Verification* – Each library should give facilities to the auditor or any other agent appointed for the purpose, for the physical verification of the books and the other materials covered by the bills to be audited.
5. *Submission to Auditor* – The certified bills and the monthly statements received by the Secretary of the Library Authority concerned will form the primary basis for audit.
6. The accounts for the income and expenditure from its own sources of income should be submitted by the Library each year to such audit as the Government may prescribe. The report of this audit will form the basis for the determination of the annual grant.

ANNEXURE I

Application Form for Recognition of Library for the Year

1. Location:
2. Name of the Library:
3. Date of Establishment:
4. Registration No. and Date:
   (Copy of the Bye-Laws to the enclosed)
5. Names of the members of the
   Managing Body:

President	1
Secretary	2
Members	3
	4
	5
	6
	7
	8

6. Name and Address of the Correspondent:
7. Date of Inspection:
8. Details of furniture: Book racks........, almirahs........, tables........, Chairs........, etc.
9. No. of books available in English . . . . ., Hindi . . . . .
10. Details of periodicals:

	Dailies	Weeklies	Fortnightlies	Monthlies	Quarterlies
1. English					
2. Hindi					
3. Others					

11. Building: Own, rented or rent-free
12. Details of Income and expenditure:
13. *Declaration on Behalf of the Management of the Library*: I hereby declare that the conditions of recognition laid down in

the rules will be fully observed and all the rules prescribed from time to time by the Director of Public Libraries which are applicable to the libraries will be fully observed and adhered to. I am prepared subject the institute together with its current endowment and trust accounts since its establishment and registers to inspection and to furnish such returns as may be required by the Department from time to time. No objectionable books and newspapers, periodicals and pamphlets will be kept in the library.

Signature of the Correspondent

ANNEXURE II

GOVERNMENT OF ....

Department of Public Libraries

Certificate of Recognition

Certified that the ________________________________ (Name of the library) at ____________ taluk ____________________ district ______________ is recognised by the Director of Public Libraries as a public library from the year ________________ in exercise of the powers conferred on him under clause _______ of subsection ______ of section ____ of the ____ Public Libraries Act, 19 ____. The continuance of this recognition shall be subject to the provisions of the _____ Libraries Rules, 19 ____ and the conditions specified below:

1. The arrangement of books in a public library shall be according to the instructions issued by the Director from time to time.
2. The library shall maintain the following records:

   (i) Constitution of the Library;
   (ii) List of Members;
   (iii) Daily Visitors Record;
   (iv) Accession Register: All books purchased or received as gift shall be accessioned within a period of ten days from the date

of receipt of the book;

(v) Book Issue Record;

(vi) Account Books (Cash Books, Ledgers, etc.);

(vii) Receipt Book;

(viii) Periodicals and Newspapers Record;

(ix) Complaint and Suggestion Book;

(x) Stock Register of furniture;

(xi) Register of Scholars and Research;

(xii) Inward and Outward Register;

(xiii) Deposit Register;

(xiv) Minutes of Meetings;

(xv) Withdrawal Register;

3. The library shall display the following notice-boards at prominent places:

   (i) the name of the library with words "Government Recognised and Free" at the end;

   (ii) the names of office-bearers and members of the Managing Committee; and

   (iii) the working hours of the library and the days on which library will remain closed.

4. The management shall supply the Director with such returns and periodical information as the Director may call for from time to time.
5. The Public Library shall spend not less than 50 per cent of the grant-in-aid on books. Provided that not less than 25 per cent of the grant shall be spent on purchase of books from not less than two lists of books issued by the Director during the year.
6. Books purchased by the public library should conform to the following requirements:

   (i) books shall be of general interest and of cultural value;

   (ii) the books should not contain anything calculated to create discontent or hatred among different communities, or communal disharmony; and

   (iii) the books should not contain undesirable pictures or any matter of doubtful taste.

7. The management shall keep the library open for inspection by the Director or any other officer authorised by him in this behalf at all times during the working hours of the library.

Director of Public Libraries
. . . . . State,

Place :
Date :

ANNEXURE III

Application for Grant-in-Aid on Behalf of the . . . . .
for the Year 19 . . .-19 . . .

1. Name and Address of the Library:

2. Name and Address of the Management:

3. Date of Establishment:

4. No. and Date of Registration:

5. No. and Date of Recognition with Director:

6. Whether it is open for all members of the society for consultation within premises without restriction of the basis of caste, creed, religion, sex and free of charge:

7. Whether it satisfies all the conditions laid down in the Act and Rules:
8. Grant required for this year

Sl. No.	Particulars	Last Year Grant:	Balance of Last Year Grant:	Grant required for this Year:
A.	*Normal Grants*			
1.	Books and periodicals			
2.	Salary of the Staff			
3.	Rents, rates, taxes			
4.	Book Building			
B.	*Special Grants*			
5.	Building construction			
6.	Library equipment			
7.	Library furniture			
C.	*Additional Grants*			
8.	Adult Education Programme			
9.	Text Book Section			
10.	Children's Section			
	Total			

9. Present accommodation whether rented or owned, full details about floor area, and other relevant factors should be given:
10. Why additional accommodation is considered essential?
11. Whether a site is available–

    (a) If so, give the measurements and full description.
    (b) If not, how the management proposes to acquire a site and complete the project within the stipulated time?

12. The estimated cost of the project:
13. How the management proposes to meet the cost of the project in excess of the grant?

    Production of evidence in this behalf.

14. Whether the plans including the site plan and estimates have been approved, and if so by whom? A copy of certificate given by such approving authority should be forwarded with the application in case the plans and estimates are not countersigned by such authority in token of approval

15. The agency by which the work is proposed to be carried out

16. Whether the management is willing to execute an agreement to utilise the grant for the purpose for which it is given and to refund the same with interest thereon at such rate as Government may fix from time to time in case the management fails to utilise the grant for the purpose within the stipulated time.

17. Whether the management is agreeable to abide by rules framed by Government for this purpose from time to time.

18. Whether all the Registers and accounts are open for

Inspection.

19. Whether you are prepared to submit any return or information received by the Department.

Declaration: On behalf of the management of the library, I hereby declare that the conditions of aid laid down in the Public Libraries Act and Rules are being and will continue to be fully observed expecting those rules from which the institution has been specially exempted by the Director in his proceedings RC No. . . . . Dt. . . . . and that I am prepared to subject the institution together with its current endowment and trust accounts since its establishment and Registers to inspection and to furnish such returns as may be required by the Department and that I shall abide by the provisions of the Grant-in-aid code in the event of the Library being closed within 5 years from the date on which grant has been drawn.

Signature of the Applicant

Enclosures

1. A detailed note on the need of each item of grant;
2. Statement account certified by a registered auditor;
3. Statement of assets and liabilities;
4. Utilisation certificates of last year's grant.
5. Plan and estimate in case of Buildings only prepared by a qualified engineer.

To be Filled by the Office

1. Certified that the grants sanctioned for the year 19 . . . . for an amount of Rs. .... (Rupees...) are spent properly. All the items are entered in the concerned stock registers and I have verified them physically.

Inspection Officer

Grant Recommended

The Library Authority, ____________________ recommended the following grants for the year 19 ____-19 ____ after satisfying about its functioning.

A. *Normal Grants*

1. Books and periodicals Rs.:
2. Staff Salary
3. Other expenditure (i.e.) Rents, Rates, Taxes and buildings.

B. *Special Grants*

4. Building Construction
5. Library Equipment

C. *Additional Grants*

6. Adult Education Programme
7. Text Books
8. Children, Section

Total Rs.

Secretary
Library Authority

7.3 **Raja Rammohun Roy Library Foundation (RRRLF)**

1. All the public libraries managed by Government, Library Authorities, Local Bodies, voluntary organisations etc. can approach the Raja Rammohun Roy Library Foundation for grant-in-aid on the following areas.

   1. Assistance towards building up of adequate stock of books, and reading and visual materials.
   2. Assistance towards development of rural book deposit centres and mobile library service.

3. Assistance towards organisation of seminars, workshops, training courses (orientation/refresher) and book exhibitions.
4. Assistance towards storage and display of books.
5. Assistance to voluntary organisations providing public library service.
6. Assistance to public libraries below district level for increasing accommodation.
7. Assistance to children's libraries and children's sections of general public libraries.

2. Libraries willing to get assistance from the RRRLF should approach the convenor of the respective State Library Committee. Full details of assistance and procedure to the following can be had from the Director, Raja Rammohun Roy Library Foundation, Block DD 34, Section I, Salt lake, CALCUTTA-700 064.

7.4 Recognition of Library Associations and Grant-in-Aid

1. The following shall be the conditions governing the recognition of any Library Association:

   1. The Association shall be registered under the Societies Registration Act, 1860 or any Act, notified by the State Government.
   2. The aims and objects of the Association shall be:

      1. Promotion of library movement and improvement in library service in the State.
      2. Promotion of library science education and the improvement in training of librarians in the State.

         Note: Recognition of an association under these rules shall not be taken *ipso facto* as permission to start, organise or conduct any training programme, either in service, or pre-service, or both, by the association. Application shall be made specifically to the Government through the Director, for grant of permission to start, conduct, or organise any training programme, and it shall be left to the discretion of the Government, to grant or reject such application. For the purpose of recognition under these rules sub-clause (b) alone is not to be deemed as compulsory.

3. Improvement in the Status and conditions of service of librarians.
4. Publications of bulletins, periodicals, books, etc., which will tend to the realisation of the objects of the association.
5. Holding meetings, conferences and seminars.
6. Encouraging the formation of district and taluk associations.
7. Maintenance of liaison with social and cultural groups in the interest of Library movement in the State.

3. The constitution and the bye-laws of the association shall be approved by the Director with or without modification and shall among others, provide for all the following matters, namely:

   1. The powers to be exercised in the matters of finance, possession of property, etc.
   2. Subscription and other conditions for becoming members of the Association.
   3. The privileges of the membership.
   4. Election of office bearers, by ballot from among the members, their tenure of office and their powers and duties.
   5. Formation of Executive Committee, District Branches, etc., and their powers and functions.
   6. The conduct of meetings of the association, the procedure to be followed in regard to the transaction of business at such meetings and the quorum for such meetings.

4. The association shall submit such reports and furnish such information to the Director or any person authorised by him in this behalf, as the Director or the person authorised may, from time to time, require.
5. The accounts of the association or of the institutions established by it shall be open to audit by the Departmental Auditors or by any other agency as may be authorised by the Director.
6. Every year the annual accounts of the association, duly audited by an authorised agency, and the annual report shall be submitted to the Director.

3. *Grants*

1. Grants shall be sanctioned by the Government to the recognised association or to the institutions established by them subject to availability of funds.
2. The grants shall be utilised for the purpose for which they are sanctioned and the association or institution shall at its expense obtain from the agency authorised to audit the accounts of the association or institution a certificate to this effect and furnish it along with the audit report and the annual report.
3. If the Government have reasons to believe that any of the conditions laid down in Rules 1 and 2 are not fulfilled by the association or if any of its office bearers disobey provisions of the . . . Public Libraries Act, 19.... or the rules made thereunder or abuse their position, the Government may call on the association to show cause against derecognition of the association and withdrawal of aid, and after considering the replies received if any and after consulting the Director, pass such orders as they may deem fit.

7.5 General Rules

1. In all the cases of financial assistance under grant-in-aid the management shall be registered under the directions of the State Government. No such registration is necessary in case of statutory bodies like Library Authorities, Local Bodies, Cooperative Societies, religious endowments etc.
2. The accounts of the managements should be audited by an agency approved by the Government.
3. The management should submit the *Utilisation Certificate*, soon after the grant is spent for the purpose.
4. The managements should be kept open for the inspection of the higher authorities.
5. The management should submit any information on the grants released, utility to the public etc. or returns if any, to the Director promptly.

ANNEXURES

10. *Bibliographies*

- 10.1 Union Bills/Acts – Books
- 10.2 State Bills/Acts – Books
- 10.3 General Articles
- 10.4 Model Bills/Acts
- 10.5 Articles – State-wise
  - Andhra Pradesh
  - Arunachal Pradesh
  - Assam
  - Bihar
  - Delhi
  - Goa
  - Gujarat
  - Haryana
  - Himachal Pradesh
  - Jammu and Kashmir
  - Karnataka
  - Kerala
  - Madhya Pradesh
  - Manipur
  - Mizoram
  - Orissa
  - Punjab
  - Tamilnadu
  - Tripura
  - Uttar Pradesh
  - West Bengal
  - Union Territories
    - Lakshadweep
- 10.6 Chronology of Library Legislation
- 10.7 Committees and Commissions
- 10.8 Conferences and Seminars

ANNEXURE 10.1

Bibliography — Union Bills and Acts

BOOKS

Advisory Committee for Libraries (1958) Report, (Ed.) 2. Delhi: Manager of Publication, 1961. p. 124.

B.S. Kesavan. *India's National Library*. Calcutta: National Library, 1961. p. 218.

Calcutta National Library. *The National Library of India 1903 – 1978.* (Released on the occasion of the Platinum Jubilee). Calcutta: National Library, 1978. p. 72.

F.M. Gardner. *Public Library Legislation : A Comparative Study.* Paris: UNESCO, 1971. p. 285.

Gopal Rao Ekbote. *Public Library System.* Hyderabad: Ekbote Brothers, 1987. p. 377.

H.R. Sood. *The National Library, Calcutta; A brief note.* Calcutta: National Library, 1983. p. 44.

National Policy on Library and Information System a presentation. New Delhi: Committee on National Policy on Library and Information System. Department of Culture, Ministry of Human Resource Development, Government of India, May 1986. p. 42.

P.N. Kaula. *The National Library of India: A critical study, Bombay*: Somaiya Publications, 1970. p. 175.

Review Committee on the National Library Calcutta, 1969. Report. New Delhi: Ministry of Education and Youth Services, 1970. 5 pl, p. 179.

R.L. Mittal, *Public Library Law: An International Survey*. Delhi: Metropolitan Book Company, 1971. p. 624.

S.R. Ranganathan. *Library Development Plan, Thirty Year Programme for India with draft Library bills for the Union and Constituent States.* Delhi : Delhi University Press, 150. p. 462.

——., *Indian Library Manifesto.* New Delhi: ABC Publishing House, 1990. p. 118.

——., *A Neelameghan* (Eds). Public Library System, Bangalore: Sarada Ranganathan Endowment for Library Science, 1972. p. 253.

Uma Majumder. *India's National Library: Systematisation and Modernisation.* Calcutta: National Library, 1987, XII, p. 244.

V.C. Scott O'connor. *An Eastern Library. An Introduction to the Khuda Baksh Oriental Public Library, Patna. 1985*, 3rd Ed. p. 92.

V. Venkatappaiah. *Indian Library Legislation.* Vol. I – Union Library Bills and Acts. Delhi : Daya Publishing House, 1990. p. 16, 179.

ANNEXURE 10.2

Bibliography – State Bills and Acts

BOOKS

Andhra Pradesh Public Libraries Act, 1960, Hyderabad : Education Department, Government of Andhra Pradesh, 1979. p. 18.

Andhra Pradesh Public Libraries Act, 1960, Hyderabad : Asia Law House, 1986. p. 111.

Andhra Pradesh Public Libraries Act with commentary and rules, orders etc., Hyderabad : Andhra Pradesh Public Library Association, 1976.

F.M. Gardner. *Public Library Legislation – A comparative study*, Paris: UNESCO, 1971. p. 285.

Gopal Rao Ekbote. *Public Library System*. Hyderabad : Ekbote Brothers, 1987. p. 377.

K. Bala Satyanarayana. *The Law of Public Libraries in India*. Allahabad, Law Book Co., 1962.

Kerala Public Libraries Act, 1989. Trivandrum : Government of Kerala, 1989.

K.M. Ujlambkar, *Salient Features of Maharashtra Public Libraries Act, 1967*. Pune : Padmashri S.R. Ranganathan Smarak Samiti, 1986. p. 16.

Souvenir brought out on the occasion of II National Seminar on the *Role of Public and School Libraries*, 1990. p. 140. (This contains Manipur, Kerala and Haryana Acts etc.).

Madras Public Libraries Act, 1948. Madras : Government of Madras, 1952.

Maharashtra Public Libraries (Recognition for Grant-in-aid and Building and Equipment, and Grants) Rules 1970. Bombay : Government of Printing and Stationery, 1971. p. 22.

Mysore Public Libraries Act, 1965 and the Rules and Notifications thereunder, Bangalore : Director of Printing, Stationery and Publications, 1967, p. 82.

Pandey S.K. Sharma. *Public Libraries in India*. New Delhi : E.S.S. Publications, 1985. pp. VIII, p. 202.

P.N. Kaula. (ed) *Library Movement in India*. Delhi : Delhi Library Association, 1958.

—— *Herald of Library Science.* Library Legislation Number VII N(3) July 1972. pp. 215-321.

R.K. Rout (ed.) *Library Legislation in India.* New Delhi : Reliance Publishing House, 1986. pp. XIV, 376.

R.L. Mittal : *Public Library Law. An International Survey.* Delhi : Metropolitan Book Co., 1971. p. XII, 624.

S.N. Sadhu and B.N. Saraf : *Library Legislation in India : A Historical and Comparative Study.* New Delhi : Sagar Publications, 1967. pp. XVI, 285.

S.R. Ranganathan. *Model Library Act, 1931.* Madras Library Association.

— *Five Laws of Library Science*, ed 2. Bombay : Asia Publishing House, 1957. p. 449.

— *Indian Library Manifesto,* New Delhi : A B C Publishing House, 1990. p. 118.

— *Library Legislation.* Handbook to Madras Library Act. Madras : Madras Library Association, 1953. p. 312.

— *Model Public Library Bill,* 1941.

— and A. Neelameghan (eds.), *Public Library System in India, Sri Lanka, U.K. and U.S.A. : Comparative Library Legislation.* Bangalore : Sarada Ranganathan Endowment for Library Science, 1972. p. 253.

State Administrative Reports of the Constituent States, prepared by the concerned departments.

Reports of the committee appointed by the Government of Andhra Pradesh in February, 1976, to review the working of the Andhra Pradesh Public Libraries Act 1960, and to suggest Amendments to the Act, 1978. p. 134.

Report of the Committee on Private Libraries. Department of Public Libraries, Government of Andhra Pradesh, 1978. p. 37.

Report of the Library Development Committee, 1939. Bombay Education Department, 1984 (Reprint)

V. Venkatappaiah, *Indian Library Legislation* — Vol. II, *State Library Bills and Acts*. Delhi : Daya Publishing House, 1990. pp. 8, 326.

— *Model Public Libraries Act, 1989*, Delhi : Indian Library Association, 1990. pp. 75 (A Working Document of the National Seminar on Model Public Libraries Act held on 14 February, 1990 at New Delhi).

— *Public Library System* : Waltair : Andhra University, 1982. p. 64.

ANNEXURE 10.3

General Articles

BIBLIOGRAPHY

A.C. Ray. Limitation of some Library concepts. *Indian Lin.* 16 (2) 1961. pp. 106-8.

A.K. Mukherjee. Public Library System: a Statistical approach regarding its use and expenditure. *J Ind Lib Asson.* 5(1-3) 1963, p. 60.

Anis Khurshid : Growth of libraries in India. *Inter-national Library Review,* 4, 1972. p. 45.

A. Landenson. Major Legislative trends: *Lib J* 99, 1974.

A.R. Hewitt. Indian Public Library Law. *J. I.L.A.,* 4(3-4), July—Oct. 1962, pp. 7-28.

B. Patnaik. Library legislation in India : An assessment. In. P.B. Mangla (eds) *Fifty years of librarianship in India.* Delhi: I.L.A, 1983. pp. 330-33.

B. Halt Library needs of India. *Lib Her* 2(1) 1956, pp. 16-18.

B.S. Kesavan, Comments on the Public Library Development Plan for 4th Plan Period as envisaged by S.R. Ranganathan. *I.L.A. Bul.* 1(1) 1965, pp. 73-76.

C.C. Rochell. Library Development and Legislation: A call for unity. *Lib J.* 104; 1979; pp. 1856-62.

C.S. Krishnamurthy. Library legislation in India: A comparative survey. *Lib Her* 1969, 11 (1-2), pp. 102-11.

— Library Legislation in India. In P.N. Kaula, (ed) *Library Movement in India.* Delhi : Library Association, 1958, pp. 32-41.

D.G. Ghugre. Library Legislation in India. In N.B. Sen, (ed) *Development of Libraries in New Delhi.* New Delhi : New Book Society of India, 1965. pp. 138-143.

E.P. Hoftman. Legislation to increase public funding needs support of all. *Pa Lib Assn Bul.* 31, 1976. p. 71.

G.L. Trehan. Modern Public Library Movement and Library Legislation.

— A second look at the Library Legislation in India. *I.L.A. Bul,* XVII; (1) Jan-Mar, 1981; pp. 11-15.

H.A. Khan. Public Library Development : Policies, Problem and Performance, *Timeless Fellowship,* V 10, 1975-76; pp. 20-33.

H.K. Majumdar. Library Movement in India. *Lib Her.* 2, 1959, 8-11.

J.B. Khanna. Library legislation : A necessity. *Her Lib Sc.* 1963, 2(2), pp. 92-94.

J. Mishra. History of library legislation in India. *Lib His Rev* 1975. 2(2), pp. 13-62.

K.D. Puranik. Data for study of library legislation. In. S.R. Ranganathan, (ed) *Public Library provision and documentation problems.* Delhi, I.L.A., 1951. pp. 24-38.

K. Ramakrishna Rao. Library development in India. *Ind Lib.* 16(2) Sept 1961. p. 85.

K.R. Bharadwaj. Library legislation in India: A viewpoint. *I.L.A. Bul.* 1981, 1791), pp. 18-20.

Indian Library Association. All India Library Association. 14th (11th-15th April, 1964) Patna. Proceedings. Delhi, I.L.A. 1965.

M.A. Gopinath. History of Library Legislation in India. In S.R. Ranganathan and A. Neelameghan (eds) *Public Library System.* p. 32.

— March of library legislation in India. In S.R. Ranganathan and A. Neelameghan, (eds) *Library services for all.* Bangalore: Mysore Library Association, 1966. pp. 42-60.

— History of Library Legislation in India. In S.R. Ranganathan and A. Neelameghan (eds) *Seminar on Public Library System 1972.* p. 27.

M.A. Nayeem. Library legislation: A proposal. *I.L.A. Bulletin* 1981. 17(1), 5-10.

— Library legislation in India. In All India Public Library Convention, Nov 16-18, 1978. Souvenir. Delhi: I.L.A. 1978. pp. 30-34.

M.J. Dalal and C.B. Limaye. A second look at library legislation *I.L.A. Bul* 1981, 17(1). pp. 1-4.

M.V.R. Rau and K. Radhakrishnan. Coordinate Library Movement *IASLIC Spl Suppl.* 6(2) 1966. pp. 110-21.

N.C. Chakravorty. Finance for Public Library Services in India. Pros. of XIV All India Library Conference Patna, April 1964. pp. 84-87.

New Education Policy *vis-a-vis* Library Development Seminar (New Delhi). Feb 13, 1986. Delhi : Indian Library Association, 1986. pp. VI, 121.

P.M. Patel. Free Book Service for All. In *Free Book Service for All.* Dr. S. R. Ranganathan etc (eds). p. 81.

P.B. Mangla. Public Library Law in India. *Jl of Lib & Inf Sc* 8(1) June 1963, pp. 1-24.

P.K. Naskar. *Library legislation in India.* In Twenty Seventh All-India Library Conference, Hyderabad, January 9-12, 1981. Papers. Delhi: I.L.A. 1981.

P.N. Kaula. A peep into the Indian Library Law. *Her Lib Sc.* 1964, 3(4), pp. 317-21.

— Chronology of Public Library Service in India. *Her Lib Sc.* 1972, 11(3), pp. 217-19.

— Evaluation of Public Library Service in India. *Her Lib Sc.* 3(2-3), April-July 1964. pp. 108-121.

— Library Legislation in India. *Her Lib Sc* 10(2) 1972. pp. 107-110.

— Library Movement in India: Golden Jubilee. *Lib Her* 2(4) 1961. pp. 172-3.

— Recent Development of Libraries in India. *Library World,* 61, 1977, pp. 1964-65.

P.S. Patnaik, Public Library Provision in the Fourth Five Year Plan *I.L.A. Bul.* 1(1) 1965. pp. 67-72.

R.B. Surgh. And T. Ranganathan Rural Library System. *Lib Sc Slant Doc*, 1, 1964. pp. 374-84.

R.L. Mittal. Economics of library legislation. In All-India Public Library Convention, November 16-18, 1978. Souvenir. Delhi: I.L.A. 1978. p. 1-10.

— Dimensions of library legislation in India. International Library Movement 1979. 1(3-4) pp. 89-99.

— Implications of library legislation in India. In Punjab Library Association. Library Service Year Book and Directory, 1962. Chandigarh, *The Association,* 1962, pp. 52-55.

— Ranganathan and Library Legislation. *IASLIC Bull* 18(1), 1973. pp. 58-66.

— Ranganathan and Library Legislation. *Her Lib Sc* 12, 1973. pp. 319-26.

R.S. Sexena. Why library legislation. In Sen, N.B. (ed.) *Development of libraries in New India.* New Delhi : New Book Society of India, 1965. pp. 90-93.

— Need for library legislation. In All-India Public Library Convention, November 16-18, 1978. Souvenir, Delhi, I.L.A. 1978. pp. 11-18.

S. Das Gupta. Library Development of India. *Lib Her* 3(1), April, 1960.

S.P. Agrawal. National and Public Libraries in India; Review and Projections, *International Library Review,* 17(3), July 1985. pp. 293-312.

S.R. Ranganathan. Annual Public Library Finance, *A. Neelameghan Library Science,* 1(4), Dec. 1964.

— Federal Govt and Library Service. *The Hindu* dated 8-9-1931.

— Library Policy in Federated India. *South Indian Teacher*, 5. pp. 495-500.

— Library legislation and its factors. *Lib Her* 1(4), 1959, pp. 181-85.

— Library way for India. In P.N. Kaula, (ed) Library Movement in India. Delhi: Library Association, 1958, pp. 19-31.

— Indian Library Policy. *Educational Review,* V48, pp. 369-381.

— Library legislation and professional responsibility. *Her Lib Sc* 9(1). 1970. pp. 55-57.

— Library Movement in India 1949-50 Act. I.F.L.A. *Comons.* 1950. pp. 122-5.

— Raising the Library Man-Power. *Lib Sc,* VI(4), Dec, 1964. pp. 364-383.

S. Sohan Singh. Seminar on State Library Legislation. Proceedings of XIV All India Library Conference, Patna, April 1964. pp. 58-73.

S.N. Bhatia. History of library legislation in India and U.K. Chandigarh : Panjab University, 1963.

S.N. Srivastava. Library legislation in India. *Indian Librarian,* 22(3), 1967. pp. 148-52.

— Library Legislation in India. *International Library Review,* 4(3), 1972. pp. 329-39.

Syed Ali Hashmi. Library legislation: Its future in India. In P.B. Mangla (eds), *Fifty years of librarianship in India.* Delhi : I.L.A., 1983. pp. 343-60.

T.D. Waknis. The problem of library legislation in India. *Indian Lib* 17(4), 1963. pp. 223-28.

V.P. Mishra. Library legislation in India. In. P.B. Mangla, *Fifty years of Indian librarianship in India.* Delhi : I.L.A., 1983. pp. 361-64.

V.S. Moga. Library legislation in India. In K.C. Sogani and C. Narain, (eds). *Librarian and the libraries.* Jaipur : Shri Sammat Pustakalaya Trust, Jaipur, 1973. pp. 53-59.

V.W. Deshpande. Library legislation in India: A critical review. *I.L.A. Bul* 17(1), 1981. pp. 16-71.

ANNEXURE 10.4

Bibliography – Model Libraries Bills and Acts

ARTICLES

C.P. Shukla. A critique of the Model Public Libraries Bill. Proceedings of XIV All India Library Conference, Patna, April 1964. pp. 79-83.

C.V. Subbarao and (Mrs) K. Subbarao. Critical core-considerations of the Model Public Libraries Bill. Proceedings of the XIV All India Library Conference, April 1964, pp. 88-98.

D. Pretzer. State of the State Legislation. *Mich Libn* 42. 1976. p. 6.

Draft Model Indian Libraries Act. Calcutta : Indian Library Association, 1942.

D.R. Kalia. Model Public Libraries Bill : An Appraisal. Proceedings of XIV All India Library Conference, Patna, April 1964. pp. 74-78.

Jain H.C. The Model Public Libraries Bill: An evaluation. *Lib Her* 7(2-3), 1964. pp. 175-84.

— The Model Public Library Bill: a comparative analysis seminar on State Library Legislation at the India Library Conference, Patna, 1964.

— Model Public Libraries Bill, with amendments of the Indian Library Association. In the Proceedings of XIV All India Library Conference held in Patna, 1964.

— Model Public Libraries Bill. *Her Lib Sc* 4 Dec 1964, pp. 384-414.

P.N. Venkatachari. Comment on the Model Public Libraries Bill. Proceedings of the XIV All India Library Conference, April 1964. pp. 99-100.

S.R. Ranganathan. Comments on Model Library Bill. Poona: Maharashtra State, S.R. Ranganathan Satkar Samiti, 1964.

— Model Public Libraries Bill. *Library Science,* I(4) Dec. 1964, pp. 384-414.

— *Model Act and Madras Act in Library Legislation*. Madras: Madras Library Association, 1953. pp. 56-158.

— *Model Library Act*. Madras Library Association, 1931.

— Model Public Libraries Act — an explanation. *I.L.A.* Bul. I, pp. 54-67.

— *Model Public Library Act: In Public Library System*: Bangalore, 1972.
— A Model Library Act for India. *South Indian Teacher*. 3, pp. 548-556.
— Model 'Public Libraries Bill. Report of the Indian Library Association. Delhi: Indian Library Association, 1942, pp. 53-73.

Bibliography — Articles (State-wise)

CONSTITUTENT STATES

Andhra Pradesh

A.L. Kapoor. Andhra Pradesh Public Libraries Act, 1960. *Lib Her* 5(2), July 1962, pp. 81-96.

C.V. Subbarao. Andhra Pradesh Act: Operational deficiencies. *Lib Her* 3(4) Jan, 1961, pp. 159 165.

G.V.S.L.N. Raju. *Effect of Library Legislation on Public Library Development in Andhra Pradesh.* Andhra University thesis, 1983.

Hyderabad: Deptt. of Public Libraries. *Report of the A.P. Seminar on Organisation and Administration of Public Libraries.* Ed: Dr. S.R. Ranganathan, 1962.

Hyderabad Legislative Assembly. *Debates.* Official Report, pp 1025-1058.

Hyderabad Library Association. *Hyderabad Public Libraries Act of 1955 and its salient features.*

K. Raghava Reddy. *Public Libraries in A.P. ; Salient features of recent development.* In Souvenir of the 4th IASLIC Seminar, Hyderabad. Dec, 1966, pp. 68-69.

M. Bhojreddy. *A note on the functioning of Libraries in A.P.* Hyderabad City Granthalaya Samstha, 1976 (Mimio).

N.B. Inamdar. Andhra Pradesh Public Library Act. *Library and the Librarian* 1(2), 1977. pp. 18-24.

P.N. Kaula. *Library Needs of A.P. Souvenir*, A.P. 1979.

P. Vijay Kumar. Ekbote Committee on the Andhra Pradesh Public Libraries Act, *Her Lib Sc* 1979. 18(3), pp. 40-53.

Proceedings of the First All Hyderabad Library Conference. Hyderabad Session. 25-27 December 1954. *Granthalaya* I(1) January 1955.

T.V. Ramanayya and N.R. Satyanarayana. Library Legislation: Its development on public libraries in A.P. *Her Lib Sc* 10(2), 1971. pp. 147-153.

R.S. Sastry and N.B. Inamdar. Library Legislation in India: Andhra Pradesh experiment. In Twenty Seventh All-India Conference Hyderabad, January 9-12, 1981. Papers. Delhi: I.L.A., 1981. pp. 1-19.

R. Sugra Begum and T. Ranganathan. Rural Library System. *Lib Sc,* VI(4), Dec. 1964. pp. 319-334.

S.R. Ranganathan. Andhra Pradesh Public Library Bill: Critique and amendments, *Lib Her.* 2(4), Jan. 1960 pp. 131-141.

— Why Library Legislation. *Granthalaya.* VI(2) Feb. 1955. pp. 1-2.

V. Venkatappaiah. A New look at the Public Library System in A.P. AP Public Libraries Act 1979. Hyderabad: A.P. Public Association.

— Andhra Pradesh needs a comprehensive library Legislation. Golden Jubilee Souvenir of the Deptt. of Library Science, Andhra Pradesh University.

— Libraries and the Library Movement in A.P. *Her Lib Sc,* 3(2-3), Apr-Jul 1964. pp. 154-161.

Statement of objects and reasons by the Minister for Education, A.P. Gazettes Part IV A Extraordinary March 21, 1989.

Arunachal Pradesh

A Brief Report on the Development of Public Libraries in Arunachal Pradesh during the 7th five Year Plan. Status Reports on Development of Public Libraries in States and Union Territories 1989. p. 3.

Assam

Assam Public Libraries Bill (1971). In Public Library System. S.R. Ranganathan and A. Neelameghan (eds) 1972, pp. 254-270.

R.L. Mittal. Assam. *In Free Book Service for All*, 1968. p. 65.

S.R. Ranganathan. *Draft Library Bill and thirty year Plan for Assam* 1964.

Bihar

Asiya Hussain. The Khuda Baksh Library. *India Magazine,* August 1986. pp. 39-47.

Khuda Baksh Library, Patna. *Annual Report 1987-88.*

J. Misra. Library Movement in Bihar. *Her of Lib Sc,* 3(2-3), April-July 1964. pp. 185-193.

Library Legislation in India with reference to Bihar. In R.S.P. Singh, (ed) *Glimpses of Librarianship*, New Delhi: Janaki Pradeshan, 1981. pp. 41-52.

P.N. Gour. Bihar. *In Public Library System.* In S.R. Ranganathan and A. Neelameghan (ed), 1972. p. 185.

Ram Goswamee. State Libraries: Their organisation and function. Pros. of XIVth All India Library Conference, Patna, 1964, pp. 48-51.

R.S.P Singh. Library Legislation in India with Special reference to Bihar. In S.N. Agarwal (eds.) *Perspectives of Library and information science: Viswanathan Festschrift,* 2 Vols. Lucknow: Print House, 1982, pp. 118-27.

— Library Legislation in India with special reference to Bihar. In Twenty Seventh All India Library Conference, Hyderabad, January 9-12, 1981, Papers, Delhi, I.L.A. 1981, pp. 26-32.

— Library Legislation in India with special reference to Bihar. *I.L.A. Bulletin Supplement,* XVII(1) Jan-Mar 1981. p. 36.

Delhi

Draft Library Bill for Delhi : Need for library legislation in Delhi. *Lib Her.* 18(1-2), 1972. pp. 69-78.

J.S. Sharma. Why Delhi Needs Library Legislation. In P.N. Kaula. (ed.) Library Movement in India, Delhi, : Library Association, 1958, p. 107-116.

S.R. Ranganathan. Library Development Plan for Delhi State. *Ann Lib Sc* 1:1954, pp. 53-8.

Goa

Pia de Menezes Rodrigues. Library Movement in Goa, Souvenir of 34th All India Library Conference, 1988. pp. 57-61.

Gujarat

Draft Library Bill for Gujarat (1965). *In Public Library System.* S.R. Ranganathan and A. Neelameghan (eds) 1972. pp. 271-284.

C.P. Shukla. Gujarat Public Library Bill, 1977 : A Critique. In All India Public Convention, November 16-8, 1978 Souvenir.

Dept. of Education and Labour. Revised Rules for grant-in-aid to Public Libraries, Govt. of Gujarat 1974. Resolution No. LIB-1066-II-79369-B.

Gujarat Public Library Bill, 1977. Gujarat Bill No. 55 of 1977. Govt of Gujarat.

J.S. Kudelkar. Baroda Library Movement. 1960, Central Library, p. 78.

N.M. Rawal. Survey of the Progress of Public Libraries in Gujarat *State Libra Her,* 8(3-4), Oct, 1965, Jan. 1966, pp. 219-234.

P.C. Shah. Public Libraries and Status of Library Legislation in Gujarat. In Library Legislation in India. Ed: R.K. Rout. p. 349.

— Position of Library Legislation in Gujarat. *I.L.A.* Bulletin 12(1), 1976. pp. 35-37.

P.V. Mehta. Library Legislation and Gujarat. In All-India Public Library Convention, November 16-18, Souvenir, Delhi: I.L.A. 1978, pp. 23-29.

Haryana

Janak Raj. Library Movement in Haryana. *I.L.A. Souvenir 1988.* p. 67.

Library Movement in Haryana. In the Souvenir brought on the occasion of II National Seminar, Puna: Indian Public Library 1989. pp. 1-16.

M.L. Bhagi. Public Library Service and Draft Bill for Library Legislation, *Indian Library Movement* V 3(2-3) June-December 1976.

Himachal Pradesh

A.S. Chandel. Himachal Pradesh Public and Academic Libraries Bill: A proposed draft. In Library Legislation in India. pp. 282-293.

Jammu and Kashmir

A.A.N. Raju. Library Movement in Jammu and Kashmir. *Her Lib Sc,* 7(2) 1968, pp. 120-3.

K.N. Hasan. Library Legislation : Plan and Prospects in Jammu and Kashmir State. pp. 129-136.

Noorul Hasan Khan. Library Legislation: Plans and Prospects in Jammu and Kashmir. In S.N. Agarwal (eds) Perspectives in library and information science; *Vishwanthan Festschrift.* 2 Vols. Lucknow Print House, 1982. pp. 129-38.

— Library Legislation on the anvil: Public Libraries in Jammu and Kashmir. *I.L.A. Bulletin* 13(1-4), 1977. pp. 5-10.

P.N. Kaula. Draft Library Bill and Library Development Plan for Jammu and Kashmir, 1951.

S.M. Safi. Development of Public Libraries in J&K: A Review. In Library Legislation in India by R.K. Rout (ed) pp. 294-301.

Karnataka

C.S. Krishnamurthy. Mysore Public Libraries Act. *Libra.* 7, 1960-70. pp. 16-20.

K.S. Deshpande. Library Movement in Mysore State. *Ind Lib* 17(1) June 1962. pp. 2-3.

Mysore : Committee on Public Libraries Bill. Report. Bangalore, 1963.

P.K. Patil. Public Libraries in Karnataka— Their scope and functions. Bangalore. Department of Public Library, 1981.

Public Libraries in Karnataka: Their Scope and Development, Govt. of Karnataka, Bangalore, 1982.

P. Sadasiva Murthy. Rural Library Development in Karnataka State, *Lucknow Lib* 15(2) June 1983. pp. 57-64.

R. Anantharaman. Public Library Bangalore (1915-1965) Golden Jubilee Souvenir, Bangalore Golden Jubilee Committee, 1966.

R.V. Subrahmanyam. The Mysore Public Libraries Act. *Ind Lib* 23(12), 1968. pp. 87-95.

S.R.I. Jari. Survey of Library Development in Karnataka. In Assessment of Public Library Development in India, Seminar. University of Madras, 1986. pp. 66-67.

March of Libraries in Karnataka. Indian Library Association Souvenir, Calcutta: Bengal Library Association, 1988. p. 75.

S.R. Ranganathan. Mysore Library Grid, A vision, In S.R. Ranganathan and A. Neelameghan (Eds) Library Service for All. Bangalore: Mysore Library Association, 1966. pp. 13-25.

Kerala

C.A. Augustine. Library Legislation: Some fundamental questions. Kerala Library Association. National Library week Souvenir, 1976, pp. 99-102.

C. Achyutha Menon. Kerala Library Bill. *Janapatham* 10(8), 1979. pp. 2-5.

K.A. Isaac. Library Service in Kerala. In Ranganathan and A. Neelameghan (eds) *Public Library System*. 1972. pp. 190-4.

K. Raveendra Ansari. Kerala Public Libraries Bill 1971. An evaluation, University thesis, 1974.

M. Bavakutty. The Kerala Public Libraries Bill, 1972. An evaluation. *Lib Her* 15(3-4), 1973-74. pp. 146-50.

— Requisites for an ideal Public Library System in Kerala. *Journal of Kerala Studies*. 3, 1976, pp. 169-78.

— Libraries and Library Education in Kerala. *I.L.A. Souvenir*, 1988. p. 78.

— Library Movement in Kerala. *Libri* (Denmark) 1982.

M.N. Ramakrishnan and C.A. Augustine. Kerala in S.R. Ranganathan (ed) *Free Book Service for all, an international survey*, 1968. pp. 91-103.

P.A. John and V.K.G. Nair. Public Library Movement in Kerala. XXVth All India Library Conference, Trivandrum, Souvenir, 1979. p. 161.

T. Vasudeva Menon. Library Movement in Kerala in P.N. Kaula (ed) *Library Movement in India*, Delhi : Library Association, 1958. pp. 96-102.

S.R. Ranganathan. Library development plan with a Draft Library Bill for Kerala State. Trivandrum : Government of Kerala, 1960.

Madhya Pradesh

G.D. Bhargava. Public Library Movement in Madhya Pradesh — Retrospect and prospect. *Library Legislation in India*. pp. 325-335.

V.S. Moghe. Free Book Service for All— Madhya Pradesh. *Free Book Service for all*. pp. 106-107.

— Library Movement in Madhya Pradesh, *Her of Lib Sc* 3(2-3), April-July 1964, pp. 198-203.

Madhya Pradesh Public Libraries Bill 1970. *Public Library System*. S.R. Ranganathan and A. Neelameghan (eds) 1972, pp. 303-312.

Maharashtra

B. Ghate. Maharashtra Library Bill. *Sahitya Sahakar* 17(6), 1976, pp. 14-17.

G.S. Krishnamurty. Maharashtra Public Library Act. Libra. 6, 1968-69, pp. 7-19.

K. Menurkar. Library Legislation and Maharashtra Government, *Sahitya Sahakar* 16(11), 1967.

Maharashtra Public Libraries Act 1967. *Public Library System*. S.R. Ranganathan and A Neelameghan (eds) 1972.

Report of the Library Development Committee Bombay: Education Deptt., 1984 (Reprint).

R.S. Parkhi. Dr. Ranganathan's Plan for Library Development in Bombay. In Kaula (P.N.), (ed) *Library Science Today*. Bombay, Asia Publishing House, 1965. pp. 397-400.

S.G. Mahajan. Library Development in Maharashtra. *I.L.A. Souvenir*, Calcutta : Bengal Library Association, 1988. p. 90.

Status Report on Development of Public Libraries in Maharashtra. All India Public Library Conference on Eighth Plan perspectives of Public Library Development, New Delhi, R.R.M.L.F., 1989. p. 70.

S.R. Ranganathan. *Comments of Model Public Libraries Bill*. Poona: Maharashtra State S.R. Ranganathan Satkar Samiti, 1964. pp. 39.

— Library Development Plan with a Draft Library Bill for the Province of Bombay, Bombay : Padma Publications, 1947, p. 128.

T.D. Waknis. The Public Libraries Bill. *Ind Lib* 22(2), 1967. pp. 88-98.

Manipur

IMPHAL: Government of Manipur. Manipur Public Libraries Act, 1988. In *CLIS Observer*. V 5(&2) Jan June 1988.

N. Giridhar Singh. Development of Libraries in Manipur State. *I.L.A. Conference Souvenir* 1988, p. 99.

R.K. Dave. Library Legislation in India: A case study of Manipur State. *Her Lib Sc* 17(1), 1978. pp. 19-30.

Meghalaya

A.S. Chandel and P.K. Mitra. Library Services in Meghalaya. *I.L.A. Souvenir*, 1988. p. 100.

Mizoram

C. Lianzama. History and Development of Library Movement of Mizoram State. *I.L.A. Souvenir*, 1988.

C. Lianzama. Public Library Service in Mizoram. In Assessment of Public Library Development in India, by P. Gangadhararao and K.S. Raghavan, Madras Dept. of Library and Inf. Science, University of Madras, 1986.

Orissa

K.C. Sachoo. Public Library Movement in Orissa. *Library Legislation in India* R.K. Rout (Ed) p. 320.

M. Mahapatra. Libraries and Library Movement in Orissa. An over view. *I.L.A. Souvenir* 1988. p. 110.

Punjab

A.K. Anand and D.R. Grover. Public Library network in Punjab problems of library legislation. *I.L.A. Bulletin* 18(3-4). 1982-83.

Hakam Singh (eds). Library legislation in the Punjab. Library Circle, Kurukshetra University Library, 1972.

G.L. Trehan. Modern Public Library movement and library legislation for Punjab. Chandigarh : Library Literature House, 1967.

— A second look at library legislation. *I.L.A. Bulletin* 17(1), 1981. pp. 11-15.

— Punjab, In Ranganathan S.R., etc., Ed. *Free Book Service for all : An International Survey*, 1968. p. 149.

— Library Development in Punjab overview. *I.L.A. Souvenir,* 1988.

K. Navalani. Punjab Libraries and Library Legislation in Punjab. R.K. Rout (ed) *Library Legislation in India.*

Punjab College Librarians Association, Jalandhar. Need of library legislation in Punjab (*Punjab Library Convention Souvenir*, 1960) Jalandhar, The Association, 1960.

Punjab Library Association, *Library Service Year Book and directory,* 1962. Chandigarh, The Association, 1962.

M.L. Bhagi. Library Movement in Punjab, *Her of Lib Sci,* 3 (2-3) April-July 1964, pp. 203-206.

R.L. Mittal. Implications of library legislation in India. *Punjab Library Association, Library Service Year Book and Directory*. Chandigarh, 1962. pp. 52-53.

Sant Ram Bhatia. History of Libraries and the Library Movement in the Punjab, *Mod Lib,* 6, 1936. pp. 88-96.

R.S. Sharma. Punjab Library Movement: Golden Jubilee, *Her Lib Sc.* 6(1) 1967. pp. 48-53.

Ram Labhaya: The Punjab Central Library Scheme. An attempt towards realization. *Mod Lib,* 3. 1933. pp. 161-164.

Rajasthan

C.D. Sharma, Narendra Sharma. Library Movement in Rajasthan. *I.L.A. Souvenir*, 1988. p. 123.

— Rajasthan, S.R. Ranganathan and A. Neelameghan (eds) *Free Book Service for All*, 1968.

C.S. Champawat. Library legislation in India: The Rajasthan scene. In Twenty Seventh All India Library Conference, Hyderabad January 9-12, 1981, Papers. Delhi : I.L.A. 1981, pp. 33-38.

R.S. Goyal. Library Movement in Rajasthan. In P.N. Kaula (ed.) *Library Movement in India*. Delhi : Library Association, 1958. pp. 103-106.

Tamilnadu

Annual Reports of the Madras Library Association 1928.

B.I. Palmer, Madras Library Movement 1985-1945, *Modern Librarian,* V. 15(2), Apr-Jun 1945. pp. 52-56.

D.B. Krishna Rao. Library Movement in Madras. In P.N. Kaula (Ed) *Library Movement in India*. Delhi : Library Association, 1958, pp. 80-87.

A. Gopinath. History of Library Legislation in India. In S.R. Ranganathan, A. Neelameghan (ed.) *Public Library System*.

K.M. Sivaraman. March of library legislation in Madras. In Kaula, P.N. (ed.) *Library Science To-day*. Bombay : Asia Publishing House, 1965, pp. 387-396.

P.A. Mohan Rajan. Peep into Public Library System. Seminar on the Assessment of the Public Library System. Organised by Department of Library and Information Science. University of Madras 1986.

R.S. Saxena. Ranganathan's Model State Library Act and Madras Public Library Act, a Comparison. *Annals-ILA,* V2(5), Dec. 1964, pp. 142-144.

R. Sugra Begum. City Library System. *Library Science,* VI(4), Dec 1964, pp. 309-318.

S.R. Ranganathan. Fifteen years library development programmes for plan periods 4 to 6. *Lib Sc with a slant to Doc.* Vol. I (4) Dec. 1964 pp. 281-308.

— Public Library Development in Madras. *Madras, Local Library Authority, Souvenir,* 10th Nov. 1965.

T.N. Rajan. Library Legislation in the State of Madras. *The Journal of the Indian Library Association.* Vol. 4, (3-4) Jul-Oct 1962. pp. 60-95.

V.N. Subbarayan. Public Libraries in the Madras State. *Hindu,* 16-4-1961.

V. Thillainayagam. Tamil Nadu. In S.R. Ranganathan and A. Neelameghan (eds) *Public Library System* 1972. pp. 169-173.

Tripura

Debabrata Chakraborty. The Development of Library Service in Tripura. ILA Souvenir 1988. pp. 125-128.

Uttar Pradesh

A.P. Tripathi. Public Library Service in Uttar Pradesh. *Her Lib Sc,* VI(3), July 1962. pp. 123-126.

Magnanand. Growth of public libraries in Uttar Pradesh. In Sen, N. B. (Ed) *Development of Libraries in New India.* New Delhi: New Book Society of India, 1965, pp. 47-61.

N.B. Srivastava. Uttar Pradesh marches towards library legislation. In S.N. Agarwal etc (eds.) Perspectives in Library and Information Science: *Vishwanathan Festschrift,* 2 Vols. Lucknow. Print House, 1982. pp. 109-17.

— Uttar Pradesh marches towards library legislation. *Lucknow Librarian* 9(1-2), 1972. pp. 42-47.

P.N. Kaula. All Uttar Pradesh Library Conference. *Lib Her,* 3,4, 1961. pp. 173-80.

— Library needs of Uttar Pradesh. Her of Lib Sc. 14. 1973.

Rochana Srivastava, S.N. Agarwal, R.K. Srivastava. Library Movement in Uttar Pradesh : A State of the Art, *I.L.A. Souvenir* 1978. p. 132.

R.S. Saxena. Uttar Pradesh. In *Free Book Service for all.* S.R. Ranganathan and A. Neelameghan (eds) 1968. p. 165.

S.R. Ranganathan. Uttar Pradesh Library Act: When? *Luck Lib* 8(3-4) 1971. pp. 5-7.

— *Library Development Plan with a Draft Library Bill for the United Provinces.* Benaras, Varanasi Granthagar, 1949. p. 120.

West Bengal

Memorandum on Libraries to the Education Minister of West Bengal. *Her Lib Sc* 16 (2) July 1977. p. 423.

Nilima Devi. Library Movement in Bengal. In P.N. Kaula (ed.) *Library Movement in India.* Delhi, Library Association, 1958. pp. 76-79.

R.L. Mittal. Library Legislation for Bengal : An evaluation. *IASLIC Bul* 25 (4) 1980. pp. 181-86.

S.R. Ranganathan. *Library Personality and Library Bill*, West Bengal. Calcutta; Bengal Library Association, 1968

West Bengal Public Libraries Act 1979. *The Calcutta Gazette.* 7 Jan 1980. p. 26.

West Bengal Public Libraries Amendment Ordinance VI of 1982. Govt of West Bengal.

West Bengal Public Libraries Management Rules 1981. Govt of West Bengal.

Union Territories

Andaman and Nicobar Islands

Ajit Kumar Datta, Andaman and Nicobar Islands: Marching towards Modernised Public Library System. I.L.A. Souvenir, 1988, pp. 29-32.

Lakshadweep

K. Hamsath. Public Library Services in Union Territory of Lakshadweep. *Souvenir of XXV All India Library Conference,* Trivandrum, 1979. p. 141.

K. Sunder Rajan. Library Services in the Union Territory of Pondichery. A paper of the National Seminar on the Assessment of Public Library Development in India, 1986, organised by Department of Library and Information Science of the University of Madras.

ANNEXURE 10.6

Chronology of Library Legislation

1. *Union Library Acts Bill*

   1. Union Library Bill, 1950 (Dr. S.R. Ranganathan)
   2. Union Library Act, 1957 (Dr. S.R. Ranganathan)
   3. Model Union Libraries Act, 1972 (Dr. S.R. Ranganathan)

2. *Union Library Acts*

   1. 1887 Press and Registration of Books Act
   2. 1902 Imperial Library (Indentures Validation) Act
   3. 1948 Imperial Library (Change of Name Act)
   4. 1954 Delivery of Books and News-papers Act
   5. 1958 Indian Copy Right Act
   6. 1969 Khudabaksh Oriental Public Library Act
   7. 1975 Rampur Raza Library Act
   8. 1976 The National Library of India Act
   9. 1981 Asiatic Society Act

3. *State Model Libraries Bills and Acts*

   1. 1930 Model Library Act (Dr. S.R. Ranganathan)
   2. 1931 Draft Model Public Libraries Bill (Dr. S.R. Ranganathan)
   3. 1957 Model Library Act (Revised) (Dr. S.R. Ranganathan)
   4. 1963 Model Public Libraries Bill (Ministry of Education, Government of India)
   5. 1965 Model Pubic Libraries Bill (Planning Commission – Government of India)
   6. 1972 Model Public Libraries Act (Revised) (Dr. S.R. Ranganathan)
   7. 1972 Model State Libraries Act (Dr. S.R. Ranganathan)
   8. 1989 Model Public Libraries Act (Dr. V. Venkatappaiah)

9. 1992 Model Public Libraries Act (Revised) (Dr. V. Venkatappaiah)

4. *State Libraries Acts*

1. 1945 Kolhapur Public Libraries Act (Merged in Maharashtra State)
2. 1948 Madras Public Libraries Act
3. 1955 Hyderabad Public Libraries Act (Merged in A.P. Public Libraries Act)
4. 1960 Andhra Pradesh Public Libraries Act
5. 1965 Karnataka Public Libraries Act
6. 1967 Maharashtra Public Libraries Act
7. 1979 West Bengal Public Libraries Act
8. 1988 Manipur Public Libraries Act
9. 1989 Kerala Public Libraries Act
10. 1989 Haryana Public Libraries Act
11. 1993 Mizoram Public Libraries Act

5. *State Libraries Bills (Statewise)*

Andhra Pradesh

1953 Hyderabad Public Libraries Bill (S.R. Ranganathan)
1957 Andhra Pradesh Public Libraries Bill (S.R. Ranganathan)
1959 Andhra Pradesh Public Libraries Bill
1969 Andhra Pradesh Public Libraries (Amendment) Bill
1979 Andhra Pradesh Public Libraries (Comprehensive) Bill (Dr. V. Venkatappaiah)
1986 Andhra Pradesh Public Libraries (Amendment) Bill
1989 Andhra Pradesh Public Libraries (Amendment) Bill (Andhra Pradesh Granthalaya Parishad)
1990 Andhra Pradesh Public Libraries (Amendment) Bill

Assam

1964 Public Libraries Bill for Assam (S.R. Ranganathan)
1972 Assam Public Libraries Bill (Dr. R.L. Mittal)
1986 Assam Public Libraries Bill

Bihar

1973 Bihar Public Libraries Bill (Bihar Library Association)
1981 Bihar Public Libraries Bill (R.S.P. Singh)

Delhi

1955 Delhi Public Library Bill (P.N. Kaula)

Goa

1983 Goa Public Libraries Bill (State Library Advisory Board)
1990 Goa Public Libraries Bill K.M. Ujlambkar

Gujarat

1965 Gujarat Public Libraries Bill (Library Committee, Gujarat Government)
1969 Gujarat Public Libraries Bill (Legislative Assembly Bill No. 27 of 1970) By Manohar Sinhji P. Jadeja, M.L.A.)
1973 Gujarat Public Libraries Bill (Maneklal Gandhi)
1978 Gujarat Public Libraries Bill (Manohar Sinhji Jadeja)
1981 Gujarat Public Library Bill (Lakhani)
1990 Gujarat Library Bill (H.J. Upadhyaya)

Haryana

1972 Haryana Public Libraries Bill (M.L. Bhagi)
1982 Haryana Public Libraries Bill (Jankraj)
1988 Haryana Public Libraries Bill (N.K. Sharma)

Himachal Pradesh

1982 Himachal Pradesh Public Libraries Bill (A.S. Chandel)
1990 Himachal Pradesh Public Libraries Bill (K.M. Ujlambkar).

Karnataka

1963 Mysore Public Libraries Bill (S.R. Ranganathan for the Mysore Public Libraries Bill Committee, 1961)

Kerala

1947 Cochin State Public Libraries Bill (S.R. Ranganathan)
1947 Travancore State Public Libraries Bill (S.R. Ranganathan)
1959 Kerala Public Libraries Bill (S.R. Ranganathan)
1969 Kerala Public Libraries Bill (S.R. Ranganathan)
1979 Kerala Public Libraries Bill

Jammu and Kashmir

1951 Library Bill for Jammu and Kashmir (P.N. Kaula)
1975 Jammu and Kashmir Public Libraries Bill (M.S. Randhava)

Madhya Pradesh

1946 Central Provinces and Benaras Public Libraries Bill (S.R. Ranganathan)
1950 Madhya Pradesh Public Libraries Bill
1958 Madhya Pradesh Public Libraries Bill (S.R. Ranganathan)
1958 Madhya Pradesh Public Libraries Bill (Maulana Azad Central Library Development Committee)
1959 Madhya Pradesh Public Libraries Bill (Madhya Pradesh Library Association)
1968 Madhya Pradesh Public Libraries Bill (G.D. Bhargava and V.S. Moghe)
1970 Madhya Pradesh Public Libraries Bill (Indore Divisional Library Association)
1978 Madhya Pradesh Public Libraries Bill
1990 Madhya Pradesh Public Libraries Bill (K.M. Ujlambkar)

Maharashtra

1936 Bombay Presidency Public Libraries Bill (S.K. Bole)
1947 Library Bill for the Provinces of Bombay (S.R. Ranganathan)
1959 Bombay State Public Libraries Bill (M.V. Donde)
1965 Maharashtra Public Libraries Bill (Maharashtra Library Association

Manipur

1988 Manipur Public Libraries Bill

Mizoram

1980 Mizoram Public Libraries Bill (State Libraries)
1988 Mizoram Public Libraries Bill

Orissa

1974 Orissa Public Libraries Bill (Utkal Library Association)
1983 Orissa Public Libraries Bill (B.B. Shukla)
1988 Orissa Public Libraries Bill (Utkal Libraries Association)

Punjab

1962 Punjab Public Libraries Bill (R.L. Mittal)
1962 Punjab Public Libraries Bill (G.L. Trehan)
1964 Punjab Public Libraries Bill (Punjab Library Association)

Rajasthan

1965 Rajasthan Public Libraries Bill (Rajasthan Library Association)
1991 Rajasthan Public Libraries Bill (K.M. Ujlambkar)

Tamil Nadu

1931 Public Libraries Bill for the Presidency of Madras (Madras Library Association)
1937 Public Libraries Bill for the Presidency of Madras (Madras Library Association)
1946 Madras Public Libraries Bill (S.R. Ranganathan)

Uttar Pradesh

1948 Library bill for the United Provinces (S.R. Ranganathan)
1958 Uttar Pradesh Public Libraries Bill (S.R. Ranganathan)

1969 Uttar Pradesh Public Libraries Act (Uttar Pradesh Library Association)
1973 Uttar Pradesh Public Libraries Bill (Goswami Committee)
1983 Uttar Pradesh Public Libraries Bill (Dr. V. Venkatappaiah)
1983 Uttar Pradesh Public Libraries Bill (Viswanathan Committee)

West Bengal

1931 Bengal Public Libraries Bill (Kumar Munindra Deb Ray Mahashay)
1958 West Bengal Public Libraries Bill (S.R. Ranganathan)
1978 West Bengal Public Libraries Bill (Left Front Government)
1982 Amendment Bill to the West Bengal Public Libraries Act
1985 Amendment Bill to the West Bengal Public Libraries Act

ANNEXURE 10.7

Committees and Commissions

1939 Library Development Committee. Chairman : A.A.A. Fyze Report of the Library Development Committee, Bombay : 1939. Education Department, Bombay State, 1984 (Reprint).

1950 Library Development Plan : Thirty year programme for India, with draft library bills for the Union and the Constituent States. Prepared by Dr. S.R. Ranganathan.

1958 Advisory Committee for Libraries. Chairman K.P. Sinha. Report. Delhi : Manager Publications, 1959, (Reprint 1963)

Committee on Public Library Bill for Mysore State.

1961 Madras Library Association. Memorandum on Library Advisory Committee Report. *Lib Her*. 9, 9, 1961, pp. 72-98.

1965 India, Planning Commission. Working Group on Libraries, A Survey of Public Library Service in India : Tabulated and analysed by D.R. Kalia. Delhi, Indian Library Association, 1965, p. 7.

1969 Reviewing Committee on the National Library, Calcutta, 1969, Report. New Delhi : Ministry of Education, 1970, p. 179.

1972 Parliament Select Committee on the National Library Bill.

1978 Committee to Review the working of the A.P.P.L. Act, 1960, and to suggest amendments to Act. Chairman : Gopal Rao Ekbote. Report – Hyderabad : Govt. of A.P., 1978.

Public Libraries Official Level Committee. Chairman : S. Srinivasan, Madras : Deptt. of Education, 1978.

1979 Committee on Private Libraries. Chairman : Vavilala Gopala Krishnaiah. Report. Hyderabad : Govt. of A.P., 1979.

1980 Public Library Advisory Committee. Report. Goa, Daman and Diu, 1980.

1984 India. Planning Commission. Working Group of Planning Commission. Modernisation of Library Services and Information for the Seventh Five Year Plan 1985-90.

1986 Committee on National Policy and Library and Information system. Chairman D.P. Chattopadyaya. Report. New Delhi : Department of Culture, Ministry of Human Resource Development, Govt. of India, 1986. p. 42.

ANNEXURE 10.8

Conferences and Seminars

1930 First All Asia Educational Conference, at Varanasi. Library Service Section. First Model Library Act was discussed.

1942 Model Public Library Bill drafted by Dr. S.R. Ranganathan was discussed in the Fifth All India Library Conference held at Bombay.

1948 Special Conference on Madras Public Libraries Act, organised by Andhra Desa Granthalaya Sangham at Vijayawada.

1952 Conference at Vijayawada on the implementation of the Madras Public Libraries Act organised by Andhra Desa Library Association. Dr. S.R. Ranganathan participated in the conference.

1954 Hyderabad Public Libraries Act discussed at First All Hyderabad Library Conference.

1962 Seminar on Library Legislation, at Chandigarh, organised by Punjab Library Association.

1962 Seminar on Public Library System, organised by Department of Public Libraries, Govt. of Andhra Pradesh. Director : Dr S.R. Ranganathan.

1962 Seminar on Library Legislation at Chandigarh, organised by Punjab Library Association.

1963 Seminar on Model Public Libraries Bill at Chandigarh organised by Punjab Library Association.

1964 Seminar on Library Legislation at Patna, organised by Indian Library Association.

1964 Draft Public Libraries Bill prepared by Dr. S.R. Ranganathan discussed in Eighth All Assam Library Conference held at Gauhati.

1964 Seminar on Model Public Libraries Bill, at Delhi organised by Delhi Library Association.

1966 Punjab Public Library Bill discussed in the Sixth All India Library Conference held at Chandigarh.

1968 M.P. Public Libraries Bill discussed in Seventeenth All India Library Conference held at Indore.

1971 Haryana Public Libraries Bill drafted by Shri M.L. Bhagi, discussed in Haryana Book Festival.

1972 Seminar on Public Library System at Bangalore organised by Sarada Ranganathan Endowment for Library Science.

1979 Andhra Pradesh Public Libraries (comprehensive) Bill drafted by Dr. V. Venkatappaiah discussed in A.P. Public Libraries conference held at Hyderabad.

1981 Seminar on Second Look on Library Legislation, at Hyderabad, organised by Indian Library Association.

1982 Haryana Public Libraries Bill discussed in the Seminar Public Library System held at Kurukshetra.

1989 Seminar on Library Legislation organised by Haryana Library Association.

1989 National Seminar on Library Legislation with special reference to Uttar Pradesh, organised by Aligarh Muslim University.

Workshop on Norms, Guidelines and Standards organised by Zilla Granthalaya Samstha, West Godavari, Eluru, Andhra Pradesh.

1990 National Seminar on Model Public Libraries Act. February 14, 1990 at New Delhi organised by Indian Library Association in collaboration with the Raja Rammohun Roy Library Foundation.

1991 State Conference on Library Legislation for Orissa. Organised by Indian Journal of Information, Library and Society, Cuttack.

Seminar on Library Legislation-organised by Punjab Library Association, Chandigarh.

1993 Seminar on Library Legislation. Organised by Vavilala Samstha, Guntur, Andhra Pradesh.

INDEX